THE THIRD GOSPEL FOR THE THIRD WORLD

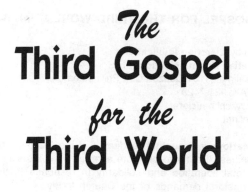

The Third Gospel *for the* Third World

VOLUME TWO–B
MINISTRY IN GALILEE
(Luke 7:1–9:50)

Herman Hendrickx, cicm

A Michael Glazier Book
THE LITURGICAL PRESS
Collegeville, Minnesota

THE THIRD GOSPEL FOR THE THIRD WORLD Vol. II-B

Copyright © 1998 by **Claretian Publications**
A division of **Claretian Communications, Inc.**
U.P. P.O. Box 4, Diliman 1101 Quezon City, Philippines
TE: 921-3984 • FAX: 921-7429
Website: http://www.cnl.net/claret
E-mail: claret@cnl.net

Claretian Publications is a pastoral endeavor of the Claretian Missionaries in the Philippines. It aims to promote a renewed spirituality rooted in the process of total liberation and solidarity in response to the needs, challenges and pastoral demands of the Church today.

Library of Congress Cataloging-in-Publication Data

Hendrickx, Herman.
 The Third Gospel for the Third World / Herman Hendrickx.
  p.   cm.
 "A Michael Glazier book."
 Includes bibliographical references.
 Contents: v. 1. Preface and infancy narrative (Luke 1:1-2:52).
 ISBN 0-8146-5870-9
 ISBN 0-8146-5871-7 Volume Two-A
 ISBN 0-8146-5872-5 Volume Two-B
 1. Bible. N.T. Luke—Commentaries I. Title.
BS2595.3.H46
226.4' 07—dc20   96-34651
                                                              CIP

Cover design by Maria d.c. Zamora

TABLE OF CONTENTS

FOREWORD

This book is the second part of the second volume of a commentary on the Gospel of Luke under the general title *The Third Gospel for the Third World*, which will eventually consist of five volumes. The first volume covering Luke's Preface (Lk 1:1-4) and Infancy Gospel (Lk 1:5-2:52) was published in September 1996. The second volume was supposed to cover Jesus' Ministry in Galilee (Lk 3:1-9:50). However, for practical reasons, the author decided to divide the said volume into two parts, namely A (Lk 3:1-6:49) and B (Lk 7:1-9:50). Volume Two-A was published in October 1997. The present Volume Two-B completes the treatment of Jesus' Ministry in Galilee.

Like the previous volumes, the present book intends to pay special, though not exclusive attention to whatever may be of particular interest to third-world readers. Again we try to deal with questions raised by the social-scientific approach to the Gospels, as well as anthropological and cultural features, like matters of family, clan and tribe, matters of honor and shame, the conditions of rural and urban life, etc. We also try again to take into account the findings of recent literary criticism. The commentary makes available to a wider reading public what the author considers to have pastoral implications first and foremost in a third-world setting. But it goes almost without saying that many of these features are also of importance to committed first-world Christians.

Since this commentary endeavors to bring together findings of various fields of research, several of which are rather new, it is obvious that we are very much indebted to experts in these various fields. We trust that the text notes and the bibliography will sufficiently account for the extent of this indebtedness. We intend to make available the insights of present-day Lukan scholarship to people who have no access to the books and periodical articles in which these insights are found and/or cannot afford to buy them.

Like the two previous volumes, this book is no easy reading, although the author tried to avoid becoming too technical. But the disciplines mentioned above are not exactly easy. So the reader will again have to invest time and effort in order to discover and assimilate the riches of the Third Gospel presented in this commentary. We wish that you may have the courage and stamina to bring this to a fruitful end.

THE RECEPTION ACCORDED TO JESUS' MINISTRY
(LK 7:1-8:3)

Lk 7:1-8:3 [or even Lk 6:20-8:3 (Ternant, 1971: 71)] is sometimes called "the little insertion" because it consists of material (six units) inserted at this point into the framework of Mark. Some of the content is found also in Matthew but not in Mark. More pronounced in this section of the Gospel than in earlier episodes is the ongoing negotiation of Jesus' identity by those who observe or who are the recipients of his ministry. Clearly, with the narratological crystallization of the character of Jesus' mission, the complementary question of his own identity has begun to move to center stage (Green, 1997: 282).

Lk 7:1 marks a transition in the narrative. Jesus has now concluded "all his sayings in the hearing of the people," and the focus of attention shifts to a more intense scrutiny of who Jesus is (Lk 7:1-9:50). The first series of stories appears to be collected around the identification of Jesus as the prophet. This is not a strict topical structure, since Luke appears to have continued to follow the "Q" traditions, moving from the "sermon" into the episodes of the healing of the centurion's servant (Lk 7:1-10) and the encounters with the messengers of John (Lk 7:18-35). But the note about the prophet that arises in the exchange with John's disciples (Lk 7:26) has now been supplemented with stories unique to Luke that highlight Jesus' identity as "prophet" (Lk 7:11-17,36-50). The first story in the section (Lk 7:1-

10) does not yet introduce the identification of Jesus as a prophet, unless one accepts the suggestion that Lk 7:1-10 is a reworking of 1 Kgs 17:1-16 rather than dependent on Q (Brodie, 1992: 54-71).

It has been suggested that Lk 7:1-10 deals with the larger issue of authority (Walaskay, 1983: 32; Tiede, 1988: 147-149). But it really is not clear that the focus of the pericope is upon Jesus' "authority," understood as miracle-working power. Indeed, in the story, the centurion compares himself to Jesus precisely on the characteristic of "authority"; he also stands under authority and has "authority" over others (Lk 7:8) and certainly not in the sense of being a miracle worker. What the passage affirms is that Jesus, like the centurion, has authority and his word is one that must be listened to and obeyed, just as the centurion's commands must be carried out by those below them. This is, then, yet another [beside "Lord": Lk 6:46; 7:6; and "word": Lk 6:46,47 and 7:7] thematic link back to the preceding parable (Lk 6:46-49), where the emphasis had been on hearing the "word" of Jesus and "doing" it (Lk 6:46,47). The focus, therefore, would appear to be upon the *contrast* between the authority of the centurion and the authority of Jesus. The narrative expresses that contrast in the admission of the centurion, "I am not worthy..." (Lk 7:6; Humphrey, 1991: 47-48).

In Lk 7:1-8:3 occur a series of episodes that highlight the reception accorded to Jesus by various persons or groups of persons as his ministry continues (York, 1991: 119; Johnson, 1977: 96-99; Ravens, 1988: 282-292). This series begins with the cure of the centurion's servant (Lk 7:1-10) and ends with the distinctively Lukan passage about the Galilean women-followers of Jesus (Lk 8:1-3). It will tell of his reception by a Gentile centurion, villagers of Nain, "all Judea," disciples of John the Baptist, and sinners. The keynote of the series is sounded in Lk 7:16, "'A great prophet has risen among us!' and 'God has looked favorably on his people!'" (Fitzmyer, 1981: 647-648).

The Sermon on the Plain (Lk 6:20-49) offered commentary on Jesus' earlier proclamation at Nazareth (Lk 4:16-30), where he propounded ideas that put under review the dominant hypotheses and class and social structures of his time. His stress was on God's beneficence that is to serve as a model for those committed to the kingdom. In the closing remarks (Lk 6:46-49), Jesus called attention to the importance of his words. In Lk 7:1-8:3 the performance of Jesus brings the divine beneficence to powerful expression. The same Jesus who called his disciples to "do good," even to outsiders, puts his own word into practice. The Sermon on the Plain had spoken about attitudes toward outsiders. Luke now shows through the story about the centurion how "enemies" can treat one another without acrimony. The age of the kingdom spells the end of weeping (Lk 6:21), and Jesus demonstrates the fact at Nain (Lk 7:11-17). What does it mean, not to judge (Lk 6:37)? Jesus offers an impressive answer in Lk 7:36-50. Lk 8:1-3 then terminates the series of benefactions with a summary statement of beneficence and reciprocity. Embedded between the story of the widow at Nain (Lk 7:11-17) and the recital about the generous woman (Lk 7:36-50) is the account concerning John the Baptist's quandary (Lk 7:18-28). But his experience is a dramatic exposition of Lk 6:22-23, and John the Baptist qualifies as one of the blessed (Lk 6:23). As for Jesus, his broad sympathies for outsiders necessarily brought him into conflict with strict interpretations of standing rules and regulations, and Lk 7:29-35 presents the sponsors of legal concern in striking contrast to the reponse of the general public (Danker, 1988: 156).

In the stories collected in Luke 7, the evangelist reminds the disciples of the general shape of Jesus' ministry by developing once again the themes of his inaugural sermon at Nazareth (Lk 4:16-30), but this time playing them in a different key. In the episode at Nazareth, Jesus cites the examples of Elijah and Elisha, whose ministry to Gentiles is used to warrant Jesus' own prophetic reading of Isa

61:1-2 (Lk 4:25-27). Luke 7 begins in a similar vein with
one account describing Jesus' healing of a Gentile slave (Lk
7:1-10), and the next (Lk 7:11-17) describing the raising
from the dead of a widow's son—the latter being an account remarkably similar to stories of Elijah (1 Kgs 17:17-
24) and Elisha (2 Kgs 4:32-37) referred to in Lk 4:25-27
(Ringe, 1995: 98).

The charge against Jesus of consorting with "tax collectors and sinners" plays an important role in Luke 7. The
complaint in Lk 7:34 of Jesus' association with "sinners"
serves a pivotal function in connecting the parable of the
children in the market (Lk 7:31-35) and the story of the
sinful woman (Lk 7:36-50). The parable informs the reader
as to how to evaluate the charge, that is, it is capricious
and unfounded. The story of the sinful woman then proves
that Jesus' association with "sinners" serves a positive function by producing repentance. Thus, all of Lk 7:28-32 and
7:36-50 pivots around the central charge in Lk 7:33-35 and
the purpose of this material is to vindicate the policy of
inclusiveness toward "sinners" pursued by Jesus (Neale, 1991:
137).

a. The Cure of the Centurion's Servant (Lk 7:1-10)

Following the demarcation of the completion of Jesus'
sermon (Lk 7:1), this pericope is effectively delimited by
the inverted parallelism of verses 2-3, 10:

A A centurion's slave is terminally ill (verse 2)
  B The centurion sends a delegation (verse 3)
  B' The delegations return to the centurion's house
    (verse 10a)
A' The slave is in good health (verse 10b)

The healing of a servant or son of a Gentile centurion
or royal official is recounted in Matthew, Luke, and John.
The Matthean (Mt 8:5-13) and Lukan (Lk 7:1-10) versions
are close enough that one may assume that they are based

on the same source, that is, on Q. There is indeed almost universal agreement that pericope came to Luke from Q, although there is disagreement over the amount of Lukan redaction. There is no solid reason to posit another source for this passage (Paffenroth, 1997: 41; for a comparison with Jn 4:46-54, see Hofrichter, 1987: 88-93). It is then held that "the narrative element in Lk 7:1-10 might be mainly the evangelist's composition, and the pericope in Q a short dialogue rather than a real 'story'" (Judge, 1989: 490). Very recently it has been suggested "that the segment of Q's opening section consisting of the temptation (4:1-13), the sermon (6:20b-49), and the healing of the centurion's child (7:1-10)—three form-critically distinct pericopes—was conceived of and executed as a literary whole in an editorial operation devoted to textualization of Jesus traditions within the framework of Hellenistic-Jewish parenetic genres.... The first section of Q was assembled with the intent of presenting Jesus as the fulfillment of the prophets and in his person and words the authoritative expression of the law" (Kirk, 1997: 257).

The Johannine version (Jn 4:46-54) is quite different from the Synoptic version, although the same substance underlies it. This author assumes that the Fourth Gospel was not written in direct literary dependence on the Synoptics.

Changes of place and characters mark Mt 8:5 as the text's beginning and verse 13 as its conclusion. In the Matthean version, a healing from leprosy (taken over from Mk 1:40-45) precedes the healing of the centurion's servant at the foot of the mountain, immediately after the Sermon on the Mount (Mt 8:1). In Mk 8:5 Jesus enters Capernaum, and the Gentile centurion approaches him as a supplicant. In Mt 8:14 Jesus enters Peter's house, where he heals Peter's mother-in-law (see Mk 1:29-31).

In Luke the story begins in Lk 7:1, immediately after the end of the Sermon on the Plain (which corresponds to Matthew's Sermon on the Mount). In Lk 7:11 an indica-

tion of time and change of place signal the beginning of
the story of the young man of Nain (Lk 7:11-17), which
Luke acquired from a source to which he alone had access
(often referred to as "L"). [For a detailed comparison of the
texts of Mt 8:5-13 and Lk 7:1-10, see Stenger, 1993: 100-
101.]

Since the text in Mt 8:5-13 consists almost entirely of
direct discourse, its segmentation is signaled by changes in
speaker:

  (1) encounter with the miracle worker and petition for
      healing (Mt 8:5-6);
  (2) declaration of willingness (Mt 8:7);
  (3) modified petition for healing, with justification (Mt
      8:8-9);
  (4) Jesus' words to his companions (Mt 8:10-12);
  (5) Jesus' healing words to the centurion (Mt 8:13a-d);
  (6) the healing (Mt 8:13e).

Luke's text is somewhat more complicated because it
includes additional characters and alternates between direct
and indirect discourse. Nonetheless, its segmentation is still
fairly straightforward:

  (1) connection to the preceding text and Jesus' change
      of location (Lk 7:1);
  (2) description of the situation (Lk 7:2);
  (3) the first group of emissaries sent with the petition
      for healing (indirect discourse), its justification (di-
      rect discourse) (Lk 7:3-5);
  (4) Jesus' departure with the emissaries (Lk 7:6a);
  (5) the second group of emissaries sent with the modi-
      fied petition (Lk 7:6b-8);
  (6) Jesus' words to the multitude (Lk 7:9);
  (7) return of the emissaries and recognition of the healing
      (Lk 7:10).

Among the more important differences, Matthew does

not include either of the two groups of emissaries (Lk 7:3-8,10), which is, then, either a Matthean deletion or a Lukan redactional addition. The latter solution is to be preferred (Gagnon, 1994: 128-145) notwithstanding extensively argued arguments to the contrary (Wegner, 1985: 238-255; Dauer, 1984: 39-125). The strongest argument for Lukan redaction is simply that the double-delegation motif embodies significant Lukan themes. The intervention of the Jewish elders on behalf of the centurion underscores the compatibility of the Gentile mission with the Jewish heritage on the basis of the pro-Jewish attitude of Gentile converts to the Christian faith. The creation of a second delegation both gives Jesus time to demonstrate his willingness to visit the house of a Gentile and underscores the centurion's great humility. The latter in turn illustrates the proper attitude of patrons and the socially advantaged in Luke's community toward others in the household of God (Gagnon, 1994: 144).

The petition for healing on the lips of the centurion occurs only in Matthew (Mt 8:6) and the centurion's remark, "therefore I did not presume to come to you," occurs only in Luke (Lk 7:7). Furthermore, Mt 8:11-12 does not occur in this story in Luke, who includes these verses in a different context (Lk 13:28-29). But the agreements in this material show that it does come from Q. Either Matthew inserted the verses here, or Luke deleted them from the story and put them elsewhere.

There are also less significant differences. It is not entirely clear whether Matthew is referring to the centurion's "servant" or "child" since the Greek word *pais* allows either translation. Luke clearly refers to the centurion's "servant" or "slave" (Greek *doulos*). The symptoms of the illness are portayed differently: In Matthew the sick person is "paralyzed" and "in terrible distress" (Mt 8:6). In Luke he is "at the point of death" (Lk 7:2). The remark that the slave "was dear" to the centurion (Lk 7:2) does not occur in

Matthew. Jesus' words of healing (Mt 8:13) do not occur in
Luke. Instead, the returning emissaries are involved in the
confirmation of success (Lk 7:10). Matthew mentions the
"very moment" of healing (Stenger, 1993: 102-103).

Four stages have been suggested in the evolution of Lk
7:1-10:

(1) the primary formation in Q;
(2) the adoption and modification of the Q tradition
by the tradents of Lukan *Sondergut* (Special Lukan
material = L);
(3) the adoption and redactional modification by Luke
of the version in the *Sondergut*;
(4) the Lukan displacement of the A version in favor
of the *Sondergut* version (Wegner, 1985: 161-188,250-
255; disputed by Catchpole, 1992: 529ff.).

With respect to *genre* the story exhibits the usual features of a miraculous healing: symptoms, petition for healing, words of healing (displaced in Luke by the emissaries),
and finally the recognition of the success of the healing.
That the miracle worker is not present where the healing
takes place can also be identified as a possible topos of miracle
stories. Normally "healing at a distance" is used to heighten
the sense of the miraculous, but here this topos is the point
of departure for the uniqueness of the centurion's confession of faith. The confession attributes to Jesus the power
to heal through words alone even though Jesus himself may
be physically absent. Although the centurion virtually per-
sonifies the illness in his confession of faith, likening it to
a soldier or slave (Lk 7:8), what he says remains within the
parameters of the genre, which in accord with its Jewish
background regards demonic powers as at work in illness.

But healing at a distance is not the focus of the story.
That focus is, rather, the centurion's faith. The petitioner's
faith is indeed characteristic of New Testament stories of
miraculous healing. The supplicant's faith in the miracle

worker can be the requisite for the actual words of healing. However, the relation between faith and miracle in the New Testament is a complicated one (Suriano, 1977: 1361; see also Theissen, 1983: 129-140).

But the way in which this story uses the genre features "healing at a distance" and "petitioner's faith" together transcends the genre of miraculous healings in the strictest sense. The uniqueness of this story is its focus on the particular sort of faith displayed by the centurion, that is, faith in the efficacy of Jesus' words despite his physical absence. This modification of the genre of miraculous healing manifests itself in another feature of the story as well. Although in other healing stories Jesus mentions faith, the centurion's faith here prompts Jesus to do what normally only the observers of his miracles do: He responds with astonishment to the centurion's faith. Viewed against the typical genre schema, this reaction actually shifts the miracle story's customary choral conclusion from the astonished crowd to Jesus himself. *The real miracle in the story is not the healing but the centurion's faith.* So here again the story uses an element typical of the genre, but also alters it and makes it autonomous. Another unique feature here is that the story expressly emphasizes that the petitioner is a Gentile and that his faith exceeded what Jesus found in Israel.

Among the New Testament miracle stories, the one most closely resembling this one is that of the Syrophoenician woman from the Markan tradition (Mk 7:24-30). The Gentile woman humbles herself as the centurion does. Although the story does not focus as explicitly on her faith, Jesus does refer to her words of petition, and again the healing takes place at a distance. It seems that these two stories represent a *subgenre of miraculous healings* (Stenger, 1993: 106-107).

Some scholars classify the pericope as a pronouncement story (Bultmann, 1963: 38-39; Fitzmyer, 1981: 649), and more recently it has been called a "quest story," an account in which someone approaches Jesus in quest of something important for human well-being. The quest itself is the story's dominant concern, and the account ends by noting whether the quest is successful. A quest account focuses on the person who comes to Jesus, unlike other pronouncement stories where Jesus' saying is the point. In Luke 7, the quest is indirect since messengers for another are involved (Tannehill, 1986: 111-116). It has also been referred to as an "apophthegmatic miracle story" (Wegner, 1985: 537).

Verse 1:   After Jesus had finished all his sayings in the hearing
                of the people,
                he entered Capernaum.

The introductory words "After Jesus had finished all his sayings" provide more than just a transition from the preceding sermon. They suggest another step in the mission Jesus came to fulfill because the word "finished" translates *eplērōsen* ("fulfilled"). "In the hearing of the people" echoes "you who hear me" (Lk 6:27) and establishes the reliability of the witnesses from Galilee who would later bear testimony to the truth about Jesus' words and deeds (Liefeld, 1995: 103). The narrative lens is so narrowly focused on Jesus that he seems to enter Capernaum alone (Green, 1997: 283).

From the plain Jesus journeys to Capernaum. From the reference to this town one should not draw any conclusion concerning the geographical location of the Sermon on the Plain (Ernst, 1977: 239). The reference to the Sermon on the Plain (Lk 6:20-49) stresses the power of Jesus' *word*. But the reference to Capernaum prepares Luke's audience for a recital of equally powerful *deeds* (see Lk 4:23; Danker, 1988: 157; Ernst, 1977: 238). So, Lk 7:1 marks a transition in the narrative. The focus of attention shifts to a more intense scrutiny of who Jesus is (Tiede, 1988: 147).

Verse 2:   A centurion there had a slave whom he valued highly,
                and who was ill and close to death.

Luke's version of the story stars the centurion, but he never comes on stage (Bock, 1994: 635). Instead, he is represented by some Jewish elders (Lk 7:3) and some friends (Lk 7:6-8), who convey his initial request for help, advocate on his behalf, and report to Jesus his words of confidence and respect, which Jesus calls "faith" (Lk 7:9). The centurion represents the Gentiles who without having seen him love him (1 Pet 1:8; Talbert, 1982: 79). The soldier's nationality is not clear, though Lk 7:9 makes clear that he is not Jewish. Since Galilee was not a part of a Roman province until the death of Agrippa I in A.D. 44, the centurion was probably not on direct assignment from Rome but may have been a veteran who assisted Herod Antipas in his police force, which was modeled along Roman lines. As an officer representing Rome, a centurion would often broker imperial resources for the local population. In this case, he has done so by building a synagogue and is thus recognized as a patron by the village elders (Malina-Rohrbaugh, 1992: 326). In any event, the word "centurion" would automatically evoke in Luke's public the image of Roman majesty and power. And such would be the case even if the centurion had historically never been a Roman officer, for Antipas ruled by the grace of Rome (Craddock, 1990: 94). It is from such perspective of Roman ascendancy and the probable perception of it by Luke and his public that the pericope concerning this centurion is here developed (Danker, 1988: 157).

Mt 8:6 tells us that the slave was paralyzed, but Luke stresses that his life is seriously endangered. The fact that the slave has a terminal illness serves to heighten the anticipated demonstration of Jesus' power.

Verses 3-5:   (3) When he heard about Jesus,
                     he sent some Jewish elders to him,
                     asking him to come and heal his slave.

(4) When they came to Jesus,
    they appealed to him earnestly, saying,
    "He is worthy of having you do this for him,
(5) for he loves our people,
    and it is he who built our synagogue for us."

"When he heard about Jesus" undoubtedly refers to his reputation as a miracle worker (Lk 4:37). "Elders" (*presbyteroi*) does not mean here merely "old men," but "elders," that is, a special group of Jewish community leaders in Capernaum (Fitzmyer, 1981: 651), that is, civil leaders rather than synagogue leaders (Plummer, 1901: 195; Schürmann, 1969: 391 note 16; Marshall, 1978: 280; Bock, 1994: 636; different: Kremer, 1988: 79). Luke's Mediterranean public would sense the author's effort to highlight the prestige of Jesus (Danker, 1988: 158).

But we must take a closer look at the motif of the emissaries in order to determine whether it was traditional and omitted by Matthew or added redactionally by Luke. In both versions of the story it is significant that a religious antithesis exists between Jesus and the centurion. That Jesus is a Jew and the centurion a Gentile provides one of the essential features to the action: It is at the behest of a Gentile that Jesus does not enter a Gentile house! Luke underscores this antithesis through the motif of two groups of emissaries. The Gentile centurion first sends as emissaries those who are more closely associated with Jesus the Jew, namely, the "elders of the Jews." When Jesus gets closer to the house (Lk 7:6b), the centurion then sends persons who are more closely associated with himself, namely, his "friends." The distance between Jesus and the centurion is thus made to seem even greater: Two sets of mediators are required to bridge the gulf (Stenger, 1993: 104). But at this stage of the narrative, in which the first emissaries request Jesus to come, the listener/reader cannot expect a second delegation asking Jesus not to come under his roof (Catchpole, 1992: 530).

The centurion seems to perceive Jesus as an itinerant healer whose services might be used to help one of the marginalized people who regularly had to rely on such healers for their medical care. The centurion is portrayed as an admirable man, both for his generosity and for his efforts to obtain healing for his slave. One aspect of the centurion's praiseworthiness is his kindness toward and good treatment of his slave, but that compassion does not extend to setting the slave free. As is often the case in Luke-Acts, Luke appears to take for granted many of the institutions and customs of his society.

The description of the centurion is remarkably similar to that of Cornelius in Acts 10:1-2. Both are Gentiles in the service of Rome, and both are close to the Jewish community—perhaps to be understood as representatives of the group of "God-fearers" from whom many early Christians came (Ringe, 1995: 99).

The human interest in the story emerges with the pleading of the Jewish elders who are willing emissaries of the centurion (Tiede, 1988: 149). The Jewish elders, who in this story are friendly to Jesus (Brawley, 1987: 112), testify to the centurion's generosity and love for the Jews, to make the case that he is "worthy" of Jesus' aid (Marshall, 1978: 280). The centurion is their benefactor and the Jews "owe him one" (Danker, 1988: 158), so they also lobby on his behalf (Bock, 1994: 637). Josephus describes Alexander the Great in similar terms, showing that one need not be a proselyte to receive such respect from Jews (Klostermann, 1929: 86; Bovon, 1991: 340 note 20). While it is possible that the Jewish emissaries intend to characterize the centurion as a "God-fearer," that is, a Gentile who is attracted by the Jewish understanding of God and by Jewish ethical thinking but has not taken the final step of becoming a "proselyte," a circumcised Gentile convert to Judaism obligated to keep the whole Mosaic Law (Hendrickx, 1996: x-xii), the emissaries' statement does not need to be so pressed

(Fitzmyer, 1981: 652). Some scholars even think that Luke implies that the centurion was not a God-fearer or proselyte, for when such a title is applicable he uses it (Walaskay, 1983: 32).

The elders refer to the centurion as one who "loves our people" or "our nation"; he respected Jewish worship and had affection for the people. When the elders in Capernaum intercede for the centurion, they commend him for building their synagogue in such a way as to imply both the approval of Jesus and the author (Brawley, 1987: 149). He has acted out his sympathy toward Judaism in an act of generosity: "he built our synagogue for us."

In Lk 7:1-10, the aspect of patronage is emphasized: The centurion donated a synagogue to the community (Moxnes, 1997: 171). The Jewish elders portray the centurion as a broker and benefactor of the people. As Rome's representative in an outpost like Capernaum, the centurion would have found himself in the role of intermediary between the local population and the demands of the Empire. It would not be unusual for such a person to adopt the religion of the local population, nor would it be unusual for him to have underwritten the building of the synagogue as a calculated maneuver to win favor among the local Jewish leadership. In any case, this is how the Jewish leaders present him to Jesus. In this manner they discharge something of their ongoing obligation to acknowledge and advertise their benefactor's generosity and eminence. In the development of this account, it is critical to recognize, then, the basis on which these elders appeal to Jesus for assistance (Green, 1997: 286-287). Luke's remark that the slave "was dear to him" (Lk 7:2, "a slave whom he valued highly"), follows along the same lines. Although antiquity certainly attests examples of personal friendship between masters and slaves, such relationships were exceptional. But here the master's attitudes transcend the prevailing social norm (Stenger, 1991: 105). Luke's church was for the most part a Gentile Christian community. Through their experience of conversion from "God-fearers" to Christians they were able to recognize themselves in the Gentile centurion. Therefore, Luke shifts the story's accent to the centurion's personality. Luke portrays him as one who is socially aware, who loves his slave, who is generous and respected by others with no loss of humility, and who, not least, has strong faith. Here the miracle recedes even further, and both the petition for healing and the actual words of healing are eliminated. Luke's portrayal thus acquires characteristics of a legend, if by "legend" we understand not an improbable story but a story that depicts a significant person whose positive character traits are exemplary for the readers. The centurion becomes a model that the reader is to emulate (Stenger, 1993: 108).

Verse 6a: And Jesus went with them,

In the Lukan form of the story, Jesus accedes to the elders' request immediately. His compassion has no racial limits. This prepares for the sending of the second delegation of "friends" (Fitzmyer, 1981: 652).

Verses 6b-8:   (6b) but when he was not far from the house,
                the centurion sent friends to say to him,
                "Lord, do not trouble yourself,
                for I am not worthy to have you come under
                my roof;
            (7) therefore I did not presume to come to you.
                But only speak the word,
                and let my servant be healed.
            (8) For I am also a man set under authority,
                with soldiers under me;
                and I say to one, 'Go,' and he goes,
                to another 'Come,' and he comes,
                and to my slave, 'Do this,' and the slave does
                it'."

While Jesus makes the final and climactic statement (Lk 7:9), the centurion, through his representatives, makes a rather long speech for a secondary character in a pronouncement story (Tannehill, 1986: 115). The first emissaries themselves judge the centurion to be worthy (Lk 7:4), but the later emissaries quote the centurion himself: "I am not worthy to have you come under my roof; therefore I did not presume to come to you." This use of the same word focuses the contrast between the appraisal of the centurion by others and his self-appraisal. His self-appraisal thus becomes an example of humility. That he sends emissaries also serves this purpose, since he does not presume to come to Jesus himself. In Matthew's version the centurion does come to Jesus, but he does not allow Jesus to enter his house; his justification is that "I am not worthy to have you come under my roof" (Lk 7:6; Mt 8:8). This sense of unworthiness recalls Peter in Lk 5:8. In fact, comparison of Lk 7:1-10 and 5:1-11 shows that Peter, a Jew, and the centurion, a Gentile, come to Jesus in the same way (Talbert, 1982: 83). The centurion is not worthy to have Jesus come into his home, but neither is he worthy to go to Jesus, a point that shows that defilement by entering the house is not the centurion's main concern (Bock, 1994: 640). Here, too, the centurion exhibits humility, but this humility functions only to anticipate Jesus' statement about faith (Mt 8:10). Though the statement about faith also occurs in Lk 7:9, that Jesus does not enter the centurion's house is amplified in Luke. This, together with the contrast between the centurion's self-appraisal and his appraisal by others, focuses the Lukan story on the centurion's "virtues": His humility is presented alongside his faith (Stenger, 1993: 104-105; Schürmann, 1969: 393 note 23; Fitzmyer, 1981: 652). But whereas traditional scholarship has made much of the "humility" of the centurion before Jesus, perhaps a better word in the context of this dialogue would be "respect" (Walaskay, 1983: 34).

　　The centurion's deference to Jesus is amazing, as well as the sensitivity to Jewish custom. He simply will not ask Jesus for extraordinary considerations, although Jesus and the elders are already on their way. The cultural dimensions of the encounter are penetrated still further when the centurion observes that because of Jesus' extraordinary authority, he need not come anyway. "It is a fascinating account in which the two principals never meet and the anticipated word of power is never pronounced... It is a lesson in cross-cultural relations. The representative of world power comes with a request to one who belongs to a troublesome minority [the Jews]. It is a lesson learned with difficulty by imperialists in secular and ecclesiastical structures" (Danker, 1988: 160).

The centurion, himself a man of considerable authority, recognizes that Jesus' word is more powerful still. Just as the centurion's slaves and the soldiers under his command obey his word, so Jesus' word has authority over the forces causing the slave's disease (Ringe, 1995: 99-100). Verse 8 points to a perception of the kind of military discipline for which Rome was highly regarded. The centurion makes a minor-to-major comparison (Fitzmyer, 1981: 652-653). Surely if he, as a member of the government's army, is obeyed, so also the spiritual forces that are subject to Jesus will obey his word (Bock, 1994: 641).

It is possible that the insertion of the delegations (especially of the second) was secondarily motivated by Luke's desire to reserve the Gentile mission for the post-resurrection epoch of the Church (see the programmatic command by the risen Christ in Acts 1:8; Conzelmann, 1960: 37; Tannehill, 1986: 114-116). Yet this can hardly be the primary motive (if indeed a motive at all) since in that event the centurion himself would be responsible for delaying the Gentile mission (Busse, 1977: 158). Luke was probably well aware that the centurion episode in Lk 7:1-10 did not constitute the start of the Gentile mission – whether Jesus met the centurion or not. It was simply an important precedent for the Gentile mission. Lk 7:7a (not paralleled in Matthew) itself provides the literary rationale both for the centurion not coming to Jesus in the first place ("I did not

presume to come to you," that is, to make the initial request for healing) and for sending the (Q) message by way
of a second delegation. The second delegation primarily makes
a point about the character of the centurion, not the source
of salvation history (Gagnon, 1994: 138-139).

Verse 9:   When Jesus heard this he was amazed at him,
                  and turning to the crowd that followed him, he said,
                  "I tell you, not even in Israel have I found such faith."

The climax of the story comes in verse 9. Jesus' response
to the request is one of surprise and commendation, especially for the centurion's confident declaration of Jesus' authority. While the emissaries praise the centurion's good
works, Jesus praises his faith (Schweizer, 1984: 131). The
centurion's faith leads Jesus to address "the crowd that followed him" ("turning"; Fitzmyer, 1981: 653; Bock, 1994:
642). The faith of the Gentile, who continually understood
himself as "unworthy" to be in Jesus' presence (Lk 7:3,6-7),
is thus contrasted with the reception given Jesus by his own
people (Tannehill, 1986: 111; York, 1991: 119). The
centurion's words evoke Jesus' affirmation that the centurion's
faith exceeds that of Israel. Faith is defined in this passage
as a plea to Jesus to offer aid in the form of his power, even
though one is unworthy to receive it (Theissen, 1983: 138).
With the concluding pronouncement of Jesus the transformation of the tradition from a miracle story into a pronouncement story or, more strictly, an "apophthegmatic
miracle story" is complete (Catchpole, 1992: 537).

Verse 10:   When those who had been sent returned to the house,
                  they found the slave in good health.

Luke reports the miracle's effect indirectly. The slave's
healing is reported without any indication of Jesus' command to be healed (Grundmann, 1963: 158; Danker 19:88:
160). Luke does not concentrate on the healing itself, but
on the the centurion's faith and the pronouncement of Jesus.

The report simply notes that when the messengers returned, the slave was healthy (Bock, 1994: 643). Jesus' power, exercised in the act performed at a distance, reveals that he too is a man of authority (Fitzmyer, 1981: 653). The concluding statement bears evidence that the centurion's faith is well placed: Jesus' word alone, even without his physical presence, has power to heal. This Gentile is the first person said to experience Jesus' healing power when Jesus is not actually present with the person being healed. The centurion's faith is an important building block in the preparation of the apostles for their ministry on Jesus' behalf. By the example of the centurion Luke intends to illustrate a faith relationship that corresponds to Jesus' summons in Lk 6:46f. (Busse, 1977: 160). The authority of Jesus' word, which they will be commissioned to carry, is sufficient even in Jesus' absence to continue the ministry of teaching and healing with which they will be entrusted (Lk 9:1-6; Ringe, 1995: 100). Thus Luke has one eye on the problems of the Church of his day, in particular, the right of the Gentile mission (Wilson, 1973: 32).

b. The Raising of a Widow and Her Son (Lk 7:11-17)

Lk 7:11-17 is a story about the raising of the dead. The delimitation of the text does not pose any difficulties. It opens with a clear change in *time*: "Soon afterwards..." (verse 11). There is also a change in topography: "...he went to a town called Nain" (verse 11). The preceding story took place in Capernaum (Lk 7:1). Both stories have many actors, but the main *actors* in the first story are: Jesus, a centurion, and and his servant. In this story we find the same Jesus, but with a widow and her dead son. It is very clear that a new story begins in verse 11. Where does the text end? In Lk 7:18 an entirely new cast of characters appears. There we read about the disciples of John and John himself. Obviously something new starts. But as often happens inside macrotexts, in this case the Gospel of Luke, this new story is not

totally independent from the material which precedes it:
"The disciples of John reported all these things to him" (Lk
7:18). The disciples of John tell John about events that are
related earlier in the Gospel of Luke. This important change
of actors suggests that we can close the story with verse 17
(Vogels, 1983: 280). Verses 11 and 17 are both considered
to be redactional (Petzke, 1990: 92), and several scholars
have detected indications of Lukan style in verses 11f. and
16f. (Schweizer, 1984: 132).

The episode at Nain occupies an important place in the
construction of Luke 7, the cornerstone of which is the cry
of the people: "God has looked favorably on his people!"
[more literally, "God has visited his people"] in Lk 7:16 and
Jesus' statement in Lk 7:22-23. God shows his favor to the
Gentiles, to the "little people" in need, to the sinners, but
resists the Pharisees and the scribes who by their pride refuse
to enter the history of salvation and God's plan (Lk 7:30;
Rochais, 1981: 19).

Lk 7:1-10 echoed the Elijah and Elisha references in Lk
4:25-27 by the introduction of the Gentile beneficiary of
Jesus' healing, and it escalated the level of healing power
beyond what Luke had previously described by having him
heal the slave at a distance. Lk 7:11-17 further heightens
the picture of Jesus' power by telling not just of the healing
of a Gentile, but of the resuscitation of someone who is
already dead.

It has long been recognized that Luke has a tendency
in his composition to generate doublets and parallels, and
part of this parallel material is recognized as "gender pairs."
Among the epic or narrative gender pairs one has identified the widow's son (Lk 7:11-17) and Jairus' daughter (Lk
8:40-56). The double message in the parallel examples of
women and men functions as an epic rejoinder to the description of the composition of a social group to whom the
epic material is addressed or belongs. Women and men be-

long to the same community; they are united by common rituals and live together in mutual material dependence (Seim, 1994b: 729-730).

There is between these two stories a certain unity and gradation (Busse, 1977: 161; Rochais, 1981: 18). Luke shows that death (Lk 7:11-17), as well as disease (Lk 7:1-10), is subject to Jesus' power: he not only heals the sick but also raises the dead (Harris, 1986: 295). This story echoes stories in which both Elijah and Elisha healed young men (1 Kgs 17:17-24; 2 Kgs 4:32-37). In the case of the Elijah story, not only is the general outline of the story the same, but the very wording of Lk 7:15, "Jesus gave him to his mother," is exactly the same as the Greek text of 1 Kgs 17:23. In both of these stories that begin Luke 7, the evangelist portrays Jesus as a prophet in the tradition of Elijah and Elisha, thereby giving his audience a framework for understanding Jesus' ministry as yet another step in God's saving presence with them (see Lk 7:17). But it is especially in Luke 9, which forms the central hinge of the Gospel, that the parallel between Jesus and Elijah is the closest. It continues, however, all the way until the ascension (Rochais, 1981: 33-35).

At the same time, Luke moves his audience to recognize ever greater dimensions of Jesus' power and authority as his ministry unfolds (Ringe, 1995: 100-101). In Nain, Jesus raises a widow's son from death like Elijah and Elisha, eliciting the response, "A great prophet has risen among us" (Lk 7:16). Luke draws attention more often than the other evangelists to the history of the ancient prophets as a foreshadowing of the work of Jesus (Lampe, 1955: 173; Penney, 1997: 44-45).

Lk 7:11-17 is also an episode that foreshadows. In Lk 7:22 Jesus will say to the messengers from John the Baptist that "the dead are being raised to life" as a manifestation of the kind of ministry in which he has been engaged. Luke is not content to illustrate that report solely with the story of the raising of Jairus' daughter, to be recounted subsequently in Lk 8:40-42,49-56. He now introduces a story of the resuscitation of a dead person so that when Jesus sends the messengers back to John in prison, his words in Lk 7:22 will already have a concrete exemplification of this phenomenon in the Lukan account itself (Fitzmyer, 1981: 655). Looking ahead to Lk 7:22, Luke inserted Lk 7:11-17 as an instance of the dead being raised (Schweizer, 1984: 129).

From a form-critical viewpoint, the episode is a *miracle story*. Lk 7:11-17 has indeed all of the usual structure of a miracle story:

(1) human interest in setting the scene (Lk 7:11-12a);
(2) detailed account of the plight of the afflicted (Lk 7:12b-13a);
(3) a dramatic encounter with the healer (Lk 7:13b-14);
(4) a clear display of the effectiveness of the miracle (Lk 7:15);
(5) a chorus of wonder or acclaim that provides a clue to the meaning of the event (Lk 7:16-17; Tiede, 1988: 151).

The pericope may be more precisely classified as a *resuscitation*. This is the first of three resuscitations that Luke has introduced into his account (see Lk 8:40-42,49-56; Acts 9:36-43). According to form, Lk 7:11-17 resembles most the stories of "healing or resurrection along the way," of which the oldest witness is an inscription at Epidaurus reporting that Asclepius healed a woman who was being carried on a stretcher (Rochais, 1981: 19-20).

A parallel to Lk 7:11-17 is often cited from Philostratus' *Life of Apollonius of Tyana* (4.45), an account about a first-century Neopythagorean sage:

A girl had just died before she was to be married and the bridegroom was following her bier, lamenting naturally his unfulfilled marriage. Since the girl belonged to a prominent family, the whole of Rome joined in his mourning. Apollonius, who happened to come by, witnessed their grief and said: "Put down the bier, for I shall put away the tears you shed for her." The crowd thought he would deliver a eulogy .... but he did nothing of the sort. Instead he merely touched the girl, said something inaudible over her, and without delay awakened her. The girl spoke out loud and returned to her own home.

However, Philostratus goes on to comment that whether Apollonius detected some spark of life in her unnoticed by others or whether her life was really extinct and was restored by the warmth of his touch, was a problem that neither he—writing some hundred years after the event—nor any of those present were able to decide. Maybe under influence of this and similar observations, the question has been asked whether Lk 7:11-17 is a real case of a raising from the dead or from unconsciousness (Obeng, 1992: 87). Luke, however, entertains no doubt that the young man was dead (Danker, 1988: 162; Fitzmyer, 1981: 656-657). The contacts between the stories are thematic rather than literary (Rochais, 1981: 20), and while there are striking similarities, the differences are equally striking (Juel, 1983: 41-43; Petzke, 1973: 371-378). One has also pointed out the parallels between Lk 7:11-17 and the raising from the dead of Tabitha/Dorcas by Peter in Acts 9:36-43 and of Eutychus by Paul in Acts 20:7-12 (Muhlack, 1979: 55-71).

The question has been raised of whether Lk 7:11-17 is an *imitation* of 1 Kgs 17:17-24. Lk 7:11-17 exemplifies Jesus' Elijah/Elisha-like ministry introduced in the Nazareth pericope (Lk 4:25-27). In Lk 4:25-26 the Lukan Jesus cited the story of Elijah's providing food for the widow and her son (1 Kgs 17:8-16). Although Lk 7:11-17 quotes no Old Testament passages, many of the story's details are probably intended to parallel the stories of Elijah raising the widow's son in 1

Kgs 17:17-24 and Elisha raising the woman's son in 2 Kgs 4:32-37. Seven parallels immediately suggest themselves: (1) "Nain" (Lk 7:11) may allude (rightly or wrongly) to the ancient city of Shunem where the woman of Elisha's miracle lived (2 Kgs 4:8). This name (from the Hebrew *Na'im* ["pleasant"] and/or Latin *Naim*) may represent an abbreviation of Shunem. In any case, Nain was situated in the proximity of the ancient site (Price, 1996: 85). (2) Both stories involve widows (Lk 7:12; 1 Kgs 17:9,17). (3) Both stories involve the death of an only son (Lk 7:12; 1 Kgs 17:17; 2 Kgs 4:32). (4) Jesus meets the grieving widow at the "gate of the town" (Lk 7:12), as Elijah had met the widow (1 Kgs 17:10). (5) Both passages describe the speaking or crying out of the resuscitated son (Lk 7:17; 1 Kgs 17:22). (6) The clause, "He gave him to his mother" (Lk 7:15) follows 1 Kgs 17:23 verbatim. (7) Although the exclamation of the astonished crowd in Nain (Lk 7:16, "A great prophet has risen") approximates the widow's exclamation (1 Kgs 17:24, "Behold, I know that you are a man of God"), it may not be a true parallel. The Targum's paraphrase of the exclamation in 1 Kgs 17:24, however, provides a very close parallel, "You are the prophet of the Lord" (Evans and Sanders, 1993: 76-77). On the basis of the parallels mentioned above and especially between Lk 7:11 and 1 Kgs 17:9-10 and between Lk 7:15 and 1 Kgs 17:23, some scholars have argued that the story is an Elijah midrash (Gils, 1957; Schnider, 1973; but different: Turner, 1996: 238-244 who suggests a reference to the Mosaic prophet).

Luke's use of the Old Testament in Lk 7:11-17 has been identified as "imitation" (Greek: *mimesis*, Latin: *imitatio*). In an age when rhetoric dominated both education and literary composition, imitation was one of the basic elements of rhetorical training and method. It is within the broad context of Hellenistic literary adaptation that the question arises of whether Lk 7:11-17 should be seen as involving an imitation of the similar text which is associated with Elijah.

This calls for an analysis of the similarity in question (see Brodie, 1986: 247,249-259).

Should Luke's treatment of the text be categorized as a form of *imitatio*, or should we see nothing more than a certain coincidence of methods, and imagine that Luke knew little or nothing of the theory and practice of imitation? It is highly probable that Luke learned rhetoric, which was pervasive in first-century education. And if Luke learned, then he must also have learned imitation. But does this mean that Luke's narrative is exclusively based on the Elijah text? Apparently not. There are elements in Luke's text that cannot be explained on the basis of the older narrative. In particular it has been noted that, unlike in the Old Testament, Luke's account contains carefully balanced references to two crowds (one accompanying Jesus, the other the widow) and two territories ("the whole of Judea" and "all the surrounding country"). If one is correct in reading the account of the word going forth to the two territories as a reference to the spread of the word among Jews and Gentiles (Schürmann, 1969: 404), and if the two crowds represent a similarly delicate reference to Jews and Gentiles—the narrative implies that they merge and become the "all" glorifying God (Lk 7:16a)—then Luke's text, apart from its use of 1 Kgs 17:17-24, involves interweaving of a specifically New Testament theme—the glory-filled union of Jews and Gentiles around the death-defeating word of Christ. It may seem, from certain points of view, that the use of the Old Testament in Lk 7:11-17 should be described not as an imitation but rather as *midrash*. After all, the use of rather similar techniques in Luke 1-2 is often described as midrash (Laurentin, 1957: 92-119). In so far as "midrash" may be used broadly to refer to any adaptation or updating of the Old Testament, then Lk 7:11-17 as well as being called an imitation, may also be described loosely as a midrash; and there is nothing inherently impossible or incongruous about the combination of Jewish and Hellenistic literary techniques (Kurz, 1980: 192-195; Brodie, 1986: 262-263).

Luke-Acts is similar to other New Testament documents in claiming three common forms of external proof: the evidence of miracles, scriptural citation or allusion, and the inclusion of witnesses. The internal proof consists of the way in which important events combine all three as an argument for legitimacy. Lk 7:11-16 includes the miracle, the allusion to scripture, and supporting witnesses. In this case, a specific citation is not necessary, as the obvious typology with Elijah/Elisha is evident by the acclaim of the witnesses themselves: "A great prophet has risen among us!" (Lk 7:16; Denova, 1997: 101-102).

Verse 11:   Soon afterwards he went to a town called Nain,
             and his disciples and a large crowd went with him.

The opening formula, "Soon afterwards he went to" is very similar to Lk 8:1, "Soon afterwards he went on..." (Lk 8:1) and a similar expression is found in Lk 9:37. It is, therefore, highly probable that the formula comes from Luke (Rochais, 1981: 21-22). Nain was a town in southern Galilee, a few kilometers southwest of Nazareth, and forty kilometers from Capernaum, the place last mentioned in Lk 7:1. It is mentioned only here in the Bible. As in Lk 6:19-20, the disciples are distinguished from the crowd, perhaps to set up a contrast with John's disciples (Lk 7:18; Danker, 1988: 161). "Disciples" here does not refer to the Twelve but to the "great crowd of his disciples" (see Lk 6:17 and 6:13; Schnyder, 1978: 78).

Verse 12:   As he approached the gate of the town,
             a man who had died was being carried out.
             He was his mother's only son, and she was a widow;
             and with her was a large crowd from the town.

Luke calls attention to the "gate of the town," for the dead were buried outside the town. The most important person in the "entering group" is clearly Jesus. The disciples are called "his" disciples. These disciples and the crowd "accompany" Jesus. The main person in the "leaving group" is without doubt the widow. The dead man is identified in terms of his relation to her as "his mother's only son," and the townspeople are said to be "with her" (Vogels, 1983: 286-287).

This is the first mention of the dead in Luke-Acts. The centurion's slave had been at the point of death (Lk 7:2), but this young man was already dead. The Way of Life meets the way of death (Grundmann, 1966: 159; Schnyder, 1978: 82). The prince of life confronts a victim of death (Harris, 1986: 296). The word *monogenēs*, "only son," occurs in the Synoptic Gospels only in Luke, and specifically in three miracle stories (Lk 7:12; 8:42; 9:38; Klein, 1987: 36).

The clause "and she was a widow" is almost identical to that in Lk 2:37 (Rochais, 1981: 23). Widows were the women who suffered most in contemporary society (Scheffler 1993: 73). The plight of the dead man's mother is poignantly described. She had no family now and in effect was an "orphaned parent" (Bock, 1994: 649). Because a women had no identity in her husband's family until she bore a son, the male child was a source of great joy and security for a mother (Pilch, 1997: 47). The young man was the widow's sole mainstay. In a time when there was no social security, this was an especially grievous calamity (Danker, 1988: 161). There was no way out of her predicament. The son was dead; but so too was the mother. Without any significant male (husband or son) in her life to take care of her, this woman was as good as dead in her society (Pilch, 1997: 47). A widow who had lost her only son was the embodiment of a human being who did no longer have any future and hope ahead of her and faced only death. By raising her son from death, Jesus does not only give life to him, but gives full life back to the widow (Schnyder, 1978: 79,83). On the other hand, it is important to notice how the woman is central (Kluge, 1978: 203,204). The Lord saw "her" and had compassion "with her" (Lk 7:13; Vogels, 1983: 282).

The word *autē* ("she/her") is used four times in verses 12-13 (Harris, 1986: 296).

Surprisingly in a social context in which females are typically identified in relation to males, the dead man is presented as "his mother's only son." Following this the focus of attention is on her: *she* was a widow, the crowd was with *her*; Jesus saw *her*, had compassion on *her*, and finally, gave the dead man brought back to life to *her*. The interpretation of this pericope is fundamentally guided by Luke's location of the woman at the center of his story (Green, 1997: 289).

Perhaps it is significant that every example in the Gospels of Jesus performing such a miracle involves women either as the object of the miracle (Mk 5:21-43 and parallels) or as those for whom the miracle is performed (Lk 7:11-17; John 11:1-44). Luke, with his interest in pairing male and female stories of similar content and intent, presents the healing of the centurion's slave (Lk 7:1-10) followed by the present pericope. Lk 7:11-17 reflects Luke's general theme of the ministry of Jesus to women, and his special interest in the way the Gospel aided such disenfranchised groups as widows and the poor (Witherington III, 1990: 84-85).

Verse 13:   When the Lord saw her,
                he had compassion for her and said to her,
                "Do not weep."

This is the first instance in which the author refers to Jesus as "the Lord." Earlier in the Gospel that title is used of Jesus in the angel's announcement of Jesus' birth (Lk 2:11), and as a form of address that need not be seen as anything more than a respectful title, "sir" (Lk 5:8,12; 6:46; 7:6). By identifying Jesus as "the Lord," Luke prepares his audience for the miracle that follows: Like God, who is also frequently referred to by that title in the scriptures of Luke's community and in the Gospel as well, Jesus will be seen to have authority over life and death (Ringe, 1995: 101). So, that Luke writes "the Lord" is not accidental. "Lord" means master. In the presence of death, he was recognized by the community as Lord by virtue of his own resurrection and is now about to display his mastery (Danker, 1988: 161; Bock, 1994: 650).

Verse 13 constitutes the dramatic turning point and the christological high point of this episode. Luke's identification of Jesus as Lord, his remark concerning Jesus' response to the woman, and his record of Jesus' first words to the woman, "Do not weep," all point to an understanding of this account that does not in the first place accord privilege to Jesus as someone capable of powerful acts. Indeed, Jesus' miraculous power has been amply demonstrated thus far in the narrative, and tales of his powerful deeds have been broadcast throughout the region. Here Luke's focus lies elsewhere. Especially by locating the remark, "he had compassion for her," at the center of this account (Green, 1997: 291). Indeed, the Greek text of Lk 7:11-17 is organized in such a way that the words "he had compassion with her" occupy a central position. The whole story comprises 218 syllables, of which 106 precede and 105 follow the expression "he had compassion with her" (Menken, 1988: 109). This and more numerical structures (Menken, 1988: 110-111) suggest that in telling this story Luke wants to present Jesus as the compassionate benefactor of the mother rather than a performer of mighty acts—a suggestion that other approaches to the story tend to confirm (Busse, 1977: 173; Vogels, 1983: 273-292). Luke presents this miracle as a masterpiece of the compassion of Jesus.

The verb used here (*splanchnizesthai*) is very rare in the Septuagint; but it corresponds to the Hebrew *raham* that indicates a very strong sentiment, an emotion that grabs your intestines (Ternant, 1971: 73). The word occurs thrice in Luke, always in his special material ("L"), namely, Lk 7:13; 10:33; 15:20, which is the more remarkable since Luke does omit it in his reformulation of Mk 6:54 and 9:22 (Klein, 1987: 36 note 13). Luke identifies Jesus as the compassionate benefactor of this widow. That is, this is less an account of healing or raising and more a disclosure of the character of Jesus' mission and, therefore, of the nature of God's redemptive intervention (Green, 1997: 291).

Jesus' "compassion" initiates the drama, which Luke heightens by his use of direct discourse. The object of Jesus' compassion is the mother. His attention is on this woman who is a widow and whose only son, her sole means of support as well as being her whole family, is dead. Jesus' whole attention is on the woman; the storyteller seems unaware of the disciples, the crowd, the bearers, the mourners (Craddock, 1990: 96). No mention is made of faith, unlike in the preceding pericope. Jesus' words to the mother, "Do not weep," which at first seem jarringly inappropriate, remind us of Jesus' recommendation, "Do not weep," in the story of the raising of the daughter of Jairus (Lk 8:52), where Luke transforms the text found in Mk 5:39 (Rochais, 1981: 25). Only Jesus could say "Do not weep" and at the same time remove the cause of the tears. Otherwise such words would be hollow, though well meant (Liefeld, 1995: 105).

Verse 14:   Then he came forward and touched the bier,
                and the bearers stood still.
                And he said,
                "Young man, I say to you, rise!"

Jesus' words which seem at first inappropriate, and his hands placed on the bier on which the corpse was carried stop the funeral procession in its tracks. Jesus' next words, "Young man, I say to you, rise!," turn the situation around (Ringe, 1995: 102). When he addresses him, Jesus calls the deceased a "young man." But beyond this, the text provides no characteristics of the dead man. Luke gives him no personality, no character traits, no attributes other than being dead (Roth, 1997: 172).

It is remarkable that Jesus "touched the bier," for contact with the dead defiles (see Num 19:11,16; Sir 34:25-26). The "bier" is a litter on which the dead man, probably concealed only with a cloth, was being transported. As in other recitals of resuscitation (see Lk 8:54; Jn 11:53), Jesus addresses the dead man personally. The dead man is not merely a corpse, or a soul, but a person (Danker, 1988: 161-162; Marshall, 1978: 286).

Since Luke's account of this miracle at Nain has several clear reminiscences of Elijah's miracle at Zarephath, one should not rule out the possibility that Luke intended a contrast to be drawn between Elijah's expenditure of physical and spiritual effort in performing the miracle and the sublime effortlessness of the new Elijah in performing his (Harris, 1986: 297).

Verse 15:   The dead man sat up and began to speak,
              and Jesus gave him to his mother.

Three simple statements mark the healing. First, "the dead man sat up." Two terms are key. Referring to the man as *ho nekros* ("the dead man") adds a note of contrast to stress the healing. And the reference to "sat up" makes use of a term that appears elsewhere in the New Testament only at Acts 9:40, where it refers to Tabitha's resuscitation by Peter (Creed, 1957: 104). Jesus' effortless call to rise up contrasts with Old Testament examples of resuscitation. Elijah stretched himself three times over the boy he revived (1 Kgs 17:21), and Elisha touched the child with his staff and then later lay over him (2 Kgs 4:31,34-35).

Second, when the man sat up he "began to talk," a point that indicates a return to life. Again the response is somewhat different from Old Testament parallels, where in Elijah's case no response is discussed (1 Kgs 17:22) and in Elisha's case where the boy sneezed seven times (2 Kgs 4:35). A similar detail about speaking is present in Philostratus, *Life of Apollonius* 4.45 (Marshall, 1978: 286; Danker, 1988: 162; Bock, 1994: 652).

Third, "Jesus gave him [the boy] back to his mother." The Greek wording agrees verbatim with 1 Kgs 17:23, indicating that Jesus' act parallels that of the great prophet Elijah. Luke's description of the event notes the Old Testament basis for the popular assessment about Jesus as a great prophet (Lk 7:26; Bock, 1994: 652). The story had left the woman with the invitation not to weep (Lk 7:13). By restoring her boy to life and giving him back to her, Jesus gave her the power she needed not to weep (Vogels, 1983: 283).

That Luke's central concern is with the widow is evidenced by the *inclusio* formed in verses 13-15. At the beginning of this encounter, Jesus saw, had compassion for, and spoke to her; at its close, he returns her restored son to his mother. The young man's resuscitation is a concrete parable of his mother's, for with his life returned to him her life is again made whole (Green, 1997: 292).

There is no delay in the restoration of the young man's powers. The one whom death had laid low and silenced sits up and begins to speak, and the one whom death had taken away is given back to his mother. Life and family are both restored (Ringe, 1995: 102). Death destroys relationships; Jesus restores them (Danker, 1988: 162). The man speaks after being resuscitated, but the audience is told nothing of what he says because his point of view is of no concern to the narrative. The fact that he speaks simply confirms that he is alive. The dead young man is resuscitated, ostensibly because of Jesus' sympathy for the man's widowed mother (Roth, 1997: 172).

As said above, the clause "Jesus gave him [back] to his mother" agrees word for word with the Septuagint version of 1 Kgs 17:23. This is no mere Septuagintal window dressing but rather signals the key element of the story, namely that the miracle is not done in the first instance for the dead man, but for the widow herself, who is clearly the center of concern (Swidler, 1979: 215). The story succinctly illustrates Jesus' concern for women, particularly widows. It depicts Jesus as the benefactor and patron of widows, just as the Old Testament cast Yahweh in the role of the defender of widows (Ex 22:22-24), even if no man would trouble to defend them (Price, 1996: 85-86). The raising is a deed of compassion—faith is not a prerequisite, though the deed does engender the praise of Jesus as a great prophet of God. The act was also a practical one since it provided the woman with a means of support as well as a source of joy (Witherington III, 1990: 85). The widow left without kin by the death of her only son has her honor restored when Jesus raises the son from the dead (York, 1991: 168). The story is focused not so much on the raising of the dead son but on the restoration of the mother, whose place in the community is reborn when the son rises (Malina-Rohrbaugh, 1992: 330). Lk 7:11-17 has a widow-empowering function (Price, 1996: 87). In this and similar stories, e.g., in the apocryphal Acts of Peter, Acts of John, and Acts of Philip, "God looks after his widows through the agency of his wandering servants, especially insofar as the widows need a defender against the official patriarchy" (Price, 1996: 91).

Verse 16:   Fear seized all of them;
                 and they glorified God, saying,
                 "A great prophet has risen among us!" and
                 "God has looked favorably on his people!"

The disciples and the crowd that accompanied Jesus and the large crowd that accompanied the widow now unite in their glorification of God (Harris, 1986: 298; Sevin, 1995: 255). The expression "fear seized all of them" (*elaben de phobos pantas*) is found only here in the New Testament, but is similar to Lk 5:26 (parallel Mk 2:12). "Fear" is the natural reaction of people to a demonstration of unearthly power; but the recognition of the source leads also to a glorifying of God (Marshall, 1978: 286). Luke's audience for sure recalled Lk 4:25-26 and would recognize as accurate though incomplete the conclusion expressed by the crowd in Lk 7:16: "a great prophet has risen." The word play on *egeirō* establishes a connection between what Jesus does and the crowd's accolades. Jesus says to the young man, "Arise" (Lk 7:14: *egerthēti*); the bystanders glorify God with the affirmation that a great prophet "has risen" (Lk 7:16: *ēgerthē*). The word "arise," which Jesus had addressed to the young man, is now referred to Jesus (Danker, 1988: 162). The crowd's acclamation, the first time Jesus is esteemed as a prophet by characters in the narrative, confirms Jesus' comment about finding honor outside of his hometown (Lk 4:24).

The two statements of the crowd are closely parallel (Ternant, 1971: 76). Each statement must be understood in the light of the other (Harris, 1986: 298) and both should be considered as interpreting the people's "glorification" of God: "A great prophet has been raised up!" "God has looked favorably on his people" [more literally: "God has visited his people"]. The NRSV's use of the active voice, "A great prophet has risen among us!" misses the point that God is the actor in both sentences. The "divine passive" could be debated in many texts where it might not be clear just who the actor may be, but here the second sentence makes it obvious that this great prophet has been "raised up" by God, because this is God's visitation. This is the work of God and it is a divine "visitation." The theme of God's visitation occurs four times in Luke-Acts and only once in the rest of the New Testament (Ternant, 1971: 76). The concept of "visitation" was also part of the promise associated with the birth of John the Baptist, linking God's "visitation" and the "redemption" of God's people (Lk 1:68; Tiede, 1988: 152-153). Luke has certainly understood this exclamation in an eschatological sense; it refers to God's definitive and salvific visitation (Lk 1:68,78; 19:44; Rochais, 1981: 36).

The crowd's acclamations characterize Jesus as "a great prophet" and as the means by which God visits humankind. It would be a mistake to speak pejoratively of the crowd's estimation of Jesus as a prophet as though that were somehow reductionist. Whereas some interpreters insist that Luke employs the title "prophet" only as a deficient christological model, others accept it as a positive component of Luke's Christology. To support this view, one has, for instance, pointed out the echo created between the words of Cleopas, "a prophet mighty in deed and word... the one to redeem Israel" (Lk 24:19,21) and the crowd's reaction at Nain, "A great prophet has risen among us!" (Lk 7:16). If the second member of this acclamation correctly assesses the situation (see Lk 19:44; 1:68), so also must the first; and, in fact, the combination of the two places Jesus' mighty prophecy in a unique eschatological framework. This is suggested, for instance, by the adjective "great" attached to "prophet" and the eschatological implications of the divine "visitation." By attaching the Nain story to Jesus' statement to the Baptist, as the latter's prelude, Luke indicates one trajectory of his christological argument, which is: the *prophet*, acclaimed for mighty works, is the Messiah, *ho erchomenos*, "the one who is to come" (Lk 7:16,19f.). Moreover, the Q sequence inaugurated by the Baptist's question (Lk 7:18-35) embraces two crucial aspects of the ministry of Jesus which Luke associates with his *prophetic* role: it begins with a demonstration of the *mighty works* of the one who is to come (Lk 7:22) and ends on the note of the people's *rejection* of the two envoys of Wisdom (Lk 7:31; Dillon, 1978: 117-119).

Regrettably some Christian traditions, zealous to label Judaism's view of Jesus as "only a prophet" and to debate certain liberals as holding Jesus to be "only a prophet," have thereby miniaturized the image of prophet. Sometimes the rush to insist on how much more than a prophet Jesus was leaves neglected the rich meaning of the role of the prophet in the tradition of Israel. The phrase "has risen among us," which, according to some scholars may be a faint allusion to Jesus' resurrection, is more likely drawn from Deut 18:18,

"I will raise up for them a prophet like you [Moses] from among their own people."

Yet having said that, it should further be said that all Christians reading Lk 7:11-17 have their minds run ahead to the climax of the Gospel: God raises Jesus from the dead. Luke must have had similar thoughts; after all, the whole story of Jesus is narrated from the perspective of one looking back from a post-Easter perspective. But Luke would correct us by saying that while the resurrection of Jesus was the climax, it too was anticipatory in the sense that the Spirit that empowered Jesus was now to be given to the Church for its life and mission (Craddock, 1990: 97-98). The Elijah motif makes one other point when it is seen as a Lukan theme: through Jesus, God is coming to the aid of the defenseless (Evans and Sanders, 1993: 70-83).

Jesus' act of raising the dead provides Luke's audience with evidence of Jesus' status as God's agent of salvation. That this act is evidence of Jesus' status as God's eschatological agent of salvation is made explicit in the episode that immediately follows this one (Lk 7:18-23). The account of the raising of this dead man supplies Luke's audience with a narrative manifestation of one facet of Jesus' answer to the question put to him by John's disciples. When Jesus responds to the question of whether or not he is "the coming one" (Lk 7:19) by pointing to his salvific deeds (Lk 7:22), Jesus' list of salvific deeds includes raising the dead (Roth, 1997: 172).

Verse 17:   This word about him spread throughout Judea
               and all the surrounding country.

The expression "throughout all Judea" occurs also in Lk 23:5; Acts 10:37. News of what took place in southern Galilee is said to have spread to other parts of Palestine. This could be the sense of "Judea" here, because of the phrase that follows (Busse, 1977: 169; Fitzmyer, 1981: 660; Rochais, 1981: 28; Bovon, 1991: 357). The story circulates in all Judea, thus setting the eventual rejection of Jesus against a background of witness to his person as the instrument of God (Danker, 1988: 162).

This rather short text of seven verses contains in fact several stories. These stories fit into each other and join together to build a beautiful narrative. There is the story of Jesus sent by God to visit his people. This is a vast program, of which the trip to Nain is but one segment. This project can be further verified in the rest of the Gospel. The visiting of his people has been given a very concrete manifestation in the story in which Jesus wants the sorrowful widow of Nain to be consoled. The story of the restoration to life by Jesus of the dead boy, the only son of the widow, completes this story and makes the consolation possible. The miracle of Jesus' giving life to the dead boy, which strikes most readers as the central message of the text, is actually in the narrative a sub-story of another story that is itself a sub-story of still another story that seems to cover a vast program. The raising of the boy, which occupies a small part in the text, is subordinated to the consolation of the widow. Jesus' first desire when he meets the group leaving the town is to console the widow. This intervention of Jesus, a prophet sent by God, manifests God's visit to his people (Vogels, 1983: 283-285).

But let us return to the widow and her condition, which is clearly the focus of the story. She has just lost her only son. Her life is over. Who is going to take care of her? She is walking out to bury her son and bury her own life. She has no rights. She is alone, according to the law, as alone as any beggar, stranger, foreigner on the streets. Even though she walks out with her neighbors, it is unlikely that any of them will invite her in, take care of her, and assume responsibility for her future. She is now on her own. This is why Jesus has compassion with her. Her child has died. That is a usual part of life. It will happen to all of us. But what is not normal, and not acceptable to Jesus and God is what

individuals, communities—even communities who claim to
be believers—do in the face of death and isolation. Jesus
pities her. That word arises again and again in the Gospels
to describe Jesus' reaction to others' experience of injustice
and needless suffering, suffering that is continued and made
worse by others' choices and insensitivities and refusal to
look at what is happening, and change so that others might
have a chance at life, more life, any life. Pity—that emotion that reveals great sadness, even enough to make one
ill, sick, sick enough to throw up at what is happening.
That is not life, not the way God intended things to be. It
deeply distresses Jesus, and it makes him angry. The other
side of pity is anger, anger at people's insensitivity and cal-
lousness in the face of another's pain and need. It is pity
that allows Jesus to raise the widow of Nain's son from the
dead and so bring *two* people back to life in the presence
of people who could help and do not choose to, people
who do not even think to change the way society and they
treat one another in distress.

The mourners, her neighbors and friends and distant
relatives, accompany her on her way to death. They go
through the ritual of shared grief, planning to go to the
cemetery, to the ritual meal, and then go home, go about
their ways. But what does Jesus do? He stops them. He touches
the bier—he puts himself in the same place as she is—outside the community. He freely puts himself alongside her in
the place of contamination. That is enough to stop everyone.

Jesus saw a woman, a widow in the larger context of a
society that cared nothing for her, a woman lost and for-
saken, soon to be excluded from the life of the community
and city. Jesus saw her—a widow without support system, a
woman in grief, and he saw the effects of a system that
would do nothing economically, socially, religiously, or politically to help her. The widow had a lot to cry about, to
weep over. And yet, Jesus' first words are: "Do not weep."

What he sees revolts Jesus—that human beings are treated like garbage, leftovers, useless. This seeing of unnecessary suffering and death also infuriates Jesus. This seeing makes him stop the reality, interrupt reality, and give birth to something new. That is what his presence does in the world of suffering and death. "Do not cry for yourself," this is not to be accepted. It is to be stopped.

The funeral procession has interrupted Jesus on the way to somewhere and that interruption calls forth from him strong emotion, revulsion, and power of resurrection. Relationship to another in service, honoring the poor, acts of mercy, and acts that resist death and defy the injustice of the system and of an individual's acceptance of this death-dealing reality happen on the way to somewhere else. They interrupt all that we intend to do and take priority. Anyone, any unknown, any lost and forgotten person, anyone cast aside and not considered human and so to be embraced with care and mercy calls forth the power of God and resurrection in Jesus (McKenna, 1997: 157-160). This leads to the raising of the son, but—as suggested by the focus of Lk 7:11-17—also, and even first and foremost the raising of the widow, and all she stands for. So, the answer to the question of which "dead" person in this story has been restored to life seems rather clear. The central character in this story is much more likely the widowed mother rather than the deceased son (Pilch, 1997: 46).

c. Jesus' Answer to the Messengers from John (Lk 7:18-23)

No temporal or chronological markers isolate this section from the preceding narrative. On the contrary, Luke's reference to "all these things" ties this pericope directly into the antecedent material, so that the questions and issues arising in Lk 7:18-35 are firmly grounded in the portrayal of the character of Jesus' ministry, above all in Lk 7:1-17. As in Lk 7:1-10 and 11-17, so here the narration revolves around the nature of Jesus' ministry, his identity, and the responses he engenders (Green, 1997: 294).

John the Baptist's question is almost universally thought to be from Q, although verse 21 is widely acknowledged to be Lukan, and verse 20 may be as well. There is no need to

The pericope forms the first of three pericopes concerning Jesus' relationship to John: (1) the question which the imprisoned John sends to Jesus and his answer to it (Lk 7:18-23); (2) Jesus' testimony about John's role and identity (Lk 7:24-30); and (3) Jesus' judgment on his own generation's estimate of both John and himself (Lk 7:31-35). The text itself gives no specific setting to this episode. It is marked off by the close of the previous episode, the account of the raising of the dead young man of Nain, with a general statement that news about Jesus spread (Lk 7:17). The change in setting at Lk 7:36 signals a new episode.

The discourse from Lk 7:18 through 7:35 calls attention to John the Baptist personally and thematically (Mattill, 1979: 159-164). But the story of John and John's relationship to Jesus is enmeshed in a second narrative dynamic. The episode (Lk 7:18-35) begins by making an issue of how Jesus relates to the blind, the lame, lepers, the deaf mute, the dead, and the poor (Lk 7:22) as their rescuer, and ends by making an issue of Jesus' relations with tax collectors and sinners (Lk 7:29,34) as their friend (Roth, 1997: 173).

The presence and absence of John's disciples divides this larger episode (Lk 7:18-35) into two parts: Lk 7:18-23, where John's disciples are in the scene, and Lk 7:24-35, where they are not. The leading interest of Lk 7:18-23 is signaled in the word-for-word repetition of John's question. Repetition serves as a rhetorical device to impress upon the audience the importance of the question for the narrative. Therefore, what is central to this episode is the *question of who Jesus is*.

Form-critically, this pericope is to be regarded as a pronouncement story, with the pronouncement enshrined in verses 22-23 (Fitzmyer, 1981: 663), or, in other words, a saying (verses 22-23) artificially set in a narrative context (verses 18-19; Cameron, 1990: 38).

In the Matthean version (Mt 11:2-6), John, in prison, hears of "the works of the Christ," and sends a delegation of his disciples to Jesus with the question, "Are you the one who is coming, or shall we look for another?" In the Lukan version, John hears about Jesus' ministry (but no mention is made of Jesus performing "the works of the Christ") via his disciples, and sends two of them to Jesus with the same question. Luke's account is longer than Matthew's because he narrates the disciples arriving and asking the question (verse 20), and reports that in the presence of John's disciples Jesus performed many miracles before providing essentially the same answer to John's question as recorded in Matthew and uttering the identical beatitude. The emphasis in Luke upon the disciples actually witnessing the miracles of Jesus probably led Luke to compose the summary of Jesus' miracles in verse 21 and to introduce the reference to "two disciples" probably to emphasize their role as witnesses (see Deut 19:15: "the evidence of two witnesses"; Fitzmyer, 1981: 663-667; Nolland, 1989: 328). Thus, it is important for Luke's purposes to narrate the arrival of John's disciples in verse 20; so this is probably Luke's redactional material (Webb, 1991b: 279).

Verses 18-19: (18) The disciples of John reported all these things
                    to him.
               So John summoned two of his disciples
               (19) and sent them to the Lord to ask,
                    "Are you the one who is to come,
                    or are we to wait for another?"

The gossip network (see Lk 4:14-15) is reporting a new status for Jesus, and John seeks confirmation of it (Malina-Rohrbaugh, 1992: 330). The organization of Lk 7:18-23 is largely determined by the movemernt of John's disciples, who report to John, are summoned by John, are sent by John, come to Jesus, and are sent by Jesus. Their departure (verse 24) marks the onset of the next unit in the larger section, Lk 7:18-35. John has been absent since his arrest (Lk 3:19-20), though his disciples are mentioned in Lk 5:33; disciples of John will reenter the Lukan narrative in Acts 19. Here, mention of his followers helps Luke's readers to recall the two prongs of John's instruction (Lk 3:1-18)— his teaching in the area of divine election and social ethics, that will come under the spotlight in Lk 7:29-35; and his anticipation of a coming one more powerful than he, identified in Lk 3:15-17 with the Messiah. The importance of John's question is emphasized indirectly for Luke's audience by the long line of negative responses Jesus' activity has attracted already in the narrative (Green, 1997: 294-295).

Luke modifies the narrative to heighten it christologically by adding "the Lord" (compare Mt 11:2, who adds "the Christ"). It would appear that Luke is uncomfortable with Jesus' ambivalence about John's question, and that he applies an antidote as close to the beginning of the dialogue as possible. Luke has also paired the disciples John sends in order to make their witness valid, and has added verse 21, so that John's disciples are made eye-witnesses and are not dependent merely on hearsay (Wink, 1989: 121-122).

A comprehensive assessment of John the Baptist passages allows us to conclude that John's expected figure is described in terms of the coming of Yahweh himself to judge and restore his people. But John did not actually expect Yahweh himself, but rather, he expected an agent of Yahweh who, acting with God's authority and power, would come to judge and restore (Webb, 1991b: 286).

Attempts to explain John's "doubts" over the centuries have been numerous (Fitzmyer, 1981: 664-665).

Verse 20:   When the men had come to him, they said,
             "John the Baptist has sent us to you to ask,
             'Are you the one who is to come,
             or are we to wait for another?'"

Lk 7:20-21 is unique to Luke and shows the question repeated exactly in the form of Lk 7:19—repetition that demonstrates the fundamental nature of this question. John is described as "the baptizer," which summarizes how he was seen (Mt 3:1; 11:11; 14:2; 17:13; Mk 1:4; 6:14; Lk 7:33; 9:19). The envoys are portrayed as faithful, for upon their arrival they ask the very question that John gave to them (Bock, 1994: 666). The people's expectation concerning John in Lk 3:15 is repeated in the question of whether "we are to wait for another?" (Tiede, 1988: 154). John's question to Jesus as to whether he is "the one who is to come" clearly looks backward as well as forward: back to the promises in the scriptural tradition of the coming of an agent of God to renew his people, and forward to the fulfillment of that hope (Kee, 1996: 379).

Verse 21:   Jesus had just then cured many people
             of diseases, plagues, and evil spirits,
             and had given sight to many who were blind.

In a parenthetical comment, Luke gives the setting of Jesus' reply to John. The reference is unique to Luke, though Matthew implies something similar when he speaks of what John's disciples saw (Bock, 1994: 666). In verse 21 the activities of Jesus are summarized in response to the question of Jesus' eschatological role as "the one who is to come" (Kee, 1996: 380). Luke employs the phrase "in that hour," or analogous phrases—here, "just then"—at signal moments in the narrative. This is a propitious moment for the fundamental question of Jesus' identity to be raised (Green, 1997: 296).

In Luke's Gospel, Jesus' answers characteristically follow immediately upon the questions or requests put to him

(Lk 5:30-32,33-39; 6:2-4; 8:9-10; 9:38-41, etc.). In this episode, a summary report by the narrator of Jesus' activity
(Lk 7:21), that further explains "all these things" in Lk 7:18,
is inserted between the question from John's disciples and
Jesus' answer. The narrator literally interrupts the conversation between Jesus and John's disciples to point out that
Jesus has been curing diseases, exorcising evil spirits, and
healing the blind. This rhetorical device not only reminds
the audience of what activity Jesus is engaged in and heightens
the drama of the moment; it invites the audience to answer
the question posed to Jesus before Jesus does, yet answer it
in the same manner Jesus will. When Jesus himself then
makes the same connection (Lk 7:22), the narrative has
succeeded in aligning Jesus' and the audience's points of
view. Jesus' mission to the blind, the lame, lepers, the deaf
mute, the dead, and the poor is the definitive content of
an affirmative answer to John's question (Roth, 1997: 174).

Verse 22:   And he answered them,
             "Go and tell John what you have seen and heard:
             the blind receive their sight,
             the lame walk,
             the lepers are cleansed,
             the deaf hear,
             the dead are raised,
             the poor have the good news brought to them.

In the inquiry of John the Baptist, Lk 7:19 employs a
messianic periphrasis, "Are you the one who is to come?"
Jesus refuses to give a direct answer. Rather, he responds by
referring to his deeds. John can supposedly deduce from Jesus'
works that he is indeed the one who is to come (Brawley,
1987: 19-20).

    Jesus' answer to John's disciples is compact and aurally
striking. The brevity of each of the six clauses intensifies
their forcefulness. Brevity, rhyming, and rhythm all combine to heighten the stylistic level of Jesus' discourse and
therefore signal special importance to these words.

The blind see (Lk 7:21); the (lame) paralytic walks (Lk 5:17-25); lepers are cleansed (Lk 5:12-13); the dead are raised (Lk 7:12-15); and the poor are preached good news (Lk 6:20). Jesus' report of the deaf mute hearing anticipates Lk 11:14. The first and the last benefactions Jesus lists, "the blind receive their sight" and "the poor have good news brought to them," repeat benefactions promised in Lk 4:18 (Roth, 1997: 174).

The importance of the echo of Lk 4:18-19 in Lk 7:18-23 can scarcely be overestimated. It places Jesus' preaching and healing within the context of Isaiah's announcement of "the acceptable year of the Lord." Lk 7:22 highlights the messianic identity of Jesus against the background of the eschatological Jubilee release. The Jubilee release provides the background for Jesus' exorcisms and healings and for his concern with the poor and oppressed throughout Luke-Acts (Brawley, 1987: 20).

The order of the items in Jesus' response to John's question about his identity in Lk 7:22 is different from that in Lk 4:18. Preaching good news to the poor is last in Lk 7:22, whereas it is the first item in Lk 4:18. A literary precedent for this type of reversal is found in the Elijah/Elisha cycle, where the charges to Elijah are not carried out in the order given. In 1 Kgs 19:15-16, the call of Elisha is last; nevertheless, this is the first charge that Elijah proceeds to carry out (1 Kgs 19:19; Denova, 1997: 138).

The logic of the narrative may now be seen. In Lk 4:18-18, the audience finds a statement in eschatological terms of what to expect of Jesus' ministry. The Sermon on the Plain, healings, and resuscitation show Jesus in the act of carrying out that ministry. The scene with John's disciples (Lk 7:18-23) recaps Jesus' ministry to this point and connects it to Jesus' reading in the synagogue (Lk 4:18-19). Of course, this narrative logic is available only to Luke's audience, not to characters in the story (Roth, 1997: 174-175).

Those characterized to greater or lesser extents in Lk

7:18-35 are Jesus, John, Pharisees, lawyers, tax collectors, and the people. Their characterization is organized around two subplots: John's uncertainty about Jesus, and opposition to John and Jesus by members of "this generation" (Lk 7:31). The blind, the lame, lepers, the deaf mute, the dead, and the poor neither speak nor act, except to the extent that it reflects their healing (Roth, 1997: 175).

Lk 7:22 does not mold the reader's understanding of what it means to be the Messiah as much as it underscores the audience's image of Jesus as the scripturally-depicted divine agent of salvation. Luke is in the process of reforming his audience's understanding of messiahship, but the issue around which Luke is reforming his Septuagint-competent implied audience's understanding of messiahship is the issue of the Messiah's relationship to sinners. Luke's Septuagint-informed implied audience would not expect the Messiah to be a friend of sinners (Roth, 1997: 175-176).

In Lk 7:22, the blind, the lame, lepers, the deaf mute, the dead, and the poor are spoken of for the purpose of providing Jesus' answer to John's disciples with persuasive substance. The question to Jesus from John is, in effect, "Are you the one eschatological prophet mightier than I, whom I announced was coming?"—the question echoing John's announcement in Lk 3:16, "one who is more powerful than I is coming; I am not worthy to untie the thong of his sandals." For Jesus to have said, "Yes, I am the coming one" would have been merely an assertion (albeit a reliable assertion as far as Luke's audience is concerned) by Jesus. However, to say, "Go, report to John what you saw and heard, the blind see again, the lame walk, lepers are cleansed, and the deaf mute hear, the dead are raised, the poor are preached the good news" has greater persuasive weight and therefore greater rhetorical value because it goes beyond assertion. The rhetorical effect of clustering references to these character types is to recall both Lk 4:18 and the Septuaginal image of them (Bock, 1994b: 290-291). These character types are standard recipients of God's saving activity in the Septuagint (Roth, 1997: 95-141). Therefore, Jesus' answer presupposes that his actions toward these beneficiaries demonstrate both to John and to his audience that he is the coming one. To Luke's audience, then, Jesus' words and actions toward the blind, the lame, lepers, the deaf mute, the dead, and the poor confirm him to be God's unique eschatological agent of salvation. Moreover, in Septuagint-like fashion, clustering references to these character types serves to heighten the magnificence of Jesus' saving action (Roth, 1997: 176-177).

Verse 23:   And blessed is anyone who takes no offense at me."

The force of the final verse in this section should not be overlooked. What Jesus is here depicted as saying and doing is highly controversial, since it is a direct challenge to the widespread concern among Jews of this period for maintenance of ritual and ethnic purity (Kee, 1996: 381).

Lk 7:23 raises the implied audience's expectation that some who come into contact with Jesus are and will be further scandalized by Jesus, and assures the audience that Jesus is aware of the opposition his words and actions engender. Almost immediately the audience receives clarification as to the identity of those scandalized, specifically the Pharisees and lawyers (Lk 7:30). But Pharisees and lawyers are not scandalized because Jesus bestows benefactions upon the blind, the lame, lepers, the deaf mute, the dead, and the poor. Rather, they are scandalized because Jesus consorts with tax collectors and sinners and discounts religious codes (Lk 5:21,30; 6:7; 7:34). Because their "proofs" from lifestyle are inconsistent, that is, proof that John has a demon is his asceticism and proof that Jesus is ungodly in his "gluttonism" (Lk 7:33-34), the opponents' actual point of contention with John and Jesus is shown to relate to what the two have in common. Both fraternize with tax collectors (Lk 3:12-13; 5:30; 7:29,34; Roth, 1997: 176).

The end of Jesus' answer is a beatitude uttered over the person who does not cling to preconceived ideas of him. The person who realizes that he has come as the embodiment of the blessings for humanity once announced by Isaiah and not as a fiery reformer will not find him to be a stumbling block (*skandalon*) in his/her life. None is to take offense at him (Fitzmyer, 1981: 665).

d. Jesus' Testimony to John (Lk 7:24-30)

Jesus' testimony about John is appended to the pronouncement story that preceded (Lk 7:18-23); it further defines the relationship of the two of them, to one another and to God's salvific plan. Jesus' testimony clearly relates John to God's plan of salvation; this is the burden not only of the testimony-verses proper but also of the appended comment of the evangelist (Lk 7:29-30; Fitzmyer, 1981: 670,671).

Verses 24-25: (24) When John's messengers had gone,
Jesus began to speak to the crowds about John:
"What did you go out into the wilderness to
look at?
A reed shaken by the wind?
(25) What then did you go out to see?
Someone dressed in soft robes?
Look, those who put on fine clothing and live
in luxury
are in royal palaces.
(26) What then did you go out to see?
A prophet?
Yes, I tell you, and more than a prophet.

The topic now changes from the role of Jesus to that of John (Liefeld, 1995: 107). The rhetorical questions first reveal what John was not, and his role is suggested in contrast to them. That implies that John is in prison precisely because he was not such (Fitzmyer, 1981: 673-674).

Verse 25 is the medial term of a threefold characterization of John, beginning in Lk 7:24b with the image of a shaken reed and ending in Lk 7:26 with the reference to a prophet. Rhetorical "build-up" is apparent in the way the questions are ordered. The initial description of John is taken from the realm of "nature": an inert plant whose agitated movements are due to the tumult of the wind. The final portrait is "supernatural": John would be the latest manifestation of the spirit of prophecy, whose agitation reflects the tumult of God. The logical fulcrum of this progression is the saying in Lk 7:25.

Despite the saying's obvious rhetorical importance, it has been given very little attention beyond the requisite paraphrase of the verse by thorough commentaries (e.g., Fitzmyer, 1981: 673-674). Entire books devoted to John do not discuss the saying, except for a brief note. But, again, it is verse 25 that ultimately makes the argument of Lk 7:24b-26 persuasive (Hoffmann, 1982: 217). Why this oversight?

Some unstated presuppositions are plainly operative in Lk 7:24b-26. One is why anyone would have ventured out into the ancient wilderness (*erēmos*) in the first place. Hence the opening question: "What did you go out into the wilderness to look at?" repeated then as: "What then did you go out to see?" Evidently, one could see "a reed shaken by the wind." But the fact that no further comment is made before moving on to the next possibility implies that this was unlikely to have been the reason why anyone undertook such a foray.

Sometimes, it is thought that the reference in Lk 7:24b to a buffeted reed recalls John's personal drama (Schweizer, 1975: 260). The verse is thus subjected to a metaphorical or moral interpretation. But none of these interpretations is convincing because, e.g., they say nothing about the fact that the reed is *in the wilderness* or that the persons dressed in soft robes are *in the royal palace*.

Returning to the question why anyone would have ventured into the desert, a real possibility is that they hoped to find a prophet there. The appearance at this time of different dissentient persons and communities in the uninhabited regions of Judea and Galilee is well known. The final comment made in verse 26c suggests, moreover, that most would have agreed that such a prospect was sufficiently compelling to draw them out of their towns and villages into the surrounding wilderness. In fact, it is implied, this is precisely what many people expected John to be. Not a few persons went out to see him, thinking that he was a prophet. At the same time, verse 26 makes clear that such a belief was erroneous: "Indeed, I tell you (*nai legō humin*), John is even (*kai*) more than a prophet."

Both of these first and final reasons why one might have gone out into the desert receive in verses 24b and 26 a negative reply—the first (Lk 7:24b), though factually true, because of insufficient motivation; the final (Lk 7:26), though factually true and sufficiently compelling, because erroneous. John could have been a prophet, but he wasn't.

The suggestion of Lk 7:25 that one might go out into the desert to see a man dressed in soft clothing is different from the other two sayings that surround it, insofar as Lk 7:25 does not discuss a real expectation. Certainly, none thought this way about John. The adversative imperative *idou* at the beginning of the verse, implying the self-evidence of commonsense, plus the reference to royal dwellings or palatial life later in the saying, make clear the proposition's essential irreality (Fitzmyer, 1981: 670). The usual interpretation is thus that, in Lk 7:25, between the inadequate proposal of Lk 7:24b and the improper one of Lk 7:26, a certain fantastic, because absurd, possibility was imagined (Fitzmyer, 1981: 674). Lk 7:25 would be a throwaway line.

Such an interpretation is improbable. The high degree of rhetorical craft apparent in the overall construction of Lk 7:24b-26 makes it unlikely that a throwaway line would occur at its heart. The usual interpretation of Lk 7:25 exists by default. Lacking any other idea what the verse might mean, perhaps because the ancient connotations of its discourse have been unknown, scholars simply impute whatever seems best to them (Vaage, 1994: 96-97).

Recently a new interpretation has been proposed by Leif A. Vaage, one that finds the fact significant that John in Lk 7:25 is opposed to the use of "soft robes" and that such apparel is simultaneously and conversely said to be especially at home in "royal dwellings" and palatial life.

The diction of Lk 7:25 is anomalous in the context of the synoptic tradition, the term *malakos*, "soft," occurring only here. The implied subject matter is, moreover, not a typical topic of concern. Elsewhere in the New Testament, *malakos* occurs only in 1 Cor 6:9. The related term *malakia*, found only in Matthew in the synoptic tradition, there means illness and does not address the same issues as our text.

In Lk 7:25, the word *truphē*, "luxury," is also employed. Like *malakos*, *truphē* is found only here in the synoptic tradition. In Lk 7:25, the initial reference to a man *en malakois himatiois*, "in soft robes," corresponds to the subsequent description of those *en himatismōi endoxo kai truphei*, "those who put on fine clothing and live in luxury." Use of the term *truphē* in Lk 7:25 is likely due to the evangelist. It represents a redactional interpretation of Q. That Luke, however, understood the saying in this way is not insignificant for what follows. He too saw that a particular kind of characterization was being made here. Luke's association of "softness" with "luxury" is, in fact, a commonplace of ancient moral philosophy.

The anomalous character of Lk 7:25 vis-à-vis the synoptic tradition stands in marked contrast to the fact that the same terminology (*malakos, truphē*) plus the more general theme of soft clothing and palatial life formed a standard part of the polemic waged by ancient Cynics against their own contemporary culture. Especially important in this regard are the so-called "Cynic epistles." In pseudo-Diogenes, epistle 28, for example, at the beginning of a long harangue against almost everything about "the so-called Greeks," a telling weakness is taken to be the envy that they feel whenever they see someone who has "clothing that is a little softer." In pseudo-Crates, epistle 19, an argument is mounted against calling Odysseus "the father of Cynicism," principally because he was the "softest" of all his companions. After equating in general terms this weakness of Odysseus with the enjoyment of pleasure, the discussion then settles on his clothing. In pseudo-Crates, epistle 29, and pseudo-Diogenes, epistle 12, the Cynic way of life is said to be opposed to "softness." And in Lucian's "Dialogues of the Dead" (20:8), the last of the marks of the false philosopher

have had in mind as "softness" can be found in Philo (de spec. leg. 3.40-41). Persons who practice pederasty are under discussion. Philo thinks that in many nations, such people receive rewards for this "incontinance and softness." Among other things, Philo mentions that such "hermaphrodites" could be found leading the processions at feasts, and various religious rites. Against the wishes of Philo, it would appear that the social status of many of these "softies" was quite high (Vaage, 1987: 556-557; Cameron, 1990: 42-44).

It is only when placed in the context of such debate, one spearheaded in antiquity by the Cynics, that the "throwaway line" in Lk 7:25 can be seen for the sharp statement that it is. The suggestion is made here that perhaps those who went out into the desert to John thought that they would see the sort of person otherwise excoriated by the popular philosophers for lurid living, the sort especially prone to gather in the royal court (or presidential palace?) like flies at a banquet. Perhaps they thought for some strange reason that John too would be dressed like one of these sycophants, arrayed in cloth as purple as their prose, though John in the desert could hardly have been farther away from

and more inimical to the official center of power and influence than he was (Vaage, 1994: 98-100).

It is sometimes suggested that Lk 7:25 refers obliquely
to Herod's court (Fitzmyer, 1981: 674). Such a perspective
certainly coheres with the preceding interpretation of the
saying's original rhetorical context, given that the Cynic
polemic against softness found its most ready and telling
target in the palace of contemporary tyrants and despots.
In Lk 7:25, John is characterized as one who, like the Cynics, was the very opposite of these persons.

The same interpretation of Lk 7:25 may provide a clue
as to why John and Herod were elsewhere recalled as having been such mortal enemies. Josephus assigns a political
motive for the execution of the Baptist. Like the Cynics,
John appeared programmed for conflict with the highest civil
authorities of the land, finding in them the most blatant
instance of what was wrong with the surrounding culture.

The greatest resistance to this interpretation of Lk 7:25
and its characterization of John as a social carper like the
Cynics will come from those who still want to see John as
a prophet. It is noteworthy, therefore, and not to be ignored that, immediately after Lk 7:25 in the following verse
(Lk 7:26) we read that John was "more than a prophet."
This cannot mean that he was therefore somehow really
quite a prophet or an exceptional one or a prophet as well
as something else. Rather, it must mean what is flatly stated:
that for the person(s) whose judgment is here recorded, John
was "not a prophet, but more" than that. The term "prophet"
as a generic category simply did not suffice to describe him.
An altogether different category of classification was required
(Ernst, 1989: 62).

The characterization of John in Lk 7:24b-26 is best
understood when we compare the saying as a whole, but
especially verse 25, with the similar discourse of the Cynics. The rhetorically logical fulcrum of Lk 7:25, linking the
inadequate motivation of Lk 7:24b with the negative con-

clusion of Lk 7:26, rides on a certain sense of irony or humor. Like the figure of Odysseus in pseudo-Crates, epistle
19, who only laughingly or scornfully could be called the
father of Cynicism, so it is that only with an advanced sense
of the ridiculous might one imagine John in the desert as
"a man dressed in soft robes." The sheerness of the contrast, whose impossibility borders on the inadequacy of the
preceding suggestion, cultivates a climate of negative expectation for the subsequent and seemingly better proposal
of John as a prophet.

At the level of expectation, the answer to the first question in Lk 7:24b is strictly speaking yes, but actually no.
The answer to the final question in Lk 7:26 is strictly speaking
no, even though most persons in antiquity would probably
have answered yes. The intervening question in Lk 7:25,
whose answer is both strictly speaking and likely no, makes
this inversion possible. At the same time, by virtue of its
purely negative quality, a specific profile is implied for John
in Lk 7:25, not unlike the relation that exists between a
shadow and its owner. The developed image would be precisely the opposite of what is stated. Cynic parallels to Lk
7:25, as in the photographic process, help then to visualize
concretely the sort of man we should imagine (Vaage, 1994:
97-101).

Lk 7:24b-25 is paralleled in the *Gospel of Thomas* 78:

> Jesus said, "Why have you come out to the country-
> side? To see a reed shaken by the wind? And to see
> a [person] clothed in soft garments [like your] kings
> and your princes? They are clothed in soft [garments]
> and cannot recognize truth."

Perhaps the most conspicuous feature of *Thomas'* version of this saying is the lack of an obvious reference to
John. This apparent absence is variously explained. But is
there any reason to think that John is being referred to
here in *Thomas?* It is Jesus who is the speaker; conceivably
he or his followers are implictly being characterized. Note

that the text asks why certain persons have come out to the countryside? Whereas Q's emphasis is on the identity of the one in the wilderness, on *what* it is one went to see, the single question in *Thomas* probes one's reasons for seeking the truth, away from cities or towns, out in the country. The cultural critique of "soft" clothing has already been traced in the tradition. What about the metaphor of the reed blown by the wind and the statement about failing to know truth? A passage from Lucian's *Hermotimus* (written between A.D. 160-180) indicates that the metaphor of the reed shaken by the wind is not used to connote something ephemeral or someone who is unstable (against Fitzmyer, 1981: 674). The image is rather one of accommodating pliability, and makes sense in a context that addresses how one lives one's life and where one searches for truth (Cameron, 1990: 44-45).

Verse 27:   This is the one about whom it is written,
             'See, I am sending my messenger ahead of you,
             who will prepare your way before you.'

The phrase "the one about whom it is written" as introductory formula for Old Testament quotations is also found in Qumran literature. CD 1:13: "These are the ones about whom it was written in the Book of Ezekiel, the prophet." The quotation in Lk 7:27 is derived mainly from Mal 3:1, which reads in the Septuagint: "Look, I am sending forth my messenger and he will examine (the) road before me." The Septuagint version of Ex 23:20 may also have affected the quotation here; it reads: "Look, I am sending my messenger before you that he may guard you on the road" (Fitzmyer, 1981: 674). In fact, there seems to be more than just a slight influence because the *aggelos*, "messenger," in Exodus can also be applied metaphorically to the Baptist (Ravens, 1988: 289).

The shift from "me" in Mal 3:1 to "you" is the result of an adaptation of the Old Testament text to the gospel tradition. The purpose of the Old Testament quotation is to identify John as a precursor of Jesus; in this he is "more than a prophet" (Fitzmyer, 1981: 674).

Verse 27 identifies John as the precursor of Jesus (but see Bachmann, 1980: 121-155). The "you" in the quotation can in this Lukan text refer only to Jesus himself; he looks on John as the messenger ahead of him. The messenger spoken of in Mal 3:1 is identified in Mal 3:23 (4:5) as Elijah, who is to be sent before the great and awesome day of the Lord. Nothing there alludes to a "messianic" or anointed agent. So, if Jesus identifies John as the messenger sent ahead of him, that is, as precursor, it does not mean as precursor of Jesus as "Messiah" (Fitzmyer, 1981: 671-673).

Verse 28:   I tell you,
              among those born of women no one is greater than
                  John;
               yet the least in the kingdom of God is greater than
                  he."

Attention now turns to the response of the people and of their leaders to John and Jesus also (Liefeld, 1995: 107). Verse 28 gives a second reason why John is "more than a prophet." Considered as a human being John is the greatest. His superiority is affirmed but is not explained. Born of a Jewish mother (Lk 1:57), John belongs to Israel of old and had no peer in it. "Born of a woman" is an Old Testament expression for pertinence to the human race (Job 14:1; 15:14; 25:4). It is used of Jesus in Gal 4:4.

The meaning and function of verse 28 have always been a matter of much discussion. Its meaning is discussed because of two Greek comparative adjectives in it, *ho mikroteros*, "the one who is less," and *meizōn*, "greater." That the second is intended as a real comparative is clear. Many commentators take the first in the sense of a superlative (see NRSV). This is grammatically justified. The saying would thus assert the difference between status in the kingdom and one's natural status: the least in the kingdom is greater even than John, the greatest of human beings. But others have taken *mikroteros* as a real comparative and understood it to mean Jesus himself. Jesus would be "less" than John either as "younger" (in age) or because he had just asserted that John is the greatest of those born of a woman. If this second part of the verse is to be traced back to Jesus himself, the comparative sense would probably be the better. But if it is really the product of the early Christian community (in debate with the disciples of John), then the superlative sense would be better (Fitzmyer, 1981: 675).

Verses 29-30:   (29) And all the people who heard this,
               including the tax collectors,
               acknowledged the justice of God,
               because they had been baptized with John's
               baptism.
               (30) But by refusing to be baptized by him,
               the Pharisees and the lawyers rejected God's
               purpose for themselves.

In the context of Jesus' discourse regarding John the Baptist, the author inserts a narrative aside [a comment that is absent from the parallel Q material in Mt 11:7-19] of great thematic significance. [On the possibility that verses 29-30 represent Jesus' continued discourse rather than a narrative aside, see Bock, 1994: 676-677.] Here Luke explicitly and directly presents the theme of divided Israel, previously established through the words and actions of the characters (Lk 2:28-32; 5:17-6:11). At this point the author draws a sharp disjuncture between those who "acknowledged that God's way was right" and those who "rejected God's purpose for themselves." As before, the Jewish leadership acts in rejection, but here is the narrator's explicit condemnation of their negative response. It is tantamount to the rejection of "the will of God," a significant term in Luke-Acts that refers to the central divine purpose realized in past events of the biblical story and in the recent events reported in Luke-Acts (Tannehill, 1986: 176; Cunningham, 1997: 75-76).

The relation of verses 29-30 to the testimony is problematic. A number of commentators regard them as a continuation of Jesus' words (Schürmann, 1969: 422; Schneider,
1977: 172). But they are rather a comment of the evangelist, but not on Jesus' sayings. They summarize the reaction
of "all the people" and of the tax collectors (why should
they be singled out? Because they listened to John's social
teaching, Lk 3:12?) to Jesus—in this context to his testimony about John. Their reaction provides the background
to judge that of the Pharisees and the lawyers. Thus Luke
begins to pit the authorities in Israel over against the masses
of the people and those who are not so highly regarded
(Fitzmyer, 1981: 673).

The narrator does no longer remain reticent. The narrative integrates a direct evaluation between Jesus' words
about John the Baptist and the "people of this generation"
(Lk 7:31). This narrative aside serves as commentary upon
the story and evaluates the responses of different characters
to God's agents. The irony is that God did not slam the
door shut; the Pharisees and lawyers had ample opportunity
to accept God's representatives, but they rejected God's plan
and slammed the door upon themselves.

Lk 7:29-30 is the narrator's parenthetical remark following Jesus' comments on John the Baptist. The narrator
makes a clear distinction between the ordinary people and
the religious establishment based on their response to John
the Baptist. The distinction comes in the form of an aside
that provides the reader with a look into the thoughts of
those listening to Jesus. On the one hand, the reader is
given information that will help her or him form opinions
about the people, the tax collectors, the Pharisees, and the
lawyers. Lk 7:29-30 reiterates the baptism of all the people
and the tax collectors by John and makes a sharp distinction between them and the Pharisees and lawyers (Brawley,
1987: 23).

In Luke, Pharisees appear in only four pericopes, where

they are a part of the main body of the narrative (Lk 7:30; 11:39-52; 12:1; 18:10-11). More than twenty additional allusions betray an editorial perspective. Only five of the references with an editorial perspective have synoptic parallels even though twelve appear in contexts that do. This indicates that Luke devotes conscious attention to the role of the Pharisees (Brawley, 1987: 85).

The tax collectors are placed with the group that has responded in the correct fashion, a surprising alignment. The Pharisees and lawyers, on the other hand, are condemned by the narrator for their rejection of John and Jesus (Gowler, 1991: 215-218). The second level on which the aside functions relates to the reader's relationship with the narrator. The reader is dependent on the narrator for the ability to read the minds of those in Jesus' audience. Thus the aside reinforces the link between narrator and reader (Sheeley, 1992: 114-115).

The omniscient, reliable narrator creates ideological distance between the Pharisees and lawyers and the readers of the narrative. The distance is a measure of the degree of identification that the reader has for the characters. The reader, of course, is supposed to rejoice with the characters (Lk 7:29, "all the people who heard this, including the tax collectors") who justified God through their baptism by John the Baptist. On the other hand, the Pharisees and lawyers once again serve as negative examples for the reader. They have rejected the purpose of God. The paradigmatic usage of characters is achieved by the contrast between the two groups. All the people and the tax collectors recognized God's agents and responded to them positively. The Pharisees and the lawyers, on the other hand, either did not recognize and/or refused to respond to the protagonists who proclaimed God's purpose (Gowler, 1991: 215-216; compare Brawley, 1987: 59-62,204-206).

The reader is told that the Pharisees and lawyers rejected the purpose of God for themselves, since unlike the tax collectors and the people, they refused John's baptism of repentance. The roles have been reversed ironically; the tax collectors have accepted the will of God which the Pharisees rejected. The narrator leaves no doubt that they will reject Jesus as well (Sheeley, 1992: 142). The seriousness of the allegation becomes evident when the centrality of the motif of "God's purpose" in Luke-Acts is realized (Green, 1995: 22-49; Squires, 1993).

e. Jesus' Judgment of His Own Generation *(Lk 7:31-35)*

The degree to which Luke's parenthetical aside in verses 29-30 is integrated into the logic of Jesus' address to the crowds is indicated by the use of a resultative "then" at the beginning of verse 31 and by the parallelism of verses 29-30 and verses 31-35 (Green, 1997: 302).

This third episode concerning John the Baptist is in reality a saying of Jesus about his own generation of Palestinian contemporaries who have failed to understand John or himself. Like the preceding episode (Lk 7:24-30), it records sayings of Jesus which are appended to the pronouncement story of Lk 7:18-23. The unit Lk 7:31-35 is clearly composite (Cotter, 1987: 293). Actually this episode consists of a parable (verses 31-32), and explanation of the parable (verses 33-34), and an added wisdom saying (verse 35). In the Lukan context the whole constitutes an interesting reflection on the two preceding Lukan verses (Lk 7:29-30; Fitzmyer, 1981: 677).

Lk 7:31-35 is very similar to Mt 11:16-19 so that it is relatively easy to reconstruct the Q-text (Cotter, 1987: 289-293) of which, however, only the "parable" of the children at play (Lk 7:[31]32 par.) is traced back to Jesus by a considerable number of scholars (Nebe, 1989: 172).

Verses 31-32:   (31) "To what then will I compare the people of
this generation, and what are they like?
(32) They are like children sitting in the marketplace
and calling to one another.
'We played the flute for you, and you did not
dance;
we wailed, and you did not weep.'

Lk 7:31-35 is connected to verses 29-30 by the use of
oun (NRSV: "then") which does not occur in the parallel
in Mt 11:16. The key to this section, which is offered in
verses 29-30 in connection with people who either accept
or reject John, is now illustrated in a parable. The parable
refers not only to John but also to Jesus. Verse 30 is being
elaborated chiastically in verses 31-34, as is verse 29 in verse
35 (Du Plessis, 1986: 124).

Verses 31-35 have a great impact upon the characterization of the Pharisees. The unit is clearly composite: (a)
verses 31-32: a simile for "this generation"; (b) verses 33-
34: a protest saying about the unfair judgment of John and
Jesus; (c) verse 35: a proverb of hope for the justification of
Wisdom by her children (Cotter, 1989: 66).

The introductory formula, "To what then will I compare the people of this generation, and what are they like?,"
is found again in Lk 13:18,20. Jesus' phrase "the people of
this generation" cannot designate, at this point in the narrative, all the people, otherwise it would directly contradict
the words of the narrator in verse 29. The phrase must designate the "Pharisees and lawyers" (and their followers) of
verse 30. Therefore the Pharisees and lawyers are the ones
who arbitrarily rejected all of God's advances. They rejected
John the Baptist and Jesus for diametrically opposing reasons (Lk 7:32-34). No messenger of God has met with their
approval. Three interpretations dominate the discussion of
the parable: (1) The children who call out to each other
represent "this generation," which stresses the capricious-
ness of the behavior; (2) the children (this generation) call
out to Jesus and John the Baptist, who refuse to change

their lifestyle (Creed, 1957: 108; see also Marshall, 1978: 300); (3) John the Baptist and Jesus call out to others and they get no response (Fitzmyer, 1981: 679; Leaney, 1958: 145; Schürmann, 1969: 423-425; Zeller, 1977: 252-257; Neale, 1991: 137-138).

Gowler considers the second possibility the more likely; if the comparison follows the order of verses 33-34, the connection is clear: John did not dance, and Jesus did not weep. The lines are clearly drawn between the two opposing groups of Lk 7:29-30 (Gowler, 1991: 216-217). But Neale adopts the first option mentioned above. He believes that the saying was a proverb, probably already known in popular form (Bultmann, 1972: 199; Grundmann, 1966: 167), that should be understood without recourse to allegory. The children in the parable cannot agree and each group petulantly insists on its own way. Play is rather comically paralyzed by the selfishness of all concerned. The two call to one another (*allēlois*), alternately suggesting different games; first piping for a mock wedding and then weeping as in a funeral. A simple parallelism is the interpretative key to the caricatured complaint repeated by Jesus after the proverb (Lk 7:33-34). "Sitting in the marketplace" is the key to understanding the groups of children; one group "sits" and refuses to go along with the other (Fitzmyer, 1981: 680).

Two examples from the Talmud, one recounting complaints of boys who cannot join a wedding round-dance, the other the protests of girls because the boys won't join them in mourning a dead grasshopper (Jeremias 1963a: 161), provide important parallels to Lk 7:32. But, while the talmudic stories do confirm the image of petulant children, and do refer to complaints featuring dancing and mourning, they don't clear up the real difficulty with the image in Lk 7:32, namely, why the children are seated and why their complaints are described with so formal a verb as *prosphōnein* ("calling"). One has proposed that the children who complain are seated in a type of pout because their playmates will not comply with their whims. But the difficulty remains because if the children are complaining that their friends won't follow their lead, how will sitting down and "addressing" complaints to them be effective? This type of behavior is only expected if now the formerly uncooperative playmates want the seated children to join them. And that is not communicated in the simile (Cotter, 1989: 67).

Proposals that the simile refers to squabbling children in the marketplace have not been able to move smoothly to the application of the image in verses 33-34, maybe because one has not quite understood the similitude. If we should re-examine the word-cluster "sitting down," "in the marketplace" and the verb *prosphōnein*, it is surprising to discover that it is the world of the judicial courts which is evoked, not the world of the child.

The English word "marketplace" does not adequately communicate the multivalent significance of the Greek *agora*. As "the center of public life" it was not only the hub of commercial enterprise, but also the place of social interchange, religious festivities, and civic events. The word is also frequently employed in reference to the courts (e.g., Acts 16:19; Cotter, 1987: 298). The verb "sitting down" (*kathēmenoi*) is also especially used of courts, councils, and assemblies, and the expression *kathēmenoi en agorai* is, therefore, best rendered "to sit in judgment" (Cotter, 1987: 299,301).

Superimposing the world of children onto that dignified and prestigious world of adult/political institution creates a stinging rebuke. The children are sitting in the judges' official chairs in the marketplace, understood here as "court." There they pronounce their verdicts over their playmates. Yet no matter how their actions imitate the grown-ups, the content of their complaints expose their foolishness. They are, after all, only children. The image of the children in the judges' seats at the *agora*, and the examples of their petulant complaints have strong resonances with general Mediterranean culture.

Seen in this way the simile is a charge against this generation, not simply of immaturity or pettiness, but for carrying on a charade of wisdom while they pursue their own selfish and vacillating whims. The path of justice is completely obstructed (Cotter, 1989: 67-68). We conclude the discussion of these verses with a summary-paraphrase:

To what then, is this generation compared? It is like children sitting in judgment at the courts, who address their peers, saying, "We piped to you and you did not dance; we wailed and you did not mourn." The parable is designed to expose the self-righteousness as so much sham. No matter how "this generation" may convince itself by externals, and by the prestige of office, that it may pronounce judgment due to its supposed wisdom and integrity, its very judgments betray the superficiality it labors to hide (Cotter, 1987: 302).

Verses 33-34:   (33) "For John the Baptist has come
                          eating no bread and drinking no wine,
                          and you say,
                          'He has a demon';
                (34) the Son of Man has come
                          eating and drinking,
                          and you say,
                          'Look, a glutton and a drunkard,
                          a friend of tax collectors and sinners!'

In verses 33-34 the two extremes expressed in the children's accusations ("we piped to you and you did not dance; we wailed and you did not mourn") are applied to the rejection of John and Jesus. Notice that the issue by which they are condemned does not relate to the differences in the preaching of John and Jesus, but rather to the differences in eating and drinking habits, that is, externals. Just so, verse 32 is preoccupied with external behavior. The basis of rejection or condemnation is the non-compliance of the children's peers to their vacilllating fancy. In verses 33-34 there is an effort to capture this outrageous smugness by means of bizarre conclusions assigned to John and Jesus on the basis of their harmless personal practice. John's fasting is judged as proof that he is possessed. Jesus' eating and drinking is judged proof that he is a glutton and a drunk (Cotter, 1987: 302-303).

Many things are remarkable about Lk 7:33, although the image of John as an ascetic type ("eating no bread and drinking no wine") is not one of them. The noun "bread" sometimes means "food" generically (2 Thess 3:8,12). "Bread" and "wine" are stock terms for food. Such a depiction corresponds more or less to what is otherwise said of John the Baptist. But as far as we know, this is the only place where it is said in Q that "he has a demon." Indeed, it is the only place in the synoptic tradition where the expression "have a demon" is used (with the exception of Lk 8:27 which is redactional; cf. Mk 5:2, "an unclean spirit"). In the so-called Beelzebul controversy (Lk 11:14-23//Mt 12:22-30 = Q; cf. Mk 3:22-27) it is implied that Jesus was similarly possessed (see especially Lk 11:15//Mt 12:24; Mk 3:22), though interestingly it is only in Mk 3:22 that the evangelist says explicitly (viz, scribes from Jerusalem charge) that Jesus "has Beelzebul." In Q (11:15) one must decide whether and/or to what extent the prepositional phrase "in Beelzebul, the prince of demons" is meant hypostatically or instrumentally. Beyond these instances, the standard statement made regarding "demons" and their like in the Gospels is precisely the opposite. Far from "having" them, Jesus (and, at times, his followers) regularly expels them. Thus, while John, the "ascetic," is not an especially notable characterization, the declaration that he "has a demon" clearly runs against a number of currents. Yet the saying is clearly attested for Q, and particularly the initial literary stratum of the document, and so we must reckon in this characterization of John with a perspective from the earliest layer of tradition: one, however, not otherwise taken up (Vaage, 1989: 163-164; 1994: 87-89).

The same situation exists even more notably with regard to Lk 7:34. If we can assume that the term "Son of Man" in this saying refers to Jesus (which does not necessarily mean that Jesus referred to himself with this term), then the picture given here of him is one of a person who "eats and drinks," who is "a glutton and a drunkard, a friend of tax collectors and sinners." That he "eats and drinks" is clearly said in contrast to the preceding description of John. Otherwise, the very language of the saying, let alone its "meaning," is quite singular. [For a discussion of how we are to make sense of Lk 7:34 in comparison with other very loaded uses of the title Son of Man in Luke, see Fletcher-Louis, 1997: 239-246.]

To begin with, the terms "glutton" (*phagos*) and "drunkard" (*oinopotēs*) are found only here in the context of the New Testament. Furthermore, the term "friend" (*philos*), while common enough in itself, never occurs in Mark nor in Matthew (except for this saying from Q). Both terms "tax collector" and "sinner" appear only here indubitably in Q. Thus, just considered linguistically, 7:34 is already most peculiar. What the statement says of Jesus does not fall short of its speech. The man emerges, in current slang, as a "real party animal." "Eating and drinking," he himself commits what elsewhere in Q (17:27-28) they are said to have done whom the deluge overwhelmed at the time of Noah. Far from worrying about where his next meal would come from (as Lk 12:22 admonishes not to do), Jesus, according to Lk 7:34, apparently ate and drank well and often enough to be suspected of overindulgence. His behavior in this regard seems not to have conformed to the conventional image of religious seriousness and uprightness. Beyond these dubious personal habits, the further characterization of Jesus as "a friend of tax collectors and sinners" suggests that the company he kept was "not the best." He chose apparently to spend his time with those whom local society did not approve or laud. This is what "sinners" were in general terms.

The reference to tax collectors specifies the impropriety (Vaage, 1989: 165-166).

Jesus repeats the complaints as though they were the taunts of selfish children who cannot agree on the game they want to play. One should recognize the element of chiding humor in the proverb and thus in Jesus' commentary. In this way Jesus upbraids his opponents as petulant, dissatisfied children, for it seems nothing can please them (Jonsson, 1985: 154,169). Their childish inconsistency demonstrates their attitude toward both John and Jesus, for they found the asceticism of John distasteful and the liberties of Jesus condemnable. There is then a parallelism between the images of the proverb and the way Jesus describes his opponents; the proverb is meant only to describe the general attitude of dissatisfaction and indecision among all the "people of this generation" (Grundmann, 1966: 167; Mussner, 1959: 600ff.; Neale, 1991: 138).

The parable is applied by Lk 7:33-34 and so the objections repeated by Jesus appear as petulant "complaints" rather than serious "charges" in the sense of a legal challenge. The latter would be too serious a label and the taunts have none of the character of a serious assault. The text thus implies that these complaints should be taken no more seriously than those of such children. In response to John's ministry, great as he was among people, these "children" could do no more than dismissively announce, "He has a demon." What is more, in relation to Jesus himself their assessment is equally errant and unperceptive: "Look, a glutton and a drunkard, a friend of tax collectors and sinners." The charges are simply the product of a childish impudence and Jesus' repetition of them is an exasperated caricature of the opposition which "this generation" seemed to show to every overture from John and himself (Neale, 1991: 139).

John's ascetic life and his distance from ordinary social interaction is surely the issue here. The "un-natural" behavior of John seems to set him outside the parameters of

the orderly universe, and it does require an explanation.
On the basis of the "out of order" character of John's practice, he bears a resemblance to those who are also outside
the cosmic order due to possession by a demon. Like the
demon that controls them, these persons are seen as "out of
place" and therefore dangerous. Either eating too little or
eating without control are both extremes which signal an
absence of order. Combined with any other manifestations
of power, or demonstrations of alienation, these eating practices could warrant a charge of demonic possession (Cotter,
1989: 71,73).

The point is, of course, that John had no demon and
Jesus himself was no friend of "tax collectors and sinners"
in the sense that he shared in their dissipation, for that
presumably is the way the slander was intended. Yes, John
abstained from food and drink and yes, Jesus associated with
less desirable people, but it is the failure of his contemporaries to comprehend the purpose and intent of these actions that stirred the rebuke (Neale, 1991: 139).

The author of Luke-Acts employs the term *philoi*, "friends,"
as it functions either as a designation for believers or as a
more general term, such as the expression "friends and relatives" (however, even then it still designates a close-knit
circle). Of these occurrences of *philos* in Luke, only a few
stem from Q (Lk 7:34//Mt 11:19). In the first layer of Q as
currently conceived, there are no instances of Jesus or any
of his disciples being called a *philos*. Just as scholars have
shown that the identification of Jesus with the Son of Man
came in the second redactional layer of Q, so, too, the reference to Jesus here as a *philos* may come from this layer.
At this point *philos* carries with it a nuance of preference,
not yet appearing as a designation for a believer. A significant usage of *philoi-* and *phileō-* related words appears in
certain strands of early Christianity (especially for the author of Luke). There is a possibility that certain vocabulary
such as *phileō* and *agapaō* (like the particular designations

for disciples) are representative of different Christian communities, such as Petrine, Pauline, or early Johannine ones.
Thus *phileō* and related words may not deserve to be in quite
such a diminished position when compared with *agapaō*. Some
early Christians may even have had a greater appreciation
for the use of *philoi-* and *phileō-* related words than has previously been considered (Brock, 1997: 396, 409).

If John's *not* eating and drinking stands for his distance
from society's conventional order, Jesus' eating and drinking represents a way of wisdom that does participate in it.
If we view verse 34 apart from the influence of verse 33,
the enemies are not really drawing a conclusion on the basis
of evidence. They are contradicting the statement. For them,
Jesus does not just eat and drink, he gorges himself. The
connection between behavior and friends explains the inclusion of "friend of tax collectors and sinners" in verse 34.
This accusation intrudes on the balance created by "eating
and drinking," "glutton and drunk." But its addition communicates the enemies' heaping up of insults upon Jesus as
it also explains the sort of company that Jesus chooses for
his participation in society. The importance of one's friends
especially in an honor-shame society cannot be overempha-
sized (Cotter, 1989: 75). In the Mediterranean world, no
one would freely associate with you in covenant relationship unless your honor rating were good, and so good name
and prestige are most valuable assets (Malina, 1981: 34).

To say that Jesus' friends are tax collectors and sinners
is to claim that Jesus is as base as these people are perceived to be. Furthermore, it situates Jesus with them on
the fringes of society. Thus Jesus can hardly be considered
a sage. Just as a charge of "devil worship" is a label that
marks an enemy as dangerous and his religion as false, so
too these charges of gluttony, drunkenness, and friendships
with the basest people serve as a label, and for the same
purpose (Cotter, 1989: 76).

Whatever verses 33 and 34 may originally have meant

separately in the tradition, once they are combined the charges against Jesus are balanced against those made against John and both verses work together to expose the superficiality of the accusers. This is accomplished by demonstrating that John and Jesus representing two opposite roads to wisdom are both viciously labeled and rejected on grounds that shift with each hero. In this way verses 33-34 act together to rebut the condemnations by means of a condemnation of their own. The result is that the honor of both John and Jesus is maintained (Cotter, 1989: 77-78).

Verse 35:   Nevertheless, wisdom is vindicated by all her
                children."

Almost every word in this short verse presents difficulties. What, for instance, is meant by *edikaiōthe* (NRSV: "is vindicated")? Who is the *sophia*, "wisdom," referred to and why is it used and not *theos*, "God"? And who are the "children"? We are faced in this short verse with problems of interpretation regarding both the subject and the object as well as the predicate of the sentence. So many difficulties in one verse weaken the position of any interpreter in taking a strong stand on any solution he may offer. If one of these words should be proved to be wrongly interpreted, it might upset the whole applecart. Therefore, one has attempted to interpret the verse based on the understanding of the whole of Lk 7:1-50. What is the point that Luke wished to make in this chapter that forms a unit on its own? The clash with the Pharisees and the scribes which was interrupted by the Sermon on the Plain is taken up again in Luke 7. People are confronted to come to a decisive choice —for or against Jesus. Luke uses this confrontation to define the identity of Jesus. The whole chapter points to the fact that even though pagans, sinners, and tax collectors have accepted God's grace in Jesus, those people in Israel who should have accepted him have not done so. In Lk 7:31 Luke refers to "the people of this generation" who have

actually rejected the offer of God. Lk 7:1-50 could therefore be summarized as follows: "God has turned to his people
but only some have accepted Him while Israel's leaders (and
all who should have known better) have rejected Him." This
explains why Luke locates the pericopes about John the Baptist
(Lk 7:18-35) in the center of this series of episodes, namely
because the identity of Jesus is so clearly defined and ac-
centuated in this passage. In Lk 7:18-35 we have, on the
one hand, the issue of Jesus' relationship to John the Baptist and, on the other hand, the attitude of people toward
both of them (Du Plessis, 1986: 112-114,119).

The main features in verses 29 and 35 represent a balanced and even chiastic parallelism that can be clearly seen
in the Greek text that follows:

v. 29:   *kai pas ho laos* ....*edikaiosan ton theon*
v. 35:   *kai edikaiōthē hē sophia*......*pantōn tōn teknōn*

The way *theos* and *sophia* are used in this parallel very
strongly supports the suggestion that *sophia* refers to God
himself (Du Plessis, 1986: 124).

Seen within the context of Luke 7 as a whole it is suggested that Lk 7:35 should be understood as follows: From
all the people, who included Gentiles (Lk 7:1-10), tax collectors (Lk 7:29), and sinners (Lk 7:36-50) come the "children" of "wisdom" (Lk 7:35) who accepted God's purpose
for them (Lk 7:30) and acknowledge that God's way is right
(Lk 7:29). By acknowledging that God's way is right they
recognize and acknowledge God's plan (*boulē*, Lk 7:30) which
appears in both John and Jesus. The Pharisees, however,
reject both John and Jesus. Thus the Pharisees reject God's
purpose for them (Du Plessis, 1986: 125).

But why does Luke use *sophia* in Lk 7:35 as a periphrasis for God? It is well known that the Q-source, which Luke
uses in this pericope, has a typical *wisdom* character. Probably, behind the saying in Lk 7:35 lies the Jewish tradition
concerning wisdom as a quasi-personal *hypostasis* who

preaches to people and longs to dwell among them but is
rejected by them. If we accept that Luke quotes literally
from his source and thus uses *sophia*, it explains why he
refers to the *boulē tou theou*, "God's purpose," in verse 30
which he inserts into the Q-material. In verse 30 he comments in his own words on the reactions of people to God's
plan and therefore he refers to God with the usual Greek
term *theos*. The *sophia* refers to God whose plan is proved
to be the right one by those who accept it. Luke stays true
to his source in Lk 7:35 and uses *sophia*, but then as referring to God himself. Because of the connotation of *sophia*
it is justifiable to understand verse 35 as including the idea
of God's plan as a *wise* plan of salvation. This plan is proved
to be wise and is also experienced as a wise plan by everyone who accepts it, thus demonstrating that they are truly
the "children" of God (Du Plessis, 1986: 125-126).

Jesus dismisses the whole business with another proverb. It distinguishes itself from the preceding unit by its use
of *tekna*, "children," instead of copying the *paidiois*, "children," of verse 32. Intelligible on its own, it could have
traveled quite independently. Two passages from Jewish tradition should be mentioned in discussing this "proverb":
"Wisdom teaches her children and gives help to those who
seek her" (Sir 4:11) and "Those who accused him she showed
to be false, and she gave him everlasting honor" (Wis 10:14b).
In both passages Wisdom plays the dominant, protective,
and rescuing role for the weak and the abused. The proverb
seals the unit Lk 7:31-35 by identifying John and Jesus as
Wisdom children (Cotter, 1989: 79-80).

Jesus was prepared to let his actions about eating and
drinking speak for themselves. The sense of this proverb is
"observe my table fellowship and make your own judgments."
But Fitzmyer, for example, again allegorizes the parable and
takes the "children" of Lk 7:35 to be Jesus and John the
Baptist who are justified by the generally positive response
of the people (Lk 7:29; Fitzmyer, 1981: 679; similarly Marshall,

1978: 298,301; Danker, 1988: 168-169). But allegorizing misses the point of the story; the question at issue is specifically the complaint about Jesus' table fellowship and whether it is justified or not. Lk 7:35 refers to this and not to the larger issue of accepting or rejecting Jesus and John. Lk 7:36-50 is introduced as a prime example of how wisdom is justified by her "children." The wisdom of Jesus' actions toward "sinners" is justified by his works as shown in Lk 7:36-50 (Neale, 1991: 139-140).

Cultural scripts play an important role in the direct definitions of Jesus and John the Baptist that are offered by the people of this generation, that is, the Pharisees and lawyers. Their labeling of John the Baptist as a deviant (Hendrickx, 1997: 9-14), that is, a witchcraft accusation, indirectly presents their own characteristic refusal to acknowledge God's agents. Witchcraft societies display six basic characteristics: clearly drawn external boundaries and the resulting purity rules, confused internal relations, close and continuous interaction, poorly developed tension-relieving techniques, weak authority, and disorderly but intense conflict (Malina-Neyrey, 1988: 23-25). The concern of witchcraft societies with boundaries and purity regulations tends to lead to the expulsion of pollutants from the group. By his actions John the Baptist received condemnation from the Pharisees and faced expulsion from their social framework. Yet no real expulsion could be effected because all those concerned still believed themselves to be Jews under the lordship of God. In addition, the Pharisees in Luke-Acts do not have that authority. An accusation of demon possession, though, is an attempt to dishonor both John the Baptist and his followers (Gowler, 1991: 217-218; Malina-Neyrey, 1988: 23,28-29).

Labels are social weapons, and they function as a device to effect social distance between the accuser and the accused. The fact that Luke reports these labels as words of Jesus' enemies completely empties them of any authority

for the reader, however. Distance is not created between
the reader and Jesus, but more distance is definitely created
between the reader and Jesus' opponents. Jesus' status as a
prominent—a person who acts outside normal social bounds
but is labeled in a positive way—has already been well-es-
tablished by the narrative (Gowler, 1991: 218).

The opponents of Jesus are the recipients of only one
saving grace in these verses: the negative epithets are *told*
not *shown* to the reader. The narrative thus loses some of
its negative force, but Jesus' voice is an authoritative one,
and the report is accurate. The readers are not in doubt as
far as the veracity of the account. The opponents of Jesus –
the Pharisees and the lawyers—do not challenge Jesus directly face-to-face in the narrative. The action is recounted,
but the honor/shame contest necessarily initiated by such
labeling does not occur in the pericope. Thus, in cultural
anthropological terms, some of the sting is removed because
Jesus reports the offense verbally. In addition, the Pharisees
and lawyers are quite removed from Jesus' report. They first
have to be identified by the reader as "the people of this
generation" (Lk 7:31), the children of the parable (Lk 7:32),
and the plural "you" that speaks in verses 33-34. What the
narrator does directly—presenting the Pharisees and lawyers as rejecting the purpose of God—Jesus does only indirectly. These themes, though, will undergo further elaboration in the narrative to come, beginning in Lk 7:36-50
(Gowler, 1991: 218).

f. The Anointing Woman/Jesus' Reply to a Pharisee (Lk 7:36-50)

No temporal markers separate Luke's account of Jesus'
encounter with Simon the Phrarisee and the anointing woman
from the immediately preceding discourse. Nor are there any
major shifts in scene even though Jesus does enter into the
home of the Pharisee (verse 36); they are still in the town

of Nain (see *polis* in Lk 7:11 and 37). Topically, moreover, this new episode continues the emphases of Jesus' discourse on a number of levels. In fact, this scene serves as a concrete example of the irony of the popular indictment against Jesus as one who eats and drinks and is a friend of sinners (Lk 7:34; Green, 1997: 305-306). In the story of the "sinful woman" Luke presents a concrete case of the general picture drawn by the Lukan Jesus in verses 29-35 (Kilgallen, 1991: 314). The criticism Jesus has received (Lk 7:34) does not preclude Luke from setting down another example of Jesus' concern for sinners (Liefeld, 1995: 108). Luke makes the anointing of Jesus a fitting climax to the other events in Luke 7, beginning with the healing of the centurion's servant (Lk 7:2-10; Ravens, 1988: 286-287).

The meal at Simon's house is the first of three to be taken in the house of a Pharisee (Lk 7:36-50; 11:37-54; 14:1-24). The first is situated in Jesus' Galilean ministry. The second and the third come later, on the way to Jerusalem (Lk 9:51-19:44; LaVerdiere, 1994: 48,50).

Luke's story of the anointing of Jesus (Lk 7:36-50) has been "a hothouse for critical reconstructors." There are two reasons for this. First, the passage is so similar to the anointings of Mk 14:3-9, Mt 26:6-13, and Jn 12:1-8, and yet so different, that one inevitably wonders whether we have two separate stories or one, based on two original events or one. Some think that the differences are sufficient to require two traditions (Liefeld, 1995: 109). Second, the text by itself seems to be criss-crossed with seams and fissures. Or, to change the metaphor, the story conveys the impression of an old house once built according to an architectural pattern, but since added unto many times, spoiling the symmetry, no matter how useful the new wings may be. This has led to a number of apparent inconsistencies in the text (Price, 1997: 101-103) for which a number of outstanding scholars have sought solutions (Price, 1997: 103-109), none of which seem to be fully satisfactory.

In the gospel tradition there are four stories about a woman who anoints Jesus with perfumed oil (Mk 14:3-9; Mt 26:6-13; Lk 7:36-50; Jn 12:1-8). The stories are similar in that (1) the setting is a meal, except in Matthew, (2) those present raise objections, and (3) Jesus responds to the objection, justifying the woman's action. Although obviously similar to Mk 14:3-9, Lk 7:36-50 is different enough both in its placement and content to lead to the hypothesis of a variant version available to Luke (Paffenroth, 1997: 35). The differences are difficult to reconcile. The character of the woman ranges from "sinner" (Luke) to the exemplary Mary (John). The objections range from "waste" (Mark, Matthew), and failure to give alms instead (Mark, Matthew, John), to the fact that Jesus allowerd it to happen (Luke). The geographical and historical placements do not agree, and the nature of Jesus' response differs markedly, especially when comparing Mark and Luke. And, finally, the literary place and purpose of the story in the four Gospels is not the same (Mack, 1989: 85-106). Mark and Matthew have an anointing sequence at the end of the Gospel in preparation of Jesus' death (Mk 14:3-9; Mt 26:6-12). Luke's story is presented at the beginning of his Gospel as a model of forgiveness, and has no association with the death of Jesus (Lk 7:36-50; Denova, 1997: 130 note 10).

Scholarship is therefore generally undecided about the relationships among the four stories. There appears to be some agreement, however, that Luke's story, though quite different from Mark's, contains at least some elements dependent upon Mark. Attention has focused primarily on the stories in Mark and Luke because, both individually and as a set, they present interesting challenges to the form-critical approach to synoptic materials (Mack, 1989: 85-86).

Jacques Dupont divided the pericope into four parts: (1) the narrative of the incident of the sinful woman in Simon's house (verses 36-39); (2) the parable of the two debtors (verses 40-43); (3) Jesus' application of the parable to Simon and the woman (verses 44-47) which is capped by the ambiguous saying at verse 47; and (4) the authority of Jesus to forgive sins: this completes the circuit back to the narrative flow of the story (verses 48-50; Dupont, 1980: 262-263).

Both Mark and Luke have resisted form-critical classification. This is because each contains a mixture of characteristics normally associated with one or another of the pure types of synoptic material. In the case of Mark's story, Bultmann settled for "biographical apophthegm" (Bultmann, 1972: 37), Dibelius saw it as a "paradigm" (Dibelius, 1971: 43), and Lohmeyer recognized elements in it that reminded him of the "controversy story" (Lohmeyer, 1959: 291). Taylor called it a "story about Jesus which is on its way to become a pronouncement story" (Taylor, 1957: 529). Recent scholars in the tradition of both form and redaction criticism have conceded that the Markan story is a "singularly mixed form" (Schenke, 1971: 89) with an "entangled history" (Schweizer, 1976: 289-290).

Derrett notes that the scenes are similar in Mark and Luke, but that the objections raised in each are different. He considers it plausible that an early form of the story common to both was simply about a women's deed, found objectionable to some, to which Jesus responded in some telling way. He finds the scene of Luke to provide the clues to what was objectionable about the woman's act, and theorizes that the fragmentation of the tradition may have resulted from diverse attempts to comment on Jesus' response (Derrett, 1970: 266). He infers from Luke that the original story may have left the source of complaint "vague," but shows that it must have been some perception of the woman, her gesture with regard to Jesus, and the fact that he allowed it which challenged conventional mores. He marshalls considerable evidence to argue that her circumstances reflect those of an "ex-prostitute," and that her behavior would readily have created an embarrassing position for Jesus (Derrett, 1970: 267).

In Mark the objection is about the "waste," a marvel-ous *tour de force* that shifts attention onto an issue capable of elaboration, while allowing the flavor of unseemliness to stand. Traditional scholarship does not seem to see the humor in all that, though Derrett sees the irony. In Luke the ob-jection that the bystanders direct toward Jesus is not that he allows the woman to perform, but that he must not be a true prophet, or else he would know what kind of woman she was. This is another very clever shift in naming the issue. But most scholars rush to Jesus' defense, thankful that Luke has preserved the story so well, and that Jesus' lesson to the Pharisees is so clear! Even Derrett reads the story as history after all, assuming that the woman had been "re-leased from a life of shame" (Derrett, 1970: 268), and that "Jesus could be the soul of tact without compromising his mission as leader and teacher" (Derrett, 1970: 278; Mack, 1989: 88-89).

The major concern of Burton L. Mack (1989: 89-106) is to demonstrate and explore the rhetorical pattern of elabo-ration in the composition of Mk 14:3-9 and Lk 7:36-50. But before moving to that exploration, he discusses the four variants as narrative amplifications of a common narrative scene. He says that there are several observations to be made that relate to the question of a *chreia* [a Greek form of an-ecdote discussed in the *progymnasmata*, "preliminary exer-cises," that began to appear in the first century B.C. from the hand of Theon, and later Hermogenes] as point of de-parture for a narrative elaboration, and the conditions un-der which the author could achieve such elaboration.

He begins by listing six formal characteristics that all of the four variants have in common: (1) the scene is simi-lar, including meal, the presence of Jesus and other guests, entrance of a woman, and her action; (2) in each case some bystander raises an objection; (3) Jesus responds to the ob-jection; (4) the response consists of making several state-ments or points, culminating in a strong pronouncement;

(5) in each case we can identify specifics, peculiar to a specific Gospel's version, that enable that version to contribute significantly to the thematic and narrative development of its larger gospel content; and (6) the characterization of Jesus that the elaboration assumes or develops is highly christological. Jesus is no mere prophet or teacher (Mack, 1989: 90).

The major components of a chreia are given with the first three items above: scene, challenge, response. It is the similarity of the four descriptions of the scene that raises the question of a common story behind the accounts. We would recognize any one account as a chreia, were it to end with a single, pointed rejoinder. Instead, each of the accounts contains a complex set of sayings at this point. And it does not appear that any one of these statements would do as a single-statement response to the situation. We cannot, therefore, reconstruct an original chreia from the material at hand. But it is not difficult to imagine such a story about Jesus, given others that do come to focus in a single pronouncement (Mack, 1989: 90-91).

We can, however, take a closer look at the scene. Various authors apparently found it remarkable in and of itself, and capable of multiple readings. All variants retain the narration of the action of the woman. Commentators have noticed that her act is unmotivated, therefore surprising, and that it is uncommon given what we know of social mores in Palestine, thus enigmatic. This means that it is the action of the woman itself that not only sets the scene, but determines the scene as challenging. There are many examples of chreiai in Hellenistic literature in which someone's behavior other than that of the principal person sets the scene as challenging. We may conclude that Jesus' response will have to meet that challenge. But what was the challenge? (Mack, 1989: 91).

As the accounts now stand, a third party articulates the challenge that Jesus must address. This feature also is not uncommon in Hellenistic chreiai as a way to make precise the challenge, and set things up for the rejoinder. But here the variant traditions part way. Mark's variant directs the objection at the woman's action (as wasteful); Luke directs the objection at Jesus himself (for allowing such a thing to happen). Both, however, can be readings of the same scene. This is especially so, since the woman's action directly involved Jesus, implicating him personally in both its surprising and embarrassing aspects. If it were a chreia, Jesus' response would have to meet a complex challenge, addressing both the woman's deed and his own acceptance of it. In both Mark and Luke Jesus' extended response actually does take up both of these aspects of the challenge (Mack, 1989: 91).

Let us look now more closely at Luke's text as we have it, in order to trace the evangelist's rhetorical achievements. We will see that his outline follows the pattern of elaboration. If we follow the suggestion about an original chreia, then what we have before us is a chreia expanded into larger narrative units by a condensed elaboration taking place with the story itself. If we do not follow this suggestion, than what we have are two longer stories (Mark, Luke) featuring different elaborate responses to the same scene, both of which the authors constructed, formally, according to the same rhetoric pattern. Either way, the importance of a memorable scene and the significance of a learned pattern are both in view (Mack, 1989: 92).

Mack focuses on the stories in Mark and Luke. He traces out the pattern of elaboration in each story by identifying the rhetorical functions of each part or saying of the story. In order to enhance his thesis that these stories are expanded chreiai, he also identifies the major components of a chreia: setting, question, response. First he gives the text, the sections identified by (1) formal correlation in chreia components, (2) brief designations of the way in which the elaboration has amplified the chreia components, and (3) their rhetorical functions. Following the text he gives a brief analysis of its rhetorical logic. First he discusses Mk 14:3-9 (Mack, 1989: 93-100). Then he turns to Lk 7:36-50.

Chreia Component: Setting
Amplification: Description of Scene, Characters, Event
Rhethorical Function: *Narratio*

> (36) One of the Pharisees asked Jesus to eat with him, and he went into the Pharisee's house and took his place at table. (37) And a woman in the city, who was a sinner, having learned that he was eating in the Pharisee's house, brought an alabaster jar of ointment. (38) She stood behind him at his feet, weeping, and began to bathe his feet and to dry them with her hair. Then she continued kissing his face and anointing them with ointment.

Chreia Component: Challenge, Question
Amplification: Question specified, but not expressed
Rhetorical Function: *Quaestio*

> (39) Now when the Pharisee who had invited him saw it, he said to himself, "If this man were a prophet, he would have known who and what kind of a woman this is who is touching him—that she is a sinner."

Chreia Component: Response
Amplification: A Dialogue ensues about the matter
Rhetorical Function: Elaboration; *Argumentatio*

> *Introduction* (Ethos of Speech – Situation established)
> (40) Jesus spoke up and said to him, "Simon, I have something to say to you." "Teacher," he replied, "Speak."
>
> *Analogy* (Contains comparison by working with the topic "greater/lesser")

(41) "A certain creditor had two debtors; one owed him five hundred denarii, and the other fifty. (42) When they could not pay, he canceled the debt for both of them. Now which of them will love him more?" (43) Simon answered, "I suppose the one for whom he canceled the greater debt." And Jesus said to him, "You have judged rightly."

Example (developed through contrast)
(44) Then turning toward the woman, he said to Simon, "Do you see this woman? I entered into your house; you gave me no water for my feet, but she has bathed my feet with her tears and dried them with her hair. (45) You gave me no kiss, but from the time I came in she has not stopped kissing my feet. (46) You did not anoint my head with oil, but she has anointed my feet with ointment.

Rationale and Commentary
(47) Therefore, I tell you, her sins, which were many, have been forgiven; henceshe has shown great love. But the one to whom little is forgiven, loves little."

Conclusion
(48) Then he said to her, "Your sins are forgiven."

Chreia Component: Challenge, Question
Amplification: The question rephrased
Rhetorical Function: Redefinition of the *Quaestio*

(49) But those who were at the table with him began to say among themselves, "Who is this who even forgives sins?"

Judgment
(50) And he said to the woman, "Your faith has saved you; go in peace" (Mack, 1989: 100-101).

Luke's story is a chreia, amplified narratively by using the standard arguments in the pattern of elaboration. It has expanded the scene in order to introduce characterization appropriate to the issue that will be determined. The question of the Pharisee specifies, but does not articulate, the issue. The question implicitly objects to the action of the woman, but directs the objection toward Jesus, thus catching up the two aspects of the challenging situation. Since the Pharisee does not express the question, however, it presents an additional challenge: will Jesus even discern the objection (that the woman is a sinner; that as a prophet he should know that and should not have allowed the action to happen)? The challenge of Jesus' discernment allows Luke to develop Jesus' superiority not only in terms of his rhetorical skills, but also in terms of his special status as savior. Luke can now expand Jesus' response into a dialogue that will defend the woman (juridical issue), instruct the Pharisee (deliberative issue), and establish his own status as one who forgives sinners (epideictic issue, that is, designed especially for rhetorical effect). The latter point is the one Luke wishes to emphasize. He does this by re-introducing the challenge at the end, rephrasing it in such a way as to allow Jesus to address it explicitly (Mack, 1989: 102).

One has also pointed out in Lk 7:36-50 the use of defamiliarization, that is, the creative distorting of a familar object or a routine convention to make it appear strange and unfamiliar. Although the "strangeness" of Lk 7:36-50 is well-known, critics tend to see the odd behavior as puzzling, rather than a specific literary device by the author. In Lk 7:36-50, defamiliarization encourages the reader to voice his or her automatized views, and then, once they have surfaced, it reveals their strangeness. Hence the "power" of the subtle, yet forceful, narrative lies in its "literariness" which "makes strange" the reader's automatized perception of reality (Resseguie, 1991: 137-138,147).

Recently one has proposed to read Lk 7:36-50 as a "widow

tradition" (Price, 1996) and that it reached its present form via four stages. In the first stage, referred to as "Prophetic privilege," the statement, "You always have the poor with you, and you can show kindness to them whenever you wish; but you will not always have me" (Mk 14:7), is to be explained as the utterance of wandering prophets who came in Jesus' name and "were received as the Lord" (Didache 11:4; Theissen, 1985: 39; Price, 1996: 112-113).

In the second stage, referred to as "Scandalous fellowship," the orginal cause of complaint, the extravagant treatment of the prophet, was replaced by another cause of outrage from the same motif-field: his association with women who scandalously fawned over him in public, devotees of the Lord whom he represented in the flesh, a devotion rampant in the Apocryphal Acts (Davies, 1980: 82). Lurking behind the Pharisaic opponents of Jesus in Luke, notably Simon, we should recognize Christian proponents of ideas rejected by the evangelist (Sanders, 1987: 106, 176), the rich and respectable members of the Christian community over against their poor coreligionists whom they are inclined to despise (Stegemann, 1986: 88-89). In any case, the pericope in its second stage is understood to be a rejoinder to those who criticized the great devotion shown by women patrons to the "Christomorphic guests" (Price, 1996: 113-118).

In the third stage of development, referred to as "Merry Widows," the focus has shifted to the woman. The woman of Lk 7:36-50 is seen here as one of the "younger widows" at whom the Pastoral Epistles take aim (1 Tim 5:6,11,13). That the younger widows or virgins were the focus of outrage on the part of male ecclesiarchs is clear also from the grumpy admonitions of the Carthagian fathers Tertullian and Cyprian. Of course these must have been well-to-do women who could pay their own way. Can such women be envisioned in Lk 7:36-50, where the woman, after all, has gotten very expensive ointment from somewhere? Perhaps she is simply wealthy and willing to shower her gratitude on her favorite holy man, sparing no expense. The suspicions against the young widow are set up for Jesus to disarm. How does he do this? By simple reference to the humble service rendered him (actually the itinerants for whom he stands). It is at this point that one can place the insertion into the story of the retrojected neglect of social amenities by Jesus' host which serves to underscore the hospitality of the widow beyond the call of duty (Lk 7:44-46). The secondary character of these verses is widely recognized (Evans, 1990: 363; Dillon, 1978: 241). In making herself a servant she showed herself greater than he that remained sitting at table (see Lk 22:27). The itinerants circulated the story as a defense of themselves for receiving the extravagant attentions of their patronesses. As the itinerants told it, it was the genuineness of their prophethood that was at stake. As remoulded by the widows, their own reputations became the central concern (Price, 1996: 118-122).

In the fourth stage, Luke has harmonized the last two versions, both of which he could easily have heard. He could not brook the criticism of Simon Peter, so he became Simon the Pharisee. He added the phrase "who was a sinner" in verse 37, to make the narrative voice confirm the suspicion of Simon, which up till now had been confuted by what followed. To reapply the story, he shoved down its throat the alien parable of the two debtors (Price, 1996: 122-123). The square peg of the parable, teaching as it does that gratitude follows on forgiveness, just does not fit the round hole of the story which appears to teach that forgiveness is a reward for love, a tension which many scholars have tried in vain to talk away (Price, 1996: 123-126). Rather than the convoluted hypotheses and interpretations of a great number of scholars, it is deemed more probable that the seams in the text are like growth rings in an old tree, and that the story has grown from one defending itinerants who require special privilege at the expense of poor relief, to one defending them for accepting the scandalous devotion of grateful patronesses, to one told on behalf of those patronesses, the widows. Rather than the sensualists and sinners they are suspected of being, they prove themselves more devout than their detractors by the loving quality of the service they render to those who come in the name of Christ. Only subsequently did the redactor Luke give the story its present, most difficult form (Price, 1996: 126).

In Luke, the story concerning Simon the Pharisee and the woman who anoints Jesus illustrates the verses immediately preceding this pericope. The sinful woman, who overcomes tremendous social barriers, symbolizes those who are responding to the Gospel (Lk 7:29). Lk 7:36-50 is a story about a woman who unexpectedly finds salvation in an encounter with Jesus (Lee, 1996: 1-15, who points out the similarities with Jn 4:1-42; 7:53-8:11). Simon illustrates those who rejected the purpose of God for themselves (Lk 7:30). Yet a complicating factor has arisen. Why would one who had rejected the purpose of God invite Jesus to dinner, an apparent act of friendship? Is there still hope for the Pharisees?

Verse 36:   One of the Pharisees asked Jesus to eat with him,
               and he went into the Pharisee's house
               and took his place at table.

The temporal setting is unspecified, and the very sober spatial notations of the account are limited to the succinct localization of the action narrated (Legaré, 1987: 77). The spatial setting finds Jesus dining in a Pharisee's house. As often in Luke, direct definition is sparsely used. Indirect presentation, however, paints a vivid picture. At this stage we may call Jesus the invitee; soon we will no longer be able to do so. As far as the one who invites him is concerned, he has no proper name yet at this stage: he is a Pharisee. He is named according to the class to which he belongs: he belongs to a social respectively religious group before being somebody, an individual (Lafon, 1992: 651).

The Pharisee's invitation to Jesus, as well as Jesus' acceptance of that invitation, presents an anomaly to the reader. Why is Jesus dining with his enemies? Pharisees extend Jesus invitations to be their guest at table on three occasions (Lk 7:36-50; 11:37-54; 14:1-24). The setting at a meal in the home of Simon presupposes conviviality. The dialogue reflects the amenities of proper social relationships; Jesus politely addresses Simon; Simon reciprocates by calling Jesus "teacher" (Lk 7:40). The strong affinity between Lk 7:36-50 and the genre of Hellenistic symposium shows that Simon provides the foil for Jesus' teaching about forgiveness. Simon fulfills the role of the host in the symposium, who is typically regarded especially for his wealth and learning (de Meeus, 1961: 862-863; Delobel, 1966: 459). But more is at stake. Simon's disdain for the woman who is a sinner demonstrates Luke's awareness that the Pharisees refuse table fellowship with sinners. And so indirectly the fellowship between Jesus and the Pharisees distinguishes Jesus from the outcasts even though he often associates with them (Brawley, 1987: 100-101). The meal scenes in Luke are revelations of who Jesus is, and revelations of salvation and judgment (Okorie, 1996: 17-26).

Verses 37-38: (37) And a woman in the city, who was a sinner,
             having learned that he was eating in the
                 Pharisee's house,
             brought an alabaster jar of ointment.
          (38) She stood behind him at his feet, weeping,
             and began to bathe his feet with her tears
             and to dry them with her hair.
             Then she continued kissing his feet
             and anointing them with the ointment.

Then the anticipated *fait divers* occurs: the "and [behold]" of the narrator affixes the spotlight upon a sinful woman who wet Jesus' feet with her tears, wiped them with her hair, kissed his feet, and proceeded to anoint them. The woman's gesture, so striking in every detail, acts as a catalyst, giving direction and unity to the rest of the story (LaVerdiere, 1994: 52). The woman is called a sinner by the narrator (Lk 7:37), the Pharisee (Lk 7:39), and implicitly by Jesus (Lk 7:47).

The woman's position "behind him [Jesus] at his feet" is easy to picture in the case of a formal dinner at which the guests "reclined." The low tables would have been arranged in a horseshoe shape, with the fourth side of the oblong or square open to allow servants access to the tables. The guests would be reclining on cushions, propped on their left elbows, using their right hands to reach the food that was on the table. Their feet would be curled behind them, pointing away from the tables. The guests would be barefoot, having removed their sandals upon entering the room, and presumably having been provided with a basin and towel with which to wash their feet. In the case of highly honored guests, a servant would be assigned to wash the guest's feet. Usually only the lowliest of the servants would be assigned such a menial task. In extreme cases, the host might perform it himself, in order to demonstrate his respect for and devotion to the guest. The woman in this story, in effect, takes on the role of such a host, for she does not act under orders as a servant would, but moved by her own emotions (Ringe, 1995: 109).

Except for the presence of the unnamed woman "of the city" (Lk 7:37) identified as a "sinner" (Lk 7:37), the gender of those in attendance at Simon's meal are comparable to the previous Pharisee-hosted banquets. But what is the social identity of the woman? Four matters aid us in attempting to answer the question.

It is excluded that the woman was an adulteress, because for this she would have been meted the death penalty (Imbach, 1991: 9). Since the woman is labelled a "sinner" who has been forgiven much, some have identified her social deviancy as prostitution (Corley, 1993: 124 note 89). Others, however, have identified the social makeup of the character group "sinners" as having two elements, neither of which necessarily centers on women or women as prostitutes. Sinners are (a) Jews who fell short of Mosaic obligations (without restricting these to the Pharisaic interpretation), but who could repent and be reconciled to God; and (b) Gentiles, who were *a-nomoi* ("law-less") and *a-theoi* ("godless"), often considered hopeless in Jewish apocalyptic literature (Fitzmyer, 1981: 591). Most women at Graeco-Roman banquets were prostitutes (Corley, 1993). Accordingly, one might view the woman as a prostitute, but the connection is not direct. The same may be said of the woman's forgiveness. Her experience of being forgiven may identify her as a prostitute, but Luke also links forgiveness with Jesus' healing activity (Lk 5:17-26) as well as Jesus' prophetic role as God's servant whose mission is to set free the oppressed. The declaration of the woman's great forgiveness does neither demand nor exclude the woman's identity as a prostitute.

But does the expression a "woman of the city" (Lk 7:37) contain a clue to the woman's social identity? The phrase may simply refer to the woman's social location at the time, "a woman in the city" (NRSV). However, the phrase seems to connote more. The woman's home may have been "the streets and lanes of the city" (Lk 14:21), that is, her social location may have been among those who loved and worked within the walled off and/or sequestered areas that included an assortment of outcasts including prostitutes (Rohrbaugh, 1991: 144). If so, the phrase possibly connotes a morally negative notion such as "a public woman."

The woman is uninvited. First, she is not a matron (Corley, 1993: 28-31), that is, a wife of an invited male. Second, her silence—indeed, she says nothing, but her actions produce a wide range of discussion—probably indicates that she is not a courtesan, a prostitute having a wealthy or upper-class clientele who would be invited to carry on conversation as well as engage in "sexual sport" (Corley, 1993: 38-

48). Third, Simon, as a respected Pharisee, would not invite a courtesan at a banquet given in honor of an alleged
prophet, or have as a guest "a person of the land." Finally,
the pericope itself indicates the woman was uninvited. She
situates herself at the feet of Jesus because she learns that
Jesus "was at table in the Pharisee's house" (Lk 7:37). The
woman "crashed" the banquet. Perhaps she was from among
the crowds (Lk 8:43-48; 11:27), one of the uninvited who
passed in and out during the festivities because the door of
the living room was left open (Talbert, 1982: 86). Since
Jesus is a public figure, the door to the meal likely remains
open, so that interested people can enter, sit on the edge
of the room, and hear the discussion. The unexpressed rebuke in verse 39 is not because the woman has come to the
meal, but because she did not stay on the sidelines (Bock,
1996: 218).

The woman violates space and time boundary markers
related to Simon's house and meal. Simon's boundaries,
however, are not the basis of fellowship for Jesus whose
boundary of space is the kingdom of God and boundary of
time is the Christian fellowship meal. Hospitality of the
kingdom is based on criteria such as repentance, love, and
faith. The woman qualifies. So, by allowing the woman to
touch him, Jesus receives and reciprocates the woman's
hospitality, and simultaneously challenges Simon's worldview.
The woman's social identity is twofold: for Simon she is a
social deviant, an outcast, probably a prostitute; but for Jesus
she is a model disciple.

The Lukan reversal probably indicates both a breaking
up of conventional Graeco-Roman gender expectations at
public meal settings and the future inclusion of women at
early Christian meals. The issue is not whether the woman
actually eats with Jesus. After all this is Simon's meal in
Simon's house, both of which will be vacated by the salvation of the kingdom (Moessner, 1989: 157). The critical
issue is the giving and receiving hospitality, something Simon

has not done. Luke treats the woman with social restraint. She remains nameless and silent. There is an element of "control" because Luke is concerned for what is acceptable to the convention of the imperial world (D'Angelo, 1990: 442). However, at minimum, the incident stretches traditional social boundaries to their limit and validates the statement: "the Son of Man has come eating and drinking; and you say, 'Behold, a glutton and a drunkard, a friend of tax collectors and sinners!'" (Lk 7:34; Love, 1995: 204-207).

Verse 39:   Now when the Pharisee who had invited him saw it,
             he said to himself,
             "If this man were a prophet,
             he would have known who and what kind of a
                  woman this is who is touching him—
             that she is a sinner."

The Pharisee's disapproval is never voiced publicly; the narrator reveals his inward thoughts. Simon's thoughts reveal doubts about who Jesus is. He assumes that if Jesus were a prophet, he would know about the sinful woman and would not allow the woman to touch him. Simon's interior speech thus presents two unreal conditions in the present time (Marshall, 1978: 308): (1) Jesus is not a prophet, and (2) Jesus does not know about the woman.

Verse 40:   Jesus spoke up and said to him.
             "Simon, I have something to say to you."
             "Teacher," he replied, "Speak."

Jesus' initial response to the woman is not described by the narrator, but the focus turns from the woman to the Pharisee (Gowler, 1991: 220). This is the only instance where Jesus addresses a critic by name (Easton, 1928: 106), and one of the few occasions in which a partner in dialogue is addressed by name (Danker, 1988: 170). Moreover, the name Simon is not introduced until suprisingly late in Lk 7:40 (Schweizer, 1984: 138). It has been suggested that this is because the name was not at first that of an opponent or outsider, but a vestige of the original identity of the com- plainer as Simon Peter who would have griped at the waste of the ointment, a detail retained in Mark, where Simon has become Simon the leper! (Price, 1997: 109-110,112).

In the present Lukan story Simon is wrong. Jesus is a prophet—he answers Simon's inward thoughts, after all (Petzke, 1990: 98)—he knows about the woman (Lk 7:47) and still allows her to touch him. Jesus' address, as well as Simon's reply, both contain the titles required in polite company (Gowler, 1991: 220). Simon directly defines Jesus as "Teacher," but his inner thoughts betray the fact that he does not consider Jesus a prophet (Lk 7:39). The title "teacher" is not used by the narrator himself and does not appear in the discourse of any intimate with Jesus. It has thus been concluded that the term appears upon the lips of those persons who have an indefinite opinion of Jesus (e.g., Lk 7:40; 8:48; 18:18; 19:39; Dawsey, 1986: 6). The only exceptions to its ambivalent use are found in Lk 20:21,28,39, where the narrator notes the speaker's pretense to sincerity (Lk 20:20). Lk 20:40, though, mitigates the antagonism (Gowler, 1991: 219 note 87). The narrator defines the Phari- see as the host (Lk 7:39), but it is left to Jesus to reveal the host's name. No other direct definition occurs.

Verses 41-43a: (41)   "A certain creditor had two debtors; one owed five hundred denarii, and the other fifty.

                   (42)   When they could not pay, he canceled the debts for both of them. Now which of them will love him more?"

                 (43a) Simon answered, "I suppose the one for whom he canceled the greater debt."

The argumentation does not follow the sequence of the elaboration pattern. Luke develops the argumentation in- ductively, beginning with a parable, the analogical function of which will only become clear when the argumentation gives the rationale. With the parable, Jesus initiates a Socratic interrogation, a dialectical method of questioning in which the opponent is refuted by using his or her

A parable (*analogy*) is appropriate rhetorically for the introduction of an inductive line of argumentation. It is also appropriate narratively, as an oblique entree into a situation of inarticulated challenge. The choice of this particular parable is clever, for it gives the theme of the elaboration (forgiveness) as well as the major rhetorical topic (comparison). The general topic of comparison will allow for the development of a contrast in an example, as well as an opposition in the rationale. The conclusion also uses this topic (comparison), although not expressly. But the reader will know that the argumentation as a whole has shown the woman to be "forgiven," not (any longer?) a "sinner." A skillful use of the topic of comparison links the several parts of the elaboration rhetorically and aligns the judicial, deliberative, and epideictic issues to be resolved (Mack, 1989: 102). The parable ends with a rhetorical question; for in fact there remains only one possible answer which the Pharisee gives not without hesitation: "I suppose." He realizes that he can give only this answer, although he cannot do so wholeheartedly (Petzke, 1990: 98).

Simon's response to Jesus' question is a careful one, either demonstrating the fact that he knows he is caught in a trap or merely reflecting his Pharisaic circumspection concerning attendant details (Gowler, 1991: 220-221).

Verses 43b-44:   (43b)   And Jesus said to him,
      "You have judged rightly."
      (44)   Then turning toward the woman,
      he said to Simon,
      "Do you see this woman?
      I entered your house; you gave me no
         water for my feet,

(45)   but she has bathed my feet with her tears
       and dried them with her hair.
       You gave me no kiss,
       but from the time I came in
       she has not stopped kissing my feet.
(46)   You did not anoint my head with oil,
       but she has anointed my feet with
       ointment.

We begin our commentary on these verses by some observations regarding the translation of the text. The words *hudōr moi epi podas ouk edōkas* in verse 44b are generally translated "you gave me no water for my feet," meaning that the host was not supposed to wash the guest's feet, but just to give the guest the opportunity for a foot bath. This translation is questionable on grammatical grounds since *epi* with accusative does not mean "for." Moreover, in verse 45a and verse 46a we are not dealing with actions that the host should make possible, but actions that he himself has failed to perform for his guest. This suggests a similar interpretation in verse 44b which would then read: "You did not pour water on my feet" or "you did not wash my feet." This constitutes then a clear contrast with "she has bathed my feet with her tears" (Hofius, 1990: 171-173).

In the relatively late Christian apocryphal *Testament of Abraham* 3:7ff.; 6:6 it is stated that Abraham washes his guests' feet, although in Gen 18:4 we read that Abraham offered his guests water to wash their feet. The change may be explained by New Testament influence which presents Abraham, following Jesus' example (Jn 13:1ff.) or in the sense of 1 Tim 5:10 as an example of the real, Christian hospitality and is, therefore, no evidence for a traditional Jewish custom. The same is true for *Joseph and Asenath* 20:1ff., which narrates that Asenath prepared a great meal for Joseph and insists that she herself will wash his feet, thereby demonstrating that she loves Joseph "as herself."

The stories mentioned above contain an important consequence for the interpretation of Lk 7:44-46. Verse 44b does not refer to the Pharisee's failure to comply with a well-known duty of hospitality, and verses 44-46 as a whole do not mean to say that the sinful woman has performed the duties of hospitality the Pharisee omitted. It is also beside the point to say that Jesus does not chide the Pharisee for a general lack of hospitality, but for the failure to show him special signs of hospitality reserved for selected guests and special occasions (as held by Bovon, 1991: 384). The words *hudor moi epi podas ouk edōkas*—as well as the parallel clauses in verses 45a and 46a—mean rather that Simon has not done anything that can be interpreted as an expression of love, and that thereby he has shown that he altogether lacks such love. Against this background the woman's expressions of love take on their real stature. Verses 44-46, therefore, do not state a contrast between *lesser* love and *greater* love, but between the absence of all expression of love and the overpowering proof of deep love. The tension between verses 41-43, 47, on the one hand, and verses 44-46, on the other, is due to the generally accepted fact that verses 44-46 did not belong to the story from the beginning (Hofius, 1990: 173-176; Manns, 1987: 1-3).

Jesus affirms Simon's correct answer and goes on to apply the parable to the current situation: Simon and the sinful woman are analogous to those two debtors. The response of the woman to Jesus is in stark contrast to Simon's: (1) Simon did not supply water for Jesus' feet, but the woman wet them with her tears and dried them with her hair; (2) Simon gave no kiss of greeting, but the woman kept on kissing Jesus' feet; (3) Simon did not anoint Jesus' head with oil, whereas the woman anointed his feet with ointment.

The parable and its application function in the first instance to vindicate the woman. But then the vindication of the woman exonerates Jesus. The question of Jesus' prophetic identity in the mind of Simon is clearly answered. Jesus does know who and what sort of woman is touching him. The identity of Jesus as a prophet (Lk 4:16-30), which is certainly a programmatic theme for Luke-Acts, emerges here as it will again later (Lk 13:31; Brawley, 1987: 21).

Cultural Scripts in Lk 7:36-50. One of the controversies surrounding this pericope involves matters of the cultural environment: Did Simon commit a grievous outrage against Jesus or did he merely not go above and beyond the duties of a host? Cultural anthropology cannot answer the specific questions concerning Simon's offense—hospitality codes vary from place to place, culture to culture, and era to era—but modern readers can examine the issues of hospitality that underlie Simon's actions.

Honor/Shame. The dialogue between Simon and Jesus is an honor/shame contest. Simon can be seen as initiating the debate: his inward speech is an indirect affront (Lk 7:39). Jesus, however, answers the silent challenge and makes the debate public (Lk 7:40-42). Simon responds in an attempt to retain honor (Lk 7:43), but he soon joins all the other Pharisees who have been bested by Jesus' expert verbal jousting. Once again, Jesus' actions, that seem shameful, have been successfully defended against a negative challenge to his honor. Jesus increases his honor as God's broker of heavenly blessings—in this instance, forgiveness of sins—and Simon the Pharisee's honor decreases in comparison.

The contrast between Simon and the sinful woman is also highlighted by honor/shame implications as is indicated by the stress upon the parts of the body in the narrative. The head, for example, is a primary symbol of a person's honor, and honor is shown when the head is anointed by another. Washing someone's feet, however, is a shameful task. Simon did not anoint Jesus' head with oil, nor did he supply water for the washing of Jesus' feet. Jesus does not suggest that Simon should have washed his feet, only that he did not supply water for the task. The woman, however, did not even dare to anoint Jesus' head; instead she wiped his *feet* with the hair of her *head*—the shameful task is done with an honored part of her body—kissed his feet, and anointed them. The stress upon her humiliation is shown by the sevenfold repetition of the word *feet* in these few verses. Her shamefulness is also shown by letting down her hair. For a woman to unbind her hair in the presence of men was seen as a great disgrace. The *Tosefta*, essentially a tannitic work, considered it a sufficient reason to divorce a wife. Jesus, however, accepts her completely and totally; he does not offer a rebuke. The honor she shows to Jesus is in great contrast to Simon's treatment of Jesus. The clash between Jesus and Simon, though, must be set in the more specific honor/shame context of hospitality (Gowler, 1991: 223).

The Law of Hospitality. Hospitality is founded upon ambivalence. When a person outside of a community is invited to a feast or to lodge with the host, that person temporarily undergoes a change from *stranger*—an unknown and therefore possibly dangerous person—to *guest*. The stranger's worth is often tested in this situation, but the extension of hospitality, although it does not eliminate conflict, places any conflict in abeyance and prohibits its expression. The avoidance of disrespect then becomes paramount.

A person who is a guest in the host's home for the first time is given precedence over habitual guests with whom greater familiarity exists. The treatment of any person, though, depends upon that person's social status, and the whole community gains honor when one in its community hosts a guest of high status. Individually, the host gains honor through the number and quality of guests. Honor is also gained when the host shows honor to a superior person; honor is lost, however, by neglecting to show honor to a person who deserves honor. The guests, in turn, are expected to show honor to the host (Pitt-Rivers, 1968: 12-30).

The law of hospitality could be infringed by a guest who might: (1) insult the host by any show of hostility or rivalry; (2) usurp the role of the host by taking precedence over the host; (3) refuse the food and drink offered by the host. A host could infringe the law of hospitality by: (1) insulting the guests or by showing any hostility or rivalry; (2) failing to protect the honor of a guest; (3) failing to attend to the guests or by not showing concern for their needs or wishes. Any infringement upon the law of hospitality eliminates the reciprocal relationship of giving honor to each other. An affront or insult entitles the slighted person to abandon the role of guest or host and to attempt to maintain honor. The resolution of this combat—which reflects the ambivalence that underlies the law of hospitality —may end in one of two ways: it may lead to the incorporation of the guest as an accepted friend or to the rejection of the guest (Pitt-Rivers, 1968: 29-30).

One can easily see the law of hospitality in Lk 7:36-50. Simon invites Jesus into his home for a meal. That invitation suspended any possible overt hostility between Jesus and the Pharisee. Yet a woman appears and her actions toward Jesus are both shocking and shameful. Jesus does nothing to deflect any possible offense given to his host Simon, but Simon still does not voice his own outrage. A further offense is given by Jesus when he complains about Simon's hospitality. The delayed revelation of Simon's actions, however, is effective. Jesus' speech is a response to Simon's earlier treatment of him; Simon had not offered Jesus his best and in that sense had failed as a host. Simon's reception of Jesus is at best lukewarm and at worst shameful. Simon as host was responsible for how Jesus was treated—as Jesus states: "I entered *your* house..." (*sou* is in the emphatic position). If Simon had known who Jesus was, he should have treated Jesus very differently. Yet the story ends without final response of Simon to Jesus or of Jesus to Simon. The fracas may still end in either incorporation or rejection (Gowler, 1991: 225).

Patron-Client. The invitation to dinner that Simon extends to Jesus initiates a dyadic contract between them. Jesus accepted his invitation, but then entered into a vertical dyadic contract with the "sinful women" by accepting her positive challenge. The illustrative parable (Lk 7:41-42,47) makes clear that this contract is a broker-client relationship between Jesus and the woman. As broker of God's blessings Jesus can announce that her sins have been forgiven. The point is that Jesus is open to all persons: those who have been forgiven much, or need to be, and those who have been forgiven little, or need to be. He enters into dyadic contracts with tax collectors and sinners (e.g., Lk 5:27-29) as well as with Pharisees. The contract with Simon, though, is violated by the actions of the host and the guests. Peace may eventually be restored, but the gap in the story does not allow anything more than speculation at this point (Gowler, 1991: 225-226).

Verse 47:   Therefore, I tell you, her sins, which were many,
                    have been forgiven;
              hence she has shown great love.
              But the one to whom little is forgiven, loves little."

For a long time the interpretation of verse 47 has caused difficulty. Two translations are possible. If the conjunction *hoti* has a causal sense, one should translate: "her many sins are forgiven because she has loved much." But if *hoti* is to be attached to "I tell you," one could translate: "I tell you she has loved much." In order to decide the matter it is worth remembering a Jewish tradition concerning Rahab, the midrash *Sifre Zuta Nb* 10:29 (Mann, 1987: 7-9) which affirms that "because she acted out of love, God has given her out of love." Many other Jewish texts speak of Rahab and call her "just" (Manns, 1987: 10-15). But was Luke in a position to know these rabbinic traditions regarding Rahab? We should note first of all that early Christianity showed a great interest in Rahab: Matthew 1; James 2; Hebrews 11, and the *Letter of Clement of Rome to the Corinthians* 12 witness to the interest in the figure of Rahab in various sectors of early Christianity. Has Lk 7:34 taken up the traditions concerning Rahab? Several objections can be raised against this hypothesis, but all of them can be credibly answered. If the rabbinic tradition of Rahab underlies the story of Luke, or of his source, some incoherences of the account can be explained. The themes of the love and faith of the sinful woman are no longer opposed to each other (Mann, 1987: 15-16).

The application of the parable to the story in which it exists is imperfect or, in other words, there is an imbalance between parable and greater story. First, though the parable is concerned with three characters (two debtors and a creditor), the application of the parable is concerned with only two: the greater debtor and the creditor—the lesser debtor drops. Indeed, the Pharisee does not qualify as the debtor who owed less and was forgiven less and thus will show less love. There is no suggestion that the Pharisee has been forgiven anything (nor that his debt is small). Furthermore, it is not of itself clear that verse 47c, "but the one to whom little is forgiven, loves little," should be applied to Simon; from the context, one can argue that it should not be applied to him. Simon is not the equivalent of the lesser debtor forgiven and loving; the acts of the sinful woman do not at all lessen the gratuitousness of the creditor's forgiveness. The parable of Lk 7:41-42, shown to be inapplicable, first to Simon, and, secondly, to the woman's acts of repentance to Jesus, is seen, thirdly, as unfulfilled by the woman, but unexpectedly fulfilled outside its own story—in the story of the women who followed Jesus to listen to his teaching and to help him materially in his mission (Lk 8:1-3; Kilgallen, 1991: 309-313,318).

But is the woman's love the *cause* or the *consequence* of the forgiveness of sins? The parable seems to support the latter, but verse 47a and b seem to support the former as well as the latter respectively. These "hitches" are most probably due to the fact that Luke inserted the parable into the story of Jesus' dealings with the woman sinner (Imbach, 1991: 11).

The rationale for the woman's action now appears. It is a conclusion to the inductive argumentation: "Much forgiven," "for she loved much." But it functions also as the rationale for the chreia: the woman acted that way because "her many sins were forgiven." The statement of the contrary clarifies the point: "The one who is forgiven little, loves little" (Mack, 1989: 102). If the analogy holds, Simon has been "forgiven little," but the analogy cannot be pressed. The emphasis is upon the contrasting responses of the woman and of Simon to Jesus. The contrasting responses of Simon and of Jesus to the woman are also emphasized. Simon—as well as the reader—is forced to consider the fact that there is qualitative difference between himself and the sinful woman, but only a qualitative difference (Steele, 1981: 66). Whether Simon comes to realize that fact is not revealed by the narrator. His final response is not given. This omission could occur for three possible reasons: (1) The Pharisee is just a foil to heighten the contrast, and the narrator is not concerned about his response; (2) Unresolved issues are a standard literary technique of parables (e.g., at the end of the parable of the Prodigal Son: Did the elder son ultimately enter and join the celebration?); (3) A negative response is assumed (cf. Lk 7:30).

It has been suggested that the main problem of interpretation of this pericope is that the narrative (verses 36-39) describes love as the *condition* of forgiveness while the parable (verses 40-43) describes love as the *consequence* of forgiveness (Creed, 1957: 110; Kilgallen, 1985: 675-679). Lk 7:47 seems to embody this confusion. Indeed, the two halves of Lk 7:47 do seem to form an unlikely couplet, but the answer lies in the relationship of the narrative (verses 36-39) to the parable (verses 40-43). The narrative focuses on the penitential behavior of the sinful woman. We are not told what is the actual cause of her behavior (grief over sin? or perhaps joy over forgiveness of sin?). Nevertheless, it seems fair to assume that Luke says that it is repentance that is demonstrated by her actions (Leroy, 1973: 92; Navone, 1970a: 158), but as readers we simply assume that she intends to renounce the offending behavior that first brought her to grief. This is an unspoken assumption which the reader brings, but there is no textual indicator for it. The parable, on the other hand, shifts the focus to the creditor who graciously forgives the debtors. The emphasis shifts from repentance to forgiveness, two closely related but still distinct phenomena. This is how the narrative and the parable differ.

> (a) Therefore, I tell you, her sins, which are many, are forgiven.
> (b) for she loved much;
> (c) but he who is forgiven little, loves little (Lk 7:47 RSV).

Lk 7:47 is the key to bringing these two themes together and it demonstrates Luke's (or his tradition's) special interest in repentance and forgiveness for the "sinner." The saying in verse 47 attempts to synthesize the two disparate perspectives of the narrative and the parable (Braumann, 1964: 488-489). Verse 47a,b refers to the repentance theme of the narrative at verses 36-39. The saying "for she loved much" (RSV; Greek: *hoti ēgapēsen polu*) refers to the sinful woman's actions and should be understood not as the basis of forgiveness, but as the *evidence* of forgiveness. The *hoti* conveys an evidential sense and the context of verse 47c confirms that this is the proper understanding, although the text on its own is ambiguous (Zerwick, 1963: 144-145; Fitzmyer, 1981: 687). Verse 47c, on the other hand, refers to the parable (Fitzmyer, 1981: 684) and serves to connect the narrative to the parable. The gracious forgiveness that is the point of the parable is connected to the penitent behavior of the sinful woman.

For all the difficulty of the structure of Lk 7:47, the point is simple enough: "That her sins are forgiven is evident in the fact that she acts as she does, that is, in a penitent and grateful manner. But the one who has experienced little of this gracious forgiveness lacks this attitude. Repentance and forgiveness have become the great equalizers for the "sinner" and have restored her to God's favor. The situation in Simon's house has now been turned completely on its head and the necessary reversal to "save" the "sinner" has been achieved by Luke (Neale, 1991: 145-146).

It is "natural" to consider verse 47, repeated substantially in verse 48, and verse 49 as indication that Jesus forgives (forgave) the woman's sins. As regards verse 47 as indicating that Jesus forgives (forgave), the essential objection comes from the main verb of verse 47a. First, *apheontai*, "are forgiven," is considered to be a "divine passive," that would make God the *forgiver* and, in consequence, Jesus the *announcer* of forgiveness. Second, according to some scholars, the end of Lk 7:36-50 parallels the beginning, which means that, as in the beginning Jesus was proposed (skeptically) as a prophet, he remains (and is proved to be) a prophet; like a prophet, he has an inspired perception (characteristic of a prophet) of the woman's true state, that is, forgiven. That is all Jesus is—prophet, not forgiver (Talbert, 1982: 86). But we think that Luke wants Jesus to be understood as centrally involved in the forgiveness of the woman's sins, and he presents that thought through more than one medium; he uses not only the clarity of verse 49 for this purpose, but he also so presents his entire story that he maintains the mystery of the interrelated roles of God and Jesus involved in this forgiveness (Kilgallen, 1991: 318-321).

Verse 48:   Then he said to her,
              "Your sins are forgiven."

Verses 48-50 are widely acknowledged to be Lukan composition based on reminiscences of Mark (Shramm, 1971:

43-45), particularly because they serve the Lukan interest of transforming the story into a symposium (Delobel, 1966: 415-475; Paffenroth, 1997: 36).

Since the argumentation has won the rationale by induction, it may now (re)state the rationale in a simple form as the conclusion: Her character is not that of a "sinner," as the objector had assumed; she is "forgiven." This means that the Pharisee was wrong and that Jesus has succeeded in countering one aspect of the challenge (that the woman was a sinner). He succeeded because the Pharisee had agreed to the validity of the point made by the analogy. He has also succeeded in demonstrating that he was a "prophet," thus countering the additional challenge of discernment presented by the Pharisee's doubt and silence. Because of the renewed assurance of forgiveness and the fact that the reaction of the guests is expressed in terms very similar to Lk 5:20f., many scholars consider Lk 7:48-50 a later addition (Petzke, 1990: 99).

Verse 49:   But those who were at the table with him began to
               say among themselves,
               "Who is this who even forgives sins?"

This verse, which does most to support the position that Jesus is the forgiver of sins, appears practically at the end of the story. One cannot deny the "tardiness" of this verse, but then one should not forget that Luke counts on his listener/reader to remember the question that has already been answered in direct confrontation: "Who can forgive sins but God alone?...But so that you may know that the Son of Man has authority on earth to forgive sins..." (Lk 5:21,24). Similarly, the verse contains the unsettling assessment of a new group of people who cannot be said to have been present at the words of Jesus in Lk 5:21,24. Yet, though appearing only briefly, the idea of verse 49, together with the omniscient statement of verse 50, puts the entire episode on the level of Christology—where it belongs at this stage of Luke's narrative. In other words, the christological statement, Lk 7:49, links the whole pericope, Lk 7:36-50, to the continual theme of this section in Luke's Gospel: the meaning of Jesus (Aletti, 1988: 87-109; Kilgallen, 1991: 321-322,324). But there is something else involved in this story.

Verse 49 brings into play now what had already been affirmed in Lk 5:17-26, that Jesus has power on earth to forgive sins. Luke seems to avoid unveiling the real identity of the author of forgiveness (Legaré, 1987: 98). Here, people not present in Lk 5:17-26 grope toward the true meaning of what has taken place, but they do it in the indicative mood (*aphiesin*, for it is a real act) and in the present tense (for it is recognized as something characteristic of Jesus). But verse 49 forces one to ask just how to relate that faith in Jesus with God who cleanses by means of faith in Jesus. What does this cleansing faith mean for the right identification of Jesus? Jesus is not just a prophet. He is intimately tied up with forgiveness; just how is not made clear, but one does not solve the problem by making him one who only learns of forgiveness and then hands on that knowledge to anyone who has faith in/love for him. That interpretation does not do justice to what Luke means when he writes that "God cleanses through faith in Jesus." What does do justice to this statement is the banqueters' introductory formula (Lk 7:49b): *who is this* who *de facto* has the characteristic of forgiving sins? (Kilgallen, 1991: 327-328).

Jesus is not merely a prophet, so the argumentation has not fully met the second aspect of the challenge presented by the implicating action of the chreia. Luke shrewdly lets the other guests raise the challenge. They raise it because Jesus has stated the conclusion in the form of an address to the woman: "Your sins are forgiven." The rhetorical ambivalence of this statement (conclusion/judgment) allows the guests to take it as an action of Jesus (Luke does not mind): "Who is this, who even forgives sins?" The "even" tips us off that the guests have accepted the demonstration of the prophetic character of Jesus. Now the issue has to do with the fact that the woman expressed her action of love (which demonstrated that she was forgiven) *toward* Jesus himself. Luke does not let this get out of hand. But he leaves the reader with the strong suggestion that Jesus has met the challenge of the chreia in respect to his character, if he is the one who forgives sins. And that is a judgment that Jesus cannot make for the listener/reader. So the self-defense reaches a certain self-referential limit at this point. Luke ends the story, therefore, with a reference to the woman's *faith* as the cause or basis for her salvation. But this reference occurs in another very strong pronouncement by Jesus that functions in the elaboration as the citation of an authority. To manipulate the elaboration sequence in such a way as to conclude with a statement of Jesus as the statement from an authority is Luke's carefully devised achievement: "Your faith has saved you; go in peace." The thinly veiled liturgical nuance of the dismissal, and the pronouncement of peace as the last word of a verbal battle, are touches that allow the authoritative judgment to come in the last place. Traditionally, the appeal to emotions, the argument by pathos, occupied the end of the rhetorical speech (Mack, 1989: 103).

Verse 50:   And he said to the woman,
               "Your faith has saved you; go in peace."

Another contrast is made between Simon's response to the woman and Jesus' acceptance of her. Jesus offers no rebuke, but instead affirms her action of love by saying not only, "Your sins are forgiven" (Lk 7:48) but also "Your faith saved you; go in peace." This final judgment may seem curiously enigmatic, that is, a kind of saying appropriate as a chreia response. If we follow the suggestion that Luke's story is an expanded recasting of an originally brief chreia, the process may be imagined as follows: Luke deleted the original brief response. In its place he gives the extended elaboration. But this also ends climactically in a poignant, chreia-like statement. The new pronouncement is acceptable, however, precisely because of the new characterization of Jesus. It may be argued, therefore, that Luke has expanded the chreia internally in order to achieve this new characterization. Luke's skill in the rhetorical analysis and elaboration of chreiai can be seen in this clever shift in characterization. But Luke has not elaborated the chreia on the model of a Hermogenes (Mack, 1989: 57-63) or a Plutarch. He has chosen to let Jesus speak for himself. The curious result is that Jesus, not Luke, appears as the master of·rhetoric, elaborating his own chreia (Mack, 1989: 103-104).

That Jesus' fundamental concern in Lk 7:36-50 is with the woman's restoration to the community of God's people (and not with her individualistic experience of forgiveness or assurance of divine acceptance) is suggested, first, by the fact that she is presented as already behaving in ways that grow out of her new life. In addition, Jesus addresses her with words usually reserved for the conclusion of miracles of healing: "your faith has made you whole" (Lk 8:48; 18:42; 17:19); and he sends her away "in peace." Such language cannot be limited to "spiritual" well-being or even, in other contexts, to "physical" vitality, but speaks of a restoration to wholeness, including (even if not limited to) restoration to the full social intercourse from which she has been excluded (Green, 1997: 314).

g. Women Followed Jesus (Lk 8:1-3)

Lk 8:1-3 provides a summary of yet another preaching tour (cf. the previous circuit described in Lk 4:44) as well as an interpretive heading for Lk 8:1-56 (Green, 1997: 315,317). Luke states Jesus' mission both in that passage and here as announcing the "good news of the kingdom of God" (Liefeld, 1995: 111). This brief summary is usually skimmed over as a mere introduction to the popular Parable of the Sower. Yet the refrain "kingdom of God" and a glance at Jewish customs at the time of Jesus invite us to see something more in Lk 8:2-3 than mere window dressing (Karris, 1977: 101). Lk 8:1-3 is near the middle of a series of stories that make special reference to women: Lk 7:11-17; 7:36-50; 8:1-3; 10:38-42; 13:10-17 (Witherington III, 1979: 243). The introductory verse 1 is highly Lukan in language and most likely composed by him. The list itself, however, may be considered as possibly from a pre-Lukan source (Fitzmyer, 1981: 119, 695,697; Paffenroth, 1997: 55). But some consider the whole passage redactional or a Lukan composition (Guillaume, 1979: 44-46).

This summary passage (Lk 8:1-3) concludes a section detailing Jesus' ministry of healing (the centurion's servant, the widow's son), his interaction with John the Baptist over his messianic office, and his anointing by a woman who is a sinner (Osborne, 1989: 279,280). At the same time, Lk 8:1-3 is an introduction to and illustration of the teaching of the Parable of the Sower (Lk 8:4-15; Tiede, 1988: 163). The women are the living embodiments of what happens when the sower sows his seed in soil that can receive and nurture it (Ellis, 1966: 126-127).

Syntactically, these verses create a problem for translation in that they form one long sentence of three parts, Lk 8:1a, 8:1b, and 8:2-3 (Reiling and Swellengrebel, 1971: 326). Lk 8:2-3 seems to be a note added as an afterthought: Jesus and his disciples are on a tour of Galilee, as we expect them to be. And suddenly, as if to whet our curiosity, Luke adds the news that the men he has named were accompanied on their journeys by a group of colorful sounding women. Each of these women has a story, or rather, is a story (Price, 1996: 127).

The list of women could be traditional and does not appear to be derived from Mark's list (Mk 15:40). Possibly, Luke himself has added the names of Joanna and/or Susanna as a result of personal knowledge or from a well-informed Palestinian source. There is little reason to question the authenticity of the information that women traveled with and served Jesus and the disciples since this conduct was unheard of and considered scandalous in Jewish circles. It is unlikely to have been invented by a Christian community that contained converted Jews and that did not wish to appear morally suspect to a Mediterranean world that was already sexually and morally indulgent. Travel for other than conventional reasons (feasts, visiting family, business) was considered deviant. Women leaving behind family responsibilities would have been considered seriously deviant (Malina-Rohrbaugh, 1992: 334).

Lk 8:1-3 stands in contrast to its historical context in early Judaism in other regards as well. We know that women were allowed to hear the word of God in the synagogue but they were never disciples of a rabbi unless their husband or master was a rabbi willing to teach them. Though a woman might be taught certain negative precepts of the law out of necessity, this does not mean they would be taught the meaning of Torah. Yet it was apparently an intended part of Jesus' ministry for women to benefit from his teaching (Lk 10:38-42) and healing (Witherington III, 1990: 110-111). Lk 8:1-3 brings together the major themes of discipleship, universalization of the gospel, good news to the poor and downtrodden (Osborne, 1979: 244). This pericope may also point out how the bonds of the family of Christ should have priority over the ties of one's family by heredity or marriage (Conzelmann, 1960: 47-48).

Verse 1:   Soon afterwards he went on through cities and
                   villages,
              proclaiming and bringing the good news of the
                   kingdom of God.
              The twelve were with him,

Luke's introductory phrase, *kai egeneto* ("and it came to pass"; NRSV: "soon afterwards"), signals a fresh development, reinforced by the express mention of "the twelve." The verbs "proclaiming" (*kerussōn*) and "bringing the good news" (*euangelizomenos*) supplement each other here. The first verb stresses a note of authority; the latter implies the idea of good tidings (see Lk 3:18; 4:43). The combination of these two verbs gives us a comprehensive picture of the whole activity of Jesus (Reiling and Swellengrebel, 1971: 326-327; Witherington III, 1979: 245). Jesus was spreading "the good news of the kingdom of God." The kingdom of God is action claiming people for the New Age and breaking down the barriers of separation, whether those are sin or legalistic walls that divide the righteous from the sinner (Danker, 1988: 172).

Reference to the Twelve is found in the primitive tradition of 1 Cor 15:5, the only place in the Pauline corpus where they are mentioned. The phrase, "the Twelve" is part of the early church tradition, being found also in Mk 3:6; 4:10; 6:7; 9:35; 10:32; 11:11; 14; 10, 17, 20, 43; in the Johannine tradition, Jn 6:67,70,71; 20:24; in "L" (Lk 8:1); and reflected in the Q-passage of Lk 22:29-30 (= Mt 19:28). Whether the association of the Twelve with the twelve tribes of Israel is primitive or not may be debated. Some writers question whether the institution of the Twelve is actually to be ascribed to Jesus himself. The problem is to explain why such companions of Jesus on his journeys would have disappeared so completely later on in the young Church. They play no special role in Jerusalem once the seven are appointed (Acts 6:1-6). But such considerations do not completely rule out the roots of the Twelve in the ministry of Jesus itself (Fitzmyer, 1981: 617). A recent study of the question concludes "when one draws together the arguments from multiple attestation of the sources and forms (Mark, L, John, Q, and pre-Pauline tradition), the argument from embarrassment, and the argument for the general flow of the New Testament traditions about the Twelve, and when one adds to these the grave difficulties under which alternative hypotheses labor, one position emerges as clearly the more probable: the circle of the Twelve did exist during Jesus' public ministry" (Meier, 1997: 672). The mention of "the Twelve" in Lk 8:1 anticipates their first independent mission in Lk 9:1-6 (Tiede, 1988: 163).

Verse 2:   as well as some women
              who had been cured of evil spirits and infirmities:
              Mary called Magdalene,
              from whom seven demons had gone out,

The women belonged to the larger group of disciples from which Jesus called the Twelve and participated fully in his ministry. The phrase "with him" in Lk 8:1-2 is a technical term for discipleship (see Lk 8:38; 9:18; 22:56; Brown, 1969: 83; Ryan, 1985: 56–59). Jesus refused to permit tradition to endorse second-class status for women. Unlike church officials of all ages who conveniently say when confronted with controversial isues, "Not in my lifetime," Jesus accepted responsibility and said, "The time is now." The implications of Lk 8:1-3 are far-reaching. Ecclesiastical leaders who search the Gospels for data that will justify their own traditional views and practices are challenged to recognize that Jesus' departures from tradition are a model for their own responsibility to face the future in a creative and innovative way (Danker, 1988: 172,174).

The first woman mentioned, Mary Magdalene, is the best known among these women, possibly because her healing was the most dramatic, that is, "seven demons" indicates an extraordinary situation. Perhaps these seven demons were the notorious gang of seven that lived in the waste places, who returned with a friend to occupy the exorcised man (Mt 12:43-45). Unfortunately, the only other reference to Mary's condition is found in the "longer ending" in Mk 16:9 (Arlandson, 1997: 162-163). There is no hint here, nor in any other portion of the Gospels, that she was the sinful woman mentioned in Lk 7:36-50. This piece

of "gossip" was first circulated by Tertullian. Moreover, demon possession was not construed as a sinful condition
(Danker, 1988: 173; Tiede, 1988: 164-165; Craddock, 1990:
107; Ringe, 1995: 112).

Surely there was a story told about Mary's torments and
deliverance, and there must be a reason why we do not
hear it (Price, 1996: 127). She, and apparently the others
mentioned, were living proof of the Gospel's power. Mary
of Magdala is commonly placed first when listed with other
women (Mk 15:40,47; 16:1; Mt 27:56,61; 28:1; Lk 24:10).
She is undoubtedly important, and so Luke wishes to mention her here. Her special devotion and witness in the resurrection narrative (Luke 24) will be seen as the proclamation of someone who has long been one of Jesus' disciples
(Witherington III, 1990: 111-112).

Mary Magdalene came from a small, unimportant town
and had been exorcised of "seven demons"; yet she is mentioned before Joanna, the wife of Herod's steward. The prominence of the former (she is always first in Luke's lists) demonstrates the reversal of status in Jesus' new order (Osborne,
1989: 280).

An important element in this passage is the social hierarchy not only between Joanna, the wife of the powerful
and wealthy retainer, and the others but between Mary and
the Twelve, mentioned one right after the other. First, the
Twelve are mentioned as such for the first time in precisely
the same context in which Mary is first mentioned along
with the female corps of disciples. Second, Mary serves as a
representative of the other women who are helped out of
their condition by Jesus. The Greek syntax in Lk 8:2-3 indicates that the "many" were also part of those who were
healed and delivered (Arlandson, 1997: 163). These women
are not part of a large crowd of disciples but have special
importance and deserve special mention. Their special role
continues. When the apostles are listed for a second time
in Acts 1:13-14, they are in prayer "together with certain

women, including Mary the mother of Jesus, as well as his brothers." Again this special group of women is mentioned along with the apostles, with Jesus' mother and brothers now added. These women, like the apostles, have the important distinction of being followers and learners during Jesus' ministry in Galilee and on the fateful journey to Jerusalem. This is an important qualification for the apostles (Acts 1:21-22; 13:31). It is also an important distinction of these special women, as shown by the mention here in Lk 8:1-3, and the repeated emphasis on their following Jesus from Galilee in Lk 23:49,55 (Talbert, 1986: 138-139).

The literary backdrop to Mary's condition and deliverance is found in Lk 6:12-16, where the calling of the Twelve is narrated. Jesus institutes a special place for them unlike that for any other male or female disciples. In the politics of space, the Twelve gather their authority and power from their proximity to Jesus. They make up the primary corps of disciples. After they are established, Luke, significantly, does not list other male disciples by name. Instead, he cites by name a group of women who make up the secondary corps. (This is why Lk 6:12-16 should be considered the background to Mary's condition and deliverance.) He inserts this passage about women as a mirror to the Twelve (Arlandson, 1997: 164). Even though women are not featured in any of the leadership roles attributed in the Gospels to the Twelve, women are clearly portrayed as present with Jesus from the beginning of his journey. Their eventual marginalization in the leadership of the Church seems to reflect the customs and social world of the emerging Christian communities rather than any exclusionary policy of Jesus (Ringe, 1995: 112).

Verse 3:   and Joanna, the wife of Herod's steward Chuza,
             and Susanna, and many others,
             who provided for them out of their resources.

Joanna appears only in Luke. Of her we are told intriguing details, details that cannot have ended here. Like Mary, Joanna is a long-standing disciple, present with Mary at the tomb and the upper room, and thereafter bearing witness. She is very unlike Mary of Magdala who came from a small town and was undoubtedly avoided by many until Jesus healed her. Joanna was the wife of Chuza who managed Herod's estate. This indicates that Jesus had penetrated Herod's own establishment. She was a woman of some means and prominence. What is especially noteworthy about her presence among Jesus' followers is that apparently she had left her home and family to become a follower and traveling companion of Jesus. Here Luke gives evidence of how the Gospel breaks down class and economic divisions, as well as social barriers, and reconciles men and women from all walks of life into one community. Luke uses Joanna as a precedent for wealthy women patrons for the missionary movement. He retrojects this arrangement into the sacred time of apostolic authorization. Hence he retains Joanna's link with Chuza so as to make clear that Joanna was a wealthy patroness (Price, 1996: 139).

The third woman, Susanna, though perhaps known to Luke's audience, is unknown to us and is not mentioned elsewhere in the Gospel. Susanna may have been named for the chaste heroine of the Greek version of the Book of Daniel. This New Testament Susanna may have had a story as colorful as that of her prototype (Price, 1996: 127).

Luke intends for us to understand that these three women were only the most prominent among "many other women" that followed Jesus (Osborne, 1989: 280). Luke indicates that Jesus' actions on behalf of these women freed them to serve both him and the disciples "out of their resources." Though it was uncommon or unknown for women to be traveling disciples of a rabbi, it was not uncommon for women to support rabbis and their disciples out of their own money, property, or foodstuffs.

Most of the discussion of the women has focused on

the question of their precise role in the entourage of Jesus. This was obviously a service of no small importance. As an itinerant exorcist and preacher Jesus did not work for a living. The same is true of the male disciples (Sim, 1989: 52). Luke says that "they provided for them out of their resources." In what did this provision consist? What did they do? There have been several answers to this question. Some suggest that the women did domestic chores for the men. Oh, to be sure, they weren't sent to the kitchen when the teaching began, but they were mainly there to—what? Roll up the sleeping bags? How many domestic chores can there have been for a wandering group of mendicant preachers? (Price, 1996: 127-128). One has referred to the use of the verb *diakoneō* in Lk 4:38-39 and 8:1-3 to defend the meaning "to serve," but the context of the two passages clearly shows that the verb cannot be meant in the same sense in both instances. Lk 4:38-39, the healing of the mother-in-law of Peter, takes place in a house and *diakoneō* is clearly meant to be taken in the sense of waiting at table or some similar aspect of hospitality. But such is not the case with Lk 8:3 where the action occurs in the open spaces as Jesus and those with him travel from village to village. Its particular nuance there must be dictated solely by its context. *Diakoneō* is best translated here as "to provide for." To translate it as "serve" implicitly imposes a condition of servitude on the discipleship of the women in Lk 8:1-3 that is not suggested in the text (Sim, 1989: 56-57). Strictly speaking, Lk 8:1-3 does not imply anything at all about the concrete discipleship roles of the women mentioned (Sim, 1989: 60).

Some understand the women more in the order of patronesses who paid the bills for Jesus and his disciples, out of their own means, but many of those who agree with this picture considered it anachronistic, retrojected into the Gospel from the situation of the early Church: The wealthy women walk with them on this journey. Are we to imagine that they carry large money-bags behind the disciples? (Schottroff,

1989: 420). Moreover, the evidence does not support the widespread view that Lk 8:1-3 refers to a few wealthy women who provided for Jesus and the Twelve. This thesis fails to recognize both the type of people with whom Jesus normally associated and the radical nature of his call to discipleship (Sim, 1989: 53). Still others think that the women are neither the retrojection of the later patronesses nor historical figures associated with Jesus, but rather a retrojection of the traveling celibate partners or sister-wives of the itinerants of the early Church (Dillon, 1978: 245). This arrangement is probably already in view in 1 Cor 9:5 (Crossan, 1991: 335).

Once we take into account the Jewish customs, attitudes, and laws that prevailed in first-century Palestinian society, it becomes possible to offer some concrete suggestions regarding the socio-economic background of the women who followed Jesus. It may be plausibly proposed that these women came mostly from the lower and poorer strata of Jewish society and that they combined what economic resources they possessed to offset the cost of Jesus' itinerant ministry. The majority of them were probably single (unmarried women, widows, divorced women and, with less certainty, former prostitutes) for only women of single status enjoyed some personal and economic independence. There were, on the other hand, some married women, like Joanna, who braved public condemnation by leaving their husbands to follow Jesus (Sim, 1989: 52-55).

Can the picture of Jesus and his men wandering through Galilee with a group of unattached women in their train possibly reflect historical memory of the life of Jesus? Although this Lukan pericope has undergone extensive editing at the hands of the third evangelist, most scholars agree that it preserves a historical reminiscence of Jesus' ministry (Sim, 1989: 51). We agree here with the statement that "the reconstruction of the Jesus movement as the discipleship of equals is historically plausible only insofar as such critical elements are thinkable within the context of Jewish life and faith" (Schüssler Fiorenza, 1983:107). If Jesus seems to be leaping out of his cultural skin, surely this means we are misreading the text, that we are applying the wrong paradigm to construe the data, or that we are dealing with an anachronism. We know of no circumsrtances in which the roving male-female band of itinerants could have flourished in Judaism. Clearly it is in the situation in the life of the Church that we should place the story of Jesus' Galilean women (Price, 1996: 132-136).

In light of what has been said, it appears that some of the purposes of this pericope are: (1) to reveal the proper response to the healing and teaching of Jesus—true discipleship involves serving the Lord and the sisters and brothers; (2) to point out that women are equally called to be disciples and witnesses as part of the universal spread of the Gospel; (3) to show that Jesus brings in the "acceptable year of the Lord" (Lk 4:19) that liberates the captives and the poor (women fitting one or both categories), and that fulfills the prophecy of Joel 3:1-5 of women speaking God's word (Wilson, 1973: 61); (4) to show the continuing loyalty of these women as disciples of Jesus—that they were prepared to be the "last at the cross, first at the tomb"; (5) to point out some women of prominence, at least known in the early Palestinian church, who were among the first to be healed and liberated to a position of equality with men; (6) to serve as an introduction and illustration of the parable that follows—that the "good soil" was not limited to a particular class, race, or sex; (7) to present Lk 8:1-3 as an example of the fulfillment of scripture Jesus read in Lk 4:18-22 (Witherington III, 1979: 247-248); (8) Lk 8:1-3 was not intended by its author to contrast with Jesus' family (Lk 8:19-21) but, together with Lk 6:13ff., 17, 20, to note the larger group of followers whom Jesus here instructs about Christian mission and who form the group of those who in Luke's view were qualified witnesses (Robinson, 1966: 133).

THE PREACHED AND ACCEPTED WORD OF GOD
(LK 8:4-21)

Lk 8:4-9:17 considers what faith looks like by calling on the disciples to cling to the word of God (Lk 8:4-21). Indeed Luke frames the parable complex (Lk 8:4-15) by the theme of the word of God: in Jesus' proclamation (Lk 8:1), and in correct hearing and doing (Lk 8:18,21; compare Lk 8:15; Reinhardt, 1995: 105). Thereby Luke thinks less of Jesus' activity as such than of the movement of God in the expansion of his word (Isa 55), especially in the time of the Church (Bovon, 1991: 398).

The Parable of the Soils commends only the ground that holds to the word with patience. Jesus goes on to declare his family to be those who obey God's word, a message he describes simply as light that will not be covered. A series of miracles follows in Lk 8:22-56, which show Jesus' power over nature, demons, disease, and death and serve as a comprehensive survey of his authority. Then in Lk 9:1-17, Jesus begins to show the Twelve how they will share in his ministry through their mission and the Feeding of the Five Thousand. Questions about Jesus surface as the disciples (Lk 8:25) and Herod (Lk 9:7-9) wrestle with who he is. This entire unit sets up a major turning point in the Gospel, Peter's Confession in Lk 9:18-20 (Bock, 1996: 228).

So, a new section of the Lukan Gospel begins here. The material which Luke had inserted, beginning at Lk 6:20, after Mk 3:19 (transposed), has come to an end, and he returns to his use of the Markan material in sequence. At Lk 8:4 Luke returns to the structure that Mark's Gospel provides (Schweizer, 1984: 144; Tiede, 1988: 165; Nebe, 1989: 174; Craddock, 1990: 106). Lk 8:4 picks up Mk 4:1 and presents a form of that Markan discourse. Unlike Mark 4 and Matthew 13, where entire chapters are devoted to kingdom teaching via parables, Luke concentrates on the one theme of faith (hearing the word and doing it; Bock, 1996: 228). The parables that Luke retains give examples of the "preaching" mentioned in Lk 8:1, but now the emphasis is much more on the word of God. In fact, the literary unit obtains its coherence by the use of terms related to hearing the word. "The word (of God)" occurs in verses 11, 12, 13, 15, and 21 and the term "to hear/listen" in verses 8, 10, 12, 13, 14, 15, 18, and 21 (Weren, 1989: 17).

As Jesus gathers disciples and gains opposition, the question about how people respond to his message surfaces. Lk 8:4-21 is presented as a basis for evaluating responses to "the word of God" that Jesus is preaching. Only the last of the four listed responses is adequate, since it involves not only hearing the word but holding it fast and bearing fruit (Lk 8:8,15). This is equivalent to "hearing the word of God and doing it" (Lk 8:21; Talbert, 1986: 146). The concluding episode about Jesus' relatives (Lk 8:19-21) rounds off the development and makes this whole section one devoted to the preached and accepted word of God (Fitzmyer, 1981: 699–700; Krämer, 1993: 30–31).

Although in Mark this section of parables (Mk 4:1-34) already referred to the preaching of the Christian Church, Luke revised it to emphasize the same reference. The section in Mark could have seemed to him a discussion of parables as a mode of Jesus' teaching, on its esoteric aspect (Mk 4:11), and on the judgment function of Jesus' preaching (Mk 4:12c). In any case Luke made changes at these points. The discussion in Luke is not on parables but on

the word of God (Nebe, 1989: 178–179). In drawing attention to a parable about Christian preaching instead of to a
parable about parables, Luke needed no other parables here.
He could therefore easily omit the Parable of the Seed Growing by Itself (Mk 4:26-29), and that of the Mustard Seed
(Mk 4:30-32), which he also had in Q. With these omitted, the concluding summary on parabolic teaching (Mk 4:33-
34) also had to go. Luke thus broke with the topical arrangement in Mark and made one unified section. The unity
of the section on Christian preaching is further defined by
its full separation from the next episode. Not only does the
passage Lk 8:19-21 conclude and so tend to separate from
the following context, but the avoidance at Lk 8:22 of Mark's
setting (Mk 4:35; cf. Mk 4:1: Jesus teaching from the boat)
and the generalization with which Luke replaced it remove
all indications that the events of Lk 8:22ff. occurred on the
same day as those of Lk 8:4ff. (Robinson, 1966: 132-133).

It has been pointed out that on three occasions, Luke
apparently omits features from Mark's parable (Mk 4:3-9;
Lk 8:4-8) which he goes on to mention in the Interpretation (Mk 4:13-20; Lk 8:11-15). First, Mark says that the
seed that fell on rocky soil sprang up quickly because it had
no depth of earth (Mk 4:5; contrast Lk 8:6). Luke omits to
mention this, for whatever reason, but he has the corresponding section in the Interpretation, "those who when
they hear, with joy they receive the word..." (Lk 8:13; Mk
4:16). Second, in Lk 8:6, the seed "withered for lack of
moisture." This is a different reason from the one in Mark
where it withers "because it had no root" (Mk 4:6). In the
Interpretation, however, Luke apparently reverts to the
Markan reason in Lk 8:13: "And these have no root; they
believe for a while." Third, the sun is the agent of scorch-
ing in Mk 4:6. This is then interpreted as "trouble or persecution." Luke does not have the sun (Lk 8:6) but he does
have "temptation" that interprets it (Lk 8:13).

Three times Luke has an interpretation to a text which

interprets features that are not in that text. He has made changes in the parable, changes that he has not been able to sustain in the interpretation. This is believed to be an example of the phenomenon of "editorial fatigue," a phenomenon that inevitably occurs when a writer is heavily dependent on another's work. In telling the same story as his predecessor, a writer makes changes in the early stages which he is unable to sustain throughout. Like continuity errors in film and television, examples of fatigue will be unconscious mistakes, small errors of detail that naturally arise in the course of constructing a narrative (Goodacre, 1998: 46,49).

a. The Parable of the Seed Among the Soils (Lk 8:4-8)

On account of a different theological interest Luke has fundamentally changed the parable chapter (compare Mk 4:1-34 and Lk 8:4-21) and made it into a section dealing with the right way of hearing the word of God and the Christian praxis that results from it: he achieves this by retaining only one parable, the Parable of the Sower (Lk 8:4-8) and its Interpretation (Lk 8:11-15). Thereby Lk 8:4-8 becomes almost an example story (see Lk 8:4: *dia paraboles*) from which can be derived an analogy for the right way of listening (see Lk 8:18: "pay attention to *how* you listen"; Fitzmyer, 1981: 718,720). Lk 8:19-21 aims then first of all at the practical consequences that result from listening to the word of God (Rauscher, 1994: 332). Lk 8:4-8 presents a Lukan form of the Parable of the Sower, the source of which is Mk 4:1-9. The main change in the parable is that it is more centered on the sowing of the seed than on the farmer (Fitzmyer, 1981: 700). Indeed, the parable is more about the fate of the seed than about the sower's action (Ringe, 1995: 113). The Lukan version of the parable and its interpretation show no interest in degrees of success, for the Markan reference to bearing thirty, sixty, and a hundred is missing. This may indicate a desire to avoid claims of superiority among the disciples, a desire that would fit the later warnings to the disciples when they become involved in disputes about greatness (Lk 9:46-48; 22:24-27; Talbert, 1986: 210).

Verse 4:   When a great crowd gathered
               and people from town after town came to him,
               he said in a parable:

Since Luke has already adapted Mk 4:1 for his introduction in Lk 5:1-3, he omits that verse here. Luke's mention of the "great crowd" (*ochlos* occurs forty-one times in Luke) helps prepare the reader for the significance of the recital that follows. In Greek we have a double genitive absolute: Jesus taught *as* the crowd gathered and *as* people came (Schurmann, 1969: 452 note 57). The crowds are often drawn to Jesus. The present tenses in the participles suggest a growth in the crowd's development, since they picture the progress of the crowd's coming and the people's gathering (Bock, 1994: 723). Luke adds that people came to Jesus "from town after town." By means of the two coordinated clauses "a great crowd gathered" and "people from town after town came to him" Luke signals the breadth of Jesus' reputation and the reach of his ministry throughout Galilee (Green, 1997: 323).

Jesus does not accept a following in terms of sheer numbers. His kingdom call is not propaganda for the rabble but an invitation to accept the rigors of discipleship (Danker, 1988: 174). Lk 8:4 makes it clear that this form of parable is addressed to the people at large, among whom one would have to reckon the Twelve and the women of Lk 8:1-3. But when the "disciples" ask Jesus for an explanation of the parable (Lk 8:9), we are not told in Luke, as we are in Mk 4:10, that they were "alone" (*kata monas*); though a contrast is, indeed, made between them and "the others," that has to be understood in its proper context (Fitzmyer, 1981: 701).

Even though the word *parabolē* was already used in Lk 4:23; 5:36; 6:39, it is here that the parable as literary form comes center stage for the first time. The word "parable," from the Greek word *parabolē*, means, literally, "that which is tossed alongside," implying a comparison, an analogy, an elaboration, or an illustration (Craddock, 1990: 107,108). Unfortunately, much unnecessary confusion has been generated in biblical study circles by persons who approach the biblical data with ready-made definitions of "parable." The result is endless discussion concerning the kinds of stories told by Jesus, with, for example, specification of similitudes and illustrations in addition to alleged pure parables. In a very general and nontechnical sense the term "parable" can be applied to any story told by Jesus in which he probes people's behavior or attitudes, especially as these involve others, or God, or both. The point is to expose the auditors to some feature of life in the world around them in such a way that they find themselves and their destiny scrutinized in a shockingly arresting manner. In some of these stories the metaphorical feature will be stronger than in others, but in every case the hearers are expected to abstract from the illustration to their own situation vis-à-vis their responsibilities toward God and/or the neighbor. Most of the stories attributed to Jesus make a single point, and the original auditors required no special education or inside information to understand them, for the story itself was the meaning. If such is the case with the story in Lk 8:4-8, it is to be interpreted without assumption of encoded details (Danker, 1988: 174-176; Craddock, 1990: 107-112).

Verse 5:   "A sower went out to sow his seed;
              and as he sowed,
              some fell on the path and was trampled on,
              and the birds of the air ate it up.

Jesus' Parable of the Sower should not have been difficult to understand. It begins in a field, with a Palestinian farmer sowing seed. Seed as a metaphor for the word was common in the ancient world (Bovon, 1991: 398). The imagery of sowing as a figure for God's giving or renewing life was common in Judaism (Isa 55:10-11; Jer 31:27; Ez 36:9; Nolland, 1989: 375-376; Bock, 1994: 732). The sower is not the center of attention; neither is particular emphasis laid on the seed. What does catch attention is the variety of soils (Liefeld, 1995: 112).

One has argued from rabbinic statements for a Palestinian custom of ploughing after sowing that would make the acts described by the parable natural (Jeremias, 1963a: 11f.). This has been contested (Drury, 1973: 367-379). Apparently, first-century Palestine was the home for various practices concerning the process of planting (Payne, 1978-1979: 123-129). The acts described may also be an instance of a deliberately bizarre element present in other parables of Jesus, which is necessary to the point. If so, before being turned into a parable of the soils by allegorical interpretation, it could have been a genuine parable of contrast, in which a sowing affords an abundant harvest contrary to all appearances and expectations (C.F. Evans, 1990: 370). Because of paths worn through the field, rocky surfaces hidden by the remaining stubble, or patches of weed, the sower of the seed does not have equal success. Only that which fell on "good soil" bore fruit (Lk 5:8; Schweizer, 1984: 144; Danker, 1988: 176; Craddock, 1990: 111). It should again be noted that the focus of the parable is already on the soils, not the seed, since the seed gets four different reactions (Bock, 1996: 230).

Although Luke's changes in the parable are chiefly stylistic, commentators generally consider the addition "his seed" (*ton sporon autou*) a reference to the first verse of the Interpretation (Lk 8:11). In Lk 8:11 Luke, in contrast with Mark and Matthew, takes the seed as point of comparison (Reinhardt, 1995: 105). And while the expression "the birds of the air" (*ta peteina tou ouranou*, literally, "the birds of heaven") is common coin with Luke, taken together with the added "was trampled upon" (*katepatēthē*) and with the Interpretation, Luke's addition of "of the air/of heaven" may be more than an "innocent" addition having no significance. Both expressions, "the birds of the air ate it up" and "was trampled on," are biblical terms indicating utter destruction, and as such may correspond with the emphasis upon destruction which Luke has added to the Interpretation by means of the clause "so that they may not believe and be saved" (Lk 8:12; Robinson, 1966: 134; Stein, 1992: 244).

Verse 6:   Some fell on the rock;
             and as it grew up, it withered for lack of moisture.

A second portion of the seed falls on rock, a thin layer of ground with limestone right under the topsoil, a condition common in the Palestinian hill country. Luke alone attributes the loss to lack of moisture. The root cannot receive water because the ground cannot hold moisture. Neither the danger of being trampled under foot (Lk 8:5) nor the lack of moisture are incorporated into the Interpretation (Schweizer, 1984: 144). Mark and Matthew speak only of the plant's lacking root, by which they mean the lack of a developed root system (Marshall, 1978: 320; Bock, 1994: 724-725). In the Interpretation (Lk 8:13) Luke returns to Mark's "had no root," which can be moralized (see Col 2:7), whereas "withered" cannot (C.F. Evans, 1990: 371).

Verse 7:   Some fell among thorns,
             and the thorns grew with it and choked it.

The third group of seeds falls in good ground, but shares that ground with greedy neighbors: thorns. These Palestinian weeds can grow up to six feet tall. They take so much nourishment from the ground that nothing else can grow around them. Despite the plowing that would have accompanied the growing season, such thistles inevitably remain.

Once again, an outside factor has intervened to prevent the seed from producing fruit. A similar warning is found in Jer 4:3: "Break up your fallow ground, and do not sow among thorns" (Bock, 1994: 725).

Verse 8:   Some fell into good soil,
                  and when it grew, it produced a hundredfold."
                  As he said this, he called out,
                  "Let anyone with ears to hear listen!"

The fourth group of seeds lands on good soil and grows to bear more seed. In contrast to the failure of the other seeds, only the last seed penetrates the soil and achieves its goal of becoming fruitful. It depicts God's word bearing fruit and growing (Isa 55:11; Acts 6:7; Schürmann, 1969: 454-455; Bock, 1994: 726).

It is striking that unlike Mark and Matthew, Luke does not differentiate various yields, but speaks only of "a hundredfold." Some scholars have wondered if thereby Luke wants to avoid "gnosticising classifications" (Schürmann, 1969: 465 note 155) or intends to oppose gradation of faith (Klauck, 1978: 199). But probably he only wants to underline how rich is the fruit in sharp contrast with the foregoing (Reinhardt, 1995: 105).

Some scholars, citing ancient works that report large yields quite in keeping with the yield of the seed that fell on good soil, state the yields of a hundredfold do not seem obviously out of the ordinary. Despite this apparent consensus among ancient writers, more sober estimates put the yield of cereal crops between fourfold and fivefold. Even the grain that gave a yield of thirtyfold in the Parable of the Sower was giving a crop that was not only exceptional, it was miraculous in first-century Palestine (McIver, 1994: 606-608).

Jesus tells the parable without explanation and then calls on his audience to hear what is said in it (verse 8b). Luke notes such calls to hear elsewhere (Lk 14:35; compare 4:23; 8:18; 9:44). This injunction underlines the importance of the parable, especially when supplied with a solemn introduction "he called out" (imperfect tense, "he repeatedly called out"; C.F. Evans, 1990: 371).

b. Why Jesus Spoke in Parables (Lk 8:9-10)

In the section of the Gospel on the word of God (Lk 8:4-21), between the Parable of the Sower (Lk 8:4-8) and its Interpretation (Lk 8:11-15) is inserted a saying of Jesus concerning "this parable" (not "[the] parables" as in Mk 4:10 and Mt 13:10).

Verse 9:   Then his disciples asked him what this parable
            meant.

In contrast to Mark (and Matthew) the question of the disciples pertains directly to the Parable of the Sower (Lk 8:5-8) that Jesus has just uttered: "His disciples asked him what *this* parable meant." Luke's revision is only natural, since Jesus will shortly provide an interpretation of the parable (Evans, 1989: 116).

The request of the disciples for an interpretation of the parable appears rather remarkable at first sight, in view of its simplicity (Green, 1997: 324-325). But the reader of Luke's Gospel must not forget that Luke is writing for the benefit of his contemporaries. In the process he eliminates the un-complimentary remark addressed by Jesus to the disciples: "Do you not understand this parable? Then how will you understand all the parables?" (Mk 4:13; Danker, 1988: 176). Lk 8:9 has substituted the singular "parable" for Mark's reference to "parables" (Mk 4:10), so that Isa 6:9-10 has to do only with the Parable of the Sower rather than with parables in general (Brawley, 1987: 76). Here is another instance where Luke's version has its own function, yet Jesus' answer using the plural "parables" in Lk 8:10 shows that the question as raised in the other Gospels is not ignored (Bock, 1994: 727).

Verse 10:   He said,
                 "To you it has been given to know the secrets of
                     the kingdom of God;
                 but to others I speak in parables, so that
                 looking they may not perceive,
                 and listening they may not understand."

The plural of *mustērion*, "mystery," "secret" (so Mk 4:11), is a word confined to this passage in the Synoptic Gospels (the idea is present in Lk 10:21//Mt 11:23; it does not occur in John). In the New Testament it is predominantly a Pauline word for the divine purpose, hitherto hidden but now published in the death and exaltation of Christ (e.g., 1 Cor 2:1). There it may owe something to the idea of a secret in Hellenistic "mystery" cults (see 1 Cor 2:6ff.), but it had already entered Judaism through the Septuagint version of Dan 2:18ff.,44ff. for the veiled announcement of the future establishment of the reign of God. A word of immense significance in biblical literature, *mustērion* is found also in extrabiblical Jewish literature. In apocalyptic literature the revelation of the secret (more commonly "secrets") of the eschatological age was a common idea (*1 Enoch* 63:3; 103:2; *4 Ezra* 12:36; C.F. Evans, 1990: 373). The basic concept of *mustērion* is that of the purpose and plan of God, which he works out phase by phase in human history and through the Church (Liefeld, 1995: 112).

The "secrets/mysteries" of the kingdom "are given" to the disciples by means of parabolic instruction. Since the parables contain mysteries, they have a positive function for those who embrace Jesus. "The others" ("the rest") is less exclusive than Mark's "those outside." To those who do not embrace Jesus, the parables are not interpreted and thus remain enigmatic. Thus, it is wrong to see the parables functioning only in a concealing role. Only when a parable remains unexplained in terms of how it relates to the kingdom does it have this function. That the disciples have access to the mysteries of God's kingdom in contrast to the crowd shows the twofold function of the parables. That the disciples are particularly blessed is seen in the emphatic position of "to you" and the perfect tense *dedotai*, which may be translated "it stands given." The passive *dedotai* makes clear that *God* has given this gift to the disciples (Fitzmyer, 1981: 707; Bock, 1994: 728).

The remark about seeing and hearing is a quotation from Isa 6:9-10. This is a saying common to the other Synoptics also (Mk 4:10-12; Mt 13:10-17). Both Luke and Matthew follow Mark by inserting these verses after the Parable of the Sower. However, both redact the Markan source differently. All three Synoptics quote Isa 6:9-10 but in a different form in all three. The quotation in Luke is the shortest but it is repeated in fuller form in Acts 28:26-27 (Lane, 1996: 150). The removal of Mark's "so that they may not turn again and be forgiven" has reduced the emphasis upon the consequences for those without insight, with the result that in Lk 8:10 the stress is now upon the gift of understanding to the disciples. They are given insight into the nature of the kingdom of God, an important theme in Luke's thought (Robinson, 1966: 135).

The saying is uttered by Jesus to explain why he speaks in parables. The disciples are contrasted to the "others" who look and do not see, listen and do not understand. The reference to "others" (*tois loipois*, literally, "the rest") is explained further in Lk 8:12. They "are those who have heard; then the devil comes and takes away the word from their hearts, so that they may not believe and be saved." They have had a chance to respond but have not (Talbert, 1986: 147). The disciples are privileged with knowledge of the mysteries/ secrets of the kingdom of God. But Luke and Matthew change the singular Markan "mystery/secret" to "mysteries/secrets." The singular of Mark implies that the mystery is a single event, the reign of God in Jesus, while the plural in Luke and Matthew means various aspects of the reign of Christ which the disciples are privileged to share

(Siegmnan, 1961: 172). The disciples are being given insight into the *nature* of the kingdom of God (Robinson,
1968: 135).

Matthew changes the problematic *hina* ("so that") of
Mark 4:12 to *hoti* but Luke retains *hina*. *Hina* normally introduces a final (purpose) clause and Lk 8:10 is often so
understood. This would suggest that Jesus deliberately spoke
in parables so that people would not understand and thus
their hearts would be hardened. But, grammatically, *hina*
may also express a result clause. This makes better sense
and it is in this sense that some scholars understand *hina*
(Fitzmyer, 1981: 708-709). Thus the hardening of people's
hearts is the result and not the purpose of speaking in parables.
Thus the words "so that" do not express purpose but tragic
realization (see Lk 8:18). The fact that many in Israel had
rejected the message required some explanation (Danker,
1988: 177). This is fulfilling scripture and fitting in with
God's plan (Nolland, 1989: 380; Lane, 1996: 150-151).

It is a saying that is difficult to understand, but it can
be understood better by reading Acts. Indeed one must read
Acts if one is to understand what Luke really intended. If
this Lukan pericope is read in the light of Acts, especially
Acts 28:23-28, where Isa 6:9-10 is once more quoted, new
possibilities of meaning emerge. Paul was preaching to the
Jews in Rome, proclaiming the good news about Jesus. Some
believed and others disbelieved and departed after Paul quoted
Isa 6:9-10. Paul applied Isaiah's prophecy to the Jews' disbelief, that they hear and do not understand, see and do
not perceive. Paul concluded therefore that the salvation
of God had been sent to the Gentiles and they would listen (Acts 28:28). The quotation then in Acts should be
understood in the light of Jewish rejection and Gentile acceptance of the message of salvation, a theme common in
Luke-Acts. That Luke wanted the same connotation to be
applied to the quotation in the Gospel seems clear from
the fact that in the Gospel Luke gives an abbreviated quo-

tation while the fuller form is given in Acts 28. Further-more, Isa 6:9-10 was understood in the early Church as a prophecy of the rejection encountered by preaching (Holtz, 1968: 35). The Gospel pericope should be reread in the light of Acts to understand the full meaning (Lane, 1996: 151).

It seems then that in Luke one of the *mustēria* given to the disciples to know was the prior preaching to and rejec-tion of Jesus' message by the Jews and the salvation of the Gentiles. The same mystery of Israel hardening its heart is similarly called a *mustērion* by Paul (Rom 11:25; Gerhardsson, 1967-1968: 190). This explains why the mission to the Gentiles was so slow to materialize in Acts even after Jesus' explicit command in Lk 24:47 to preach to all nations.

By the end of Acts, the prior preaching to the Jews and their rejection of the message has been seen on a number of occasions. The quotation from Isaiah 6 standing at the end of Acts is a summary of what has been taking place in the course of the book. That a shorter form of this quota-tion is cited in Lk 8:10 and quoted in fuller form in Acts 28 after so many illustrations of the quotation have been offered, suggests that the prior preaching to the Jews, their rejection of Jesus' message and the Gentiles' acceptance of it, is one of the *mustēria* given to the disciples to know. Therefore Lk 8:10 is fully intelligible only by reading Acts and therefore implicitly preparing for Acts (Lane, 1996: 151-152).

Luke has softened Mark here, but still verse 10 shows that Luke is struggling with a matter every teacher and preacher has faced: Why is it that in the same audience some hear and some do not? Is it intelligence? Sin? Predes-tination? God's grace? Whatever the conclusion reached, whatever the theological underpinnings of that conclusion, one thing is clear: in the crowd of auditors, some disciples ask for help in understanding. They have a great deal invested in Jesus and his ministry and Jesus will not let them walk away empty and confused (Craddock, 1990: 112).

Luke does not share Mark's view that the purpose of Jesus' parables is to prevent repentance and forgiveness. What Luke seems to be saying instead is that whereas the disciples of Jesus receive full disclosure of the details pertaining to the kingdom of God, those who have not chosen to follow Jesus receive no more than parables. The implication is that not until one becomes a disciple of Jesus will one receive all the truth. In Luke the obduracy idea is present, but it is not presented in quite the same manner as in Mark. Unlike in Mark, in Luke only a softened version of the obduracy idea is applied to the disciples. They are unable to understand fully because it was God's will that they not know more fully until the risen Christ should explain the scriptures to them (Lk 24:25-27). At no time do they oppose Jesus, and at no time does Jesus regard them as having "hardened hearts," "blind eyes," or "deaf ears." It is likely that Luke regards all of the various types of response to Jesus as part of God's ordained plan (Evans, 1989: 118,120).

The parable sheds light on the proclaiming and liberating activity of Jesus and his disciples. But the story is also a key to the effect that Luke expects his book to have on his readers, as indicated in various ways. A first indication is that Luke refers to his Gospel account by the term *logos* ("word"; Lk 1:2), and that in Acts he refers back to his first volume by the same term. Moreover, at the beginning of the Parable of the Seed (Lk 8:4) as that of the Parable of the Word (Lk 8:10), the addressees are not explicitly mentioned. This enables the readers to count themselves among the addressees. Similarly, the summons to listen (Lk 8:8) and the formulation of Lk 8:16-18 are so general that they may be considered applicable to the readers (Weren, 1989: 20).

c. The Interpretation of the Parable (Lk 8:11-15)

Having shown the danger of unbelief in verse 10, Luke now returns to the parable, explaining why the proclaimed "word of God" (Lk 8:11) fails to bring a uniform response of faith (Liefeld, 1995: 113). According to many interpreters, in Lk 8:11-15 the parable is made into an allegory (Marshall, 1978: 323), that is, a story in which each item in the narration is said to represent something else. Most scholars take this interpretation to represent the situation of the early Church in its missionary preaching to a variety of conditions (Craddock, 1990: 112). Most scholars consider the interpretation to be secondary (Marshall, 1978: 323; Page, 1995: 115). But the Interpretation of the Parable in verses 11-15 is not an interpretation in the strict sense. Many words that belong to the agrarian world of the seed return. Verse 11 reads literally: "This is the parable: the seed is the word of God." Lk 8:11-15 may be best characterized as the Parable of the Word. This Parable of the Word is constructed in a way that is parallel to the Parable of the Seed. The Parable of the Seed and the Parable of the Word are tuned in to each other. Thereby the parable is also tuned in to the life praxis of Jesus and his disciples (Weren, 1989: 18-19).

Since application of Jesus' instruction was made by teachers in the Church in accordance with the mind of Christ, under the guidance of the one Spirit, Luke does not hesitate to follow Mark in attributing the explanation to Jesus, for he is the authoritative teacher (see Lk 24:32). As for Mark, he probably found precedent in Ezekiel 14 for the association of illustration and explanation that he found in the tradition of the recital. The four classes of hearers suggest types of response encountered by the apostolic proclamation (Danker, 1988: 177).

The Interpretation of the Parable moves in ascending order, from those who retain the word for the least amount of time (those who are along the road) to those who retain it permanently (those in good soil). But this does not mean that Jesus envisages a perceptional scale, an order of seeing and hearing that one may ascend as one learns better how to see and how to hear. Quite to the contrary, only the ones who retain the word in a good heart and bear fruit truly hear and see. Even those who internalize Jesus' word long enough to begin growing fruit (those among thorns) ultimately fail, for—so Jesus claims—genuine hearing always results in fruit. It is a "closed system" in which the one with the good heart perceives the sacred and produces (an unbelievable amount of) fruit, while all others, despite any indication to the contrary, remain completely barren. This categorical scenario is made even more vivid by Jesus a few sentences later: "Then pay attention to how you listen: for to those who have, more will be given; and from those who do not have, even what they seem to have will be taken away" (Lk 8:18). The fruit (wheat) one produces is actually *more seed*, which, in turn, produces more seed in the agricultural cycle. The seed is thus both received and delivered by the good soil, much as the witness is to perceive correctly and then pass along the word she or he has heard. The word is thus both seed and fruit, and its dissemination is the highest value. All of this impresses upon the audience that the stakes are high, that hearing and seeing (reading) are not to be taken for granted, that *how* one perceives is of ultimate import, that a genuine hearer is, necessarily, both receptive and productive (Darr, 1994: 100).

The latter lesson—that perception and action are linked— is clarified and reinforced by the addition of the short pericope of Jesus' mother and brothers trying to see him, but being unable to do so because of the crowd (Lk 8:19-21). This provides the platform for Jesus to claim: "My mother and my brothers are those who hear the word of God and do it." Hearing and doing the word is one of the narrative's

most prominent themes. Authentic perception will always
result in active obedience to the word (Lk 6:46-49; 11:27-
28). One cannot be a true hearer without being a doer, for
the word is at one and the same time a proclamation of
freedom and a summons to decision, responsibility, and action. Through such rhetoric, the authorial audience learns
that there is an ethical dimension to reading this narrative,
for it requires introspection, investment, and personal response, not passive (or resistant) auditing (Darr, 1994: 100-
101).

Verse 11:   "Now the parable is this:
             The seed is the word of God.

Although Jesus continues to speak to the disciples, he
does so within the hearing of the larger crowd that has
gathered about him, because at the end of his parabolic
teaching the crowds are still present (Lk 8:19b; Green, 1997:
323,327).

The opening clause may be translated: "the parable means
this" (Marshall, 1978: 324). The sower is no longer mentioned, and so is not identified directly with Jesus (Schweizer,
1984: 145). In fact, the parable itself already focused the
reader's attention not on the sower himself but on the seed
and what happened to it (LaVerdiere, 1980: 113).

In Mark the seed is "the word," which Luke qualified
with "of God" (see Lk 5:1; 8:21), because this expression
had not yet been used absolutely, that is, without qualification (contrast Mk 1:45; 2:2). Later "the word" will be used
without qualification throughout Acts (see Acts 4:4; 6:4;
8:4; 10:36; Stein, 1992: 246). Luke situates his story in a
network of interpretation, identifying the "seed" of the farming
story with the "word of God" in the story of the realization
of God's purpose in his ministry. In identifying the seed as
the word of God, he also grounds the meaning of his ministry in the ancient story of Israel. Yahweh was active in
creation and redemption by means of his word, and the

prophets were the bearers of the word of God. In associating Jesus' ministry so intimately with the word of God (Lk 5:1) the narrative presents Jesus as the one who discloses and brings to fruition the divine purpose, in the face of which response is not only possible but mandatory (Green, 1997: 327).

That "the seed is the word of God" is an association that was also made in Judaism (Schürmann, 1969: 463 note 131; Fitzmyer, 1981: 712; Bock, 1994: 732). Luke omitted Mk 4:13 in his abbreviated account. This may have been due to his desire to omit the negative comment about the disciples (Stein, 1992: 245).

Verse 12:   The ones on the path are those who have heard;
                then the devil comes and takes away the word from
                    their hearts,
                so that they may not believe and be saved.

"The ones on the path" refers to the seed planted by the road, and the masculine form may refer to the individual seeds or the persons represented by them. Strictly speaking, it is the various types of ground that represent the different groups of people, but with an understandable looseness the people are identified rather with the plants that spring from the ground as a result of the sowing of the seed (Marshall, 1978: 325; Stein, 1992: 246).

The "devil" actually means the "slanderer," who causes confusion and thus seeks to alienate human beings from God (Schweizer, 1984: 145). The devil is identified with the birds that ate the seed along the path. The symbolic association of birds with Satan was well established in late Judaism. Indeed there is a very close parallel to this aspect of the parable in *Jubilees* 11:5-24. *Jubilees* 11:11 says that, before the time of Abraham, Prince Mastema (Satan) sent birds to eat the seed that was being sown by farmers. Then the land began to be barren (verse 13). In verses 18-24 the narrative goes on to tell how Abraham frightened the birds away and devised a method of planting the seed that prevented the birds from getting it. In addition to this story, Satan is associated with birds in the *Apocalypse of Abraham* 13:3-7 and *1 Enoch* 90:8-13. In the Parable of the Sower, the identification of the birds with Satan is not arbitrary, and it would have been reasonable for Jesus to expect that a Jewish audience would think of Satan when they heard of birds taking away the word of God (Knowles, 1995: 145-151). Oddly enough, each version of the Interpretation of the Parable refers to Satan by a different expression. Mark uses "Satan" (Mk 4:15); Matthew uses "the evil one" (Mt 13:19); and Luke uses "the devil" (Lk 8:12). There does not appear to be any significance to this variation, although it should be noted that Mark and Luke never refer to Satan as "the evil one" (Page, 1995: 114-115).

Mark focuses on Satan's role in aborting the beginnings of spiritual life and makes no reference to the responsibility of the person who hears the message. In Matthew and Luke are comments that show that the absence of fruitfulness is not due to Satan alone. Matthew qualifies the statement about hearing the message with the observation that the message is not understood (Mt 13:19). Luke follows the statement about the devil's taking the word away with the result clause "so that they may not believe and be saved" (Page, 1995: 116). In fact, this addition is the most striking divergence from Mark in Luke's interpretation. It reflects Luke's intense concern regarding salvation (Liefeld, 1995: 113). If this emphasis on utter destruction is not to be derived from Luke's version of the parable itself, and if it is not a "Paulinism" in Luke (Haenchen), then what is its origin? It seems that it is from Mk 4:12, replacing "so that they may not turn again and be forgiven," the part of the Isaiah 6 reference which Luke omitted from Lk 8:10 parallel Mk 4:12 (Robinson, 1966: 134).

Some people never seem interested—they are like the first soil. Or if they do show some interest in the word of

God, only the most bizarre elements speak to them. It is hard to reach people in whom the seed has never taken root (Bock, 1996: 233). For such people, hearing is the most that happens. There is no attraction to the message or reflection on it. Another point is important here. This text is not an existential moment-by-moment picture of how one receives the word at various times, but pictures what the word does throughout the totality of one's life. One is not pictured as moving from soil to soil at different times. Such an application might be drawn from this imagery, but it is not the point of the parable. The soil represents the different kinds of individuals viewed in terms of their whole life, not the different responses of an individual. Taking one's life as a whole, the parable is designed to produce reflection on the question, "What single type of response to the word have I given?" Or, "What various responses to the word exist among people as one looks at the whole pattern of their response?" Jesus is explaining why the word is received in a variety of ways. He notes that many obstacles prevent fruit-bearing, while faithful, patient reception produces fruit (Bock, 1994: 733-734).

Verse 13:   The ones on the rock are those who,
              when they hear the word,
              receive it with joy.
              But these have no root;
              they believe only for a while
              and in a time of testing fall away.

The second group of seed faces the first obstacle to fruitfulness: a shallow faith that cannot survive the pressure of persecution (Bock, 1994: 735). Those in verse 12 do not have faith; those in verse 13 have faith only for a while. They initially receive the word with joy. The term "receive" is a Lukan expression for responding positively toward Jesus, the gospel, or the gospel messengers (Lk 9:5,48,53; 10:8,10; 18:17). These hearers even receive the word with the proper attitude of "joy" (Lk 1:14; 2:10; 24:41,52; Stein, 1992: 246). The major point is that this belief is short-lived and unproductive because trial dissolves faith (Brown, 1969: 12-16,30-31). These two references to having faith in verses 12 and 13 are absent from the parallels to these verses in Mark and Matthew. Those with a temporary faith in verse 13 contrast with those who "hold fast the word" and bear fruit "with steadfastness" (different Mark, Matthew; Talbert: 1986: 211).

Luke's use of the word *peirasmos* ("testing") in Acts 20:19 with reference to Paul's testings (especially in light of the close association with *thlipsis* ["tribulation"; NRSV translates: "persecutions"] in Acts 20:23) indicates that in the present setting, *peirasmos* ("testing") may at least include persecution. This is further confirmed by Luke's use of *hupomonē* ("patient endurance") as a contrast to those that fall away (Lk 8:15), for the only other use of *hupomonē* in Luke-Acts is clearly in the context of suffering persecution (Lk 21:19; Cunningham, 1997: 77-78).

The emphasis on firmness and persistence marks the difference between true faith and the temporary faith of those who grow on rocky ground. The story of the storm on the lake (Lk 8:22-25), which follows the Interpretation of the Sower more quickly in Luke than in Mark, shows that the disciples do not achieve this steady faith immediately (Lk 8:25; Talbert, 1986: 211-212).

Verse 14:   As for what fell among the thorns,
              these are the ones who hear,
              but as they go on their way,
              they are choked by the cares and riches and
                  pleasures of life,
              and their fruit does not mature.

The third group of seed also fails to bear fruit. Like the second soil there is a start in faith but no perseverance. The wording's implication is that a response to the message occurs ("they go on their way"), but nothing comes to complete fruition because other matters crowd out the word's ability to do its cultivating work (Bock, 1994: 737). There is the danger that faith will be choked out "by cares and riches and pleasures of life." One has noted a similar expression in Jewish thought. CD (= Damascus Document) 4:15-5:10 speaks of a threefold obstacle in which Israel was ensnared: defiling the sanctuary, excessive wealth, and taking two women in one's lifetime—a list distinct from Jesus' in particulars but parallel in tone (Fitzmyer, 1981: 714).

If possessions are not handled as Jesus directs and if the situation of persecution is not faced steadfastly, the seed will fail to bear fruit. Possessions and persecutions will be major continuing concerns in Jesus' later instruction of the disciples. While the "time of temptation/testing" need not be restricted to situations of persecution, persecution must be a major part of the meaning of this phrase, as the use of *peirasmos* ("temptation/testing") in Lk 22:40,46; Acts 20:19 indicates. Persecution is one of the major problems for disciples, and Jesus will repeatedly seek to prepare his followers for it (see Lk 9:23-26; 12:1-12; 21:12-19). According to Lk 21:19 persecution must be met by "endurance" or "steadfastness" (*hupomonē*), and in Lk 8:15 Jesus points to the same quality as characteristic of those who bear fruit (different in Mark and Matthew). The second major danger concerns possessions. In Lk 8:14 the "cares" are anxieties for the daily needs of life that money can provide (see Lk 12:22-32; 21:34), and an interest in "pleasures" also leads one to seek the "riches" that can provide them. The conflict between discipleship and the desire for possessions and financial security is also a subject of repeated instruction to the disciples, including several comparatively lengthy speeches (see Lk 12:22-34; 16:1-13). Thus the two potential problems for disciples briefly indicated in Jesus' interpretation of the Parable of the Sower become important themes of Jesus' teaching of disciples in later chapters. The interpretation of the Parable of the Sower prepares for this (Talbert, 1986: 211).

Verse 15:   But as for that in the good soil,
              these are the ones who,
              when they hear the word,
              hold it fast in an honest and good heart,
              and bear fruit with patient endurance.

The fourth group of seed has the response that yields fruit. Luke does not mention levels of fruitfulness (contrast Mk 4:8: "thirty and sixty and a hundredfold"). He speaks simply of success. There are three keys to that response. The first is the right kind of heart: an honest and good heart (the reference to the heart is not found in Mark and Matthew). A part of Luke's Hellenistic perspective is the phrase "an honest and good heart."

In the anthropology of the first-century Mediterranean, the heart and eyes were thought of as the center of emotion-fused thought. The mouth, ears, and tongue, and lips were the locus of expression. The arms, legs, hands, and feet were the symbols for action. When all three zones are involved, as they are here, we are to understand that the total person was involved (Malina-Rohrbaugh, 1992: 334).

The terms for "honest" and "good" (see Tob 5:14 and 2 Mac 15:12) are commonly combined by Greek writers into one expression, denoting a person of exceptional merit (Danker, 1982: 319-320; 1988: 177). Among those who have heard the word in good faith ("honest and good heart"), God will cause the word to grow and prosper (Tiede, 1988: 168-169).

The second key response is holding fast to the word, which is another way to speak of faith, since the verb portrays clinging to the word.

The third response is "patient endurance." The word "patient endurance" (*hupomonē*) suggests that the four classes of hearers refer to types encountered by the apostolic proclamation. "Patience" means endurance or perseverance and describes disciples who hold out in the face of opposition (see Lk 21:19), not succumbing like the shallow-rooted people of verse 13, who fall away in time of temptation.

If it is true that the Parable of the Sower does continue Luke's concern to instruct the disciples on the correct response to persecution, then he has also introduced another facet of this theme with the use of *hupomonē*, "patient endurance," the last word of the pericope. The need of endurance in the midst of persecution will be emphatically stated in Lk 21:19: "By your endurance you will gain your souls." The witnesses to persecution in Acts also demonstrate the point. Although the word *hupomonē* does not reappear in Acts, perseverance is exhorted through the words of the chief characters (Acts 11:23; 13:43; 14:22), as well as their actions, that serve as frequent models of steadfastness and perseverance in the face of opposition (Cunningham, 1997: 78).

d. The Parable of the Lamp *(Lk 8:16-18)*

The Parable of the Lamp occurs in two different contexts in Luke, firstly in Lk 8:16 in the section on the word of God (Lk 8:4-21) and secondly in Lk 11:33 in the Travel Narrative. Unlike Mk 4:21f., Lk 8:16f. is closely connected with the preceding context (Rauscher, 1994: 221-222). There is not even a transition phrase, for these words are an explication of what the parable means for Luke's readers (Tiede, 1988: 168).

This episiode provides an excellent opportunity to observe the influence of context on the meaning of a passage: its repetition in the tradition indicates that it should be interpreted contextually in each case (Bock, 1994: 744-745). Mark tells the story in a setting of intense controversy in which the tension between Jesus and his critics extends to Jesus and his family. Mark also locates it prior to the Parable of the Sower. In Luke's location immediately *after* the Parable of the Sower, the episode illustrates the truth of the parable: hearing and doing the word of God is the way into the fellowship created by Jesus. And by removing the event from an atmosphere of controversy, and reducing it, Luke has the coming of Jesus' mother and brothers become the occasion for Jesus to teach that the family of God includes all who hear and do God's will (Craddock, 1990: 113).

The function of light is to make visible that which was previously hidden in darkness. So it will be with Jesus' message. Everything that is hidden will be made known and all secrets will be brought to light. One must therefore listen with care, since we are all accountable. There is much at stake, for whoever has, in terms of responding to revelation, will get more. On the other hand, those who do not have because they refuse to respond will lose what they seemed to have, ending up with nothing (Bock, 1996: 231).

Verse 16: "No one after lighting a lamp hides it under a jar,
  or puts it under a bed,
  but puts it on a lampstand,
  so that those who enter may see the light.

  [No one after lighting a lamp
  puts it in a cellar,
  but on the lampstand
  so that those who enter may see the light (Lk
  11:33)].

The peasant house of first-century Palestine was generally a single room. The family lived in one end, often elevated, while the other end was used for livestock at night. Such a one-room house is envisioned here, if all who enter can see the lightstand (Malina-Rohrbaugh, 1992: 335).

This parable occurs also in the other Synoptics (Mk 4:21 and Mt 5:15). There are two different traditions concerning this parable, that of Mark and that of Matthew (Q), and Luke seems to know both traditions (but see Rauscher,

1994: 42-46; 91-123, who opts for two successive stages of the Markan tradition: Mark and Deutero-Mark [Fuchs]). Lk 8:16; 11:33 and Mt 5:15 contain a number of agreements over against Mk 4:21 (Rauscher, 1994: 35-41). Commentators agree that Luke used Mark as his source for Lk 8:16, since Lk 8:16-18 follows the same order as Mk 4:21-25, and that Q is the source for Lk 11:33, but Lk 8:16 also seems to have been influenced by Q (Marshall, 1978: 328; Fitzmyer, 1981: 717; for a detailed discussion of Luke's redaction, see Rauscher, 1994: 64-90). Thereby Luke tightens the connection with what immediately precedes. Thus mention of the shining lamp follows in Lk 8:16 directly on the statement of fruitbearing (Lk 8:15), so that the lamp does not refer to the disciples' ability to understand Jesus' esoteric teaching, as it seems to do in Mark, but refers to fruitful Christian witness; "lighting" in Lk 8:16 is then analogous to "hold fast the word" in Lk 8:15. Further reference to the missionary ministry of the Church in Luke's time may be seen in the addition of "so that those who enter may see the light" (Lk 8:16; Robinson, 1966: 132-133).

So, although the metaphor field changes abruptly, Luke registers no shift in topic. The central concern of Jesus' Interpretation of the Parable of the Sower has been "how one hears." Having established the norms of hearing by which to determine authentic discipleship in verses 11-15, Jesus continues along the same lines by insisting that authentic (and inauthentic) hearing, although grounded in one's heart, is manifest in one's behavior. The truism of verse 16, with its list of bizarre attempts to conceal what is obviously meant to provide illumination, is just that, a saying with which everyone would agree. In the same way, Jesus argues, how one has heard the word of God cannot be hidden but eventually will manifest itself—either in practices appropriate to God's people (and outlined in the Sermon on the Plain, Lk 6:20-49) or in failure to do so (Green, 1997: 329).

In Mark the parable takes the form of *two rhetorical*

questions and the lamp is the *subject:* "Is a lamp brought in to be put under the bushel basket, or under the bed, and not on the lampstand?" (Mk 4:21). The twofold question form is characteristic of Semitic expression (Rauscher, 1994: 245-248). In Luke and Matthew instead, the parable takes the form of a *statement* and the lamp is the *object* of the statement, under the influence of Q. The place where the lamp is not put varies according to the versions. In Lk 8:16 it is not put under a jar or under a bed and in Lk 11:33 it is not put in a cellar [some old manuscripts add: "or under a bushel basket" (a bushel is an eight gallon measure for fruit or grain)]. In Mk 4:21 it is not put under a bushel basket or under a bed and in Mt 5:15 it is not put under a bushel basket. The "no one" (*oudeis*) at the beginning of the statement sounds apodictic (Ernst 1977: 381) and prohibitive. It is part of an unconditional demand to give up a particular possibility and to embrace a reality that is expressed in the positive part of the saying. In the apodosis the positive repectively negative consequences of the option expressed in the "no one" clause are explicitated. Basically this form schema appeals to the listeners to correct their perception of reality, their attitude, and their actions (Rauscher, 1994: 251).

It is interesting to note the reason given by the evangelists for putting the lamp on the stand. In Mark the reason is not given. In Mt 5:15 the reason is so that it gives light to all those in the house. In Lk 8:16 and 11:33 the lamp is put on the stand so that those who enter may see the light. Not just once, but twice Luke has made an addition to the parable. Lukan redaction has come into play, altering sources for his own purposes.

What is the reason for the Lukan addition: "so that those who enter may see the light" (Lk 8:16; 11:33)? In Mk 4:21 the lamp is not to be put under "the bed," while Lk 8:15 omits the article, saying the lamp is not put under "a bed." Therefore, the suggestion is that it is not the only bed in the Lukan house. Lk 8:16 and Mt 5:15 state that the lamp is put "on a stand." In Lk 11:33 the lamp is put "on the stand" (*epi tēn luchnias*). Lk 8:16 makes a grammatical correction not made in Lk 11:33, having changed the accusative to genitive: the lamp is "on a stand" (*epi luchnias*). The lampstand is not the only lampstand in the Lukan house.

The solution to the reason for this Lukan redaction cannot be that Luke had one type of house in mind as opposed to another (*pace* Dupont, 1985: 1037). There is something peculiar in Luke redacting the parable the way he did. The reason for this will be seen in reading Acts: in other words, the parable can be better comprehended by reading Acts and indeed foreshadows Acts. Of course, the parable can be understood without reading Acts, but by reading Acts it gets added meaning. But before explaining the parable in the context of Luke-Acts, it would be natural to explain it in its immediate context in both Luke 8 and Luke 11 (Lane, 1996: 132-134).

It is obvious that one lights a lamp to give light; one does not light a lamp to cover it (Jeremias, 1940: 237-240). Because of its context in Luke 8 in the section on the word of God (Lk 8:4-21), the saying of the lamp in Lk 8:16 is regarded as encouragement for the disciples in their work of evangelization (C.F. Evans, 1990: 369). In this case the shining lamp is the person who has heard the word of God and makes it visible (Nolland, 1989: 391). Lk 8:16 is connected to Lk 8:17-18 (following Mk 4:21-25) but it is best to regard Lk 8:16 as originally an independent saying that was later joined to the following verses. Even so, its present meaning is influenced by its grouping with Lk 8:17-18. According to Lk 8:17 nothing is hidden that will not be manifest, thus in this context what Jesus taught the disciples in private (Lk 8:10) will be made known (the light must be put on the stand). Verse 18 is encouragement to the disciples to listen well, because they have to proclaim openly so that others will see the light (Swartz, 1994: 53-59; Ruch, 1996: 11-17).

When Luke repeats the saying later in Lk 11:33, he obviously intends to have a different nuance or to introduce something new. Lk 11:33 is centered more on Christ. Because of its immediate context coming after the sign of Jonah, the implication is that Jesus is the sign, Jesus is the lamp shining for this generation. The enlightening lamp in Lk 11:33 may be taken as Christ whose teaching illuminates humankind. Lk 11:33 is connected to Lk 11:34-36 through the use of light imagery, but Lk 11:33 is normally considered as being of independent origin (Garrett, 1991: 101-105; Lane, 1996: 134-135).

Neither Mark nor Matthew mention the word "light" in the Parable of the Lamp. In Mark, Jesus asks if the lamp is not put on the lampstand (Mk 4:21). Although the purpose is understood, it is not stated. In Matthew the lamp is put on the stand to light up all those in the house (Mt 5:15). But in Luke the lamp is put on the stand so that those who enter may see the "light" (phōs, Lk 8:16; 11:33). There is a peculiarity about the Lukan redaction that can be comprehended better by reading Acts.

An examination of the use of phōs in Luke reveals that it is sometimes used in a literal sense (e.g., Lk 22:56; Lane, 1996: 136). The use of phōs in the literal sense clearly cannot be applied to the Gentile mission. But the three figurative uses in Lk 8:16; 11:33; 12:3 are open to this application. Indeed it seems likely that Luke was hinting at such a subtle layer of meaning in the Parable of the Lamp in view of the uses of phōs elsewhere in connection with the Gentile mission (Lk 2:32; Acts 13:47; 26:17-18; 26:23; Rauscher, 1994: 343). The light of Christ was not to be reserved only for the Jews, but was to be put on the lampstand so that all those coming into the house, the Gentiles, might see it. Both uses of the parable, Lk 8:16 encouraging disciples in spreading the word, and Lk 11:33 describing Jesus as rev-

elation, may be read with this secondary meaning. Thus in
Lk 8:16 the disciples are to listen well so that they will
make the light visible also to the Gentiles. In Lk 11:33
Jesus is the lamp shining to cast his light also on the Gentiles.

An investigation of the semantic field of illumination
in Luke-Acts demonstrates that the Jewish people is passing from vision to lack of vision and the Gentiles are passing from darkness to light. That the semantic field of illumination shows salvation advancing to the Gentiles also
lends more weight to the probability that Luke has the Gentile
mission in mind in Lk 8:16 and 11:33.

The addition of the word *phōs* is not the only piece of
Lukan redaction deserving attention. Both Lk 8:16 and 11:33
mention that the light is put on the stand so that those
who are coming in (*hoi eisporeuomenoi*) may see the light.
In the context of Luke-Acts, given that Luke is writing in
the time of the Church, *hoi eisporeuomenoi* can reasonably
be taken to allude to those who in the second volume are
invited in to see the light, that is, the Gentiles. Although
the verb *eisporeuomai*, "to go/come in," normally refers to
persons physically moving into a house or city (Lk 19:30;
22:10), Luke does use it elsewhere in a figurative sense for
entering the kingdom (Lk 18:24), which adds weight to the
suggestion that Luke could use it in a figurative sense elsewhere, namely Lk 8:16 and 11:33. Furthermore, in Acts 14:27
Luke describes the Gentiles entering the Church as coming
through a door of faith: "God opened a door of faith to the
Gentiles." Therefore, in Lk 8:16 and 11:33 the third evangelist most likely envisaged the Gentiles entering through a
door of faith and seeing the light, receiving salvation (Lane,
1996: 136-137), although the matter has not been given
much attention by scholars, being for the most part raised
and taken for granted (Fitzmyer, 1981: 939) or raised and
dismissed (Marshall, 1978: 329) in the space of one sentence.

Verse 17:   For nothing is hidden that will not be disclosed,
              nor is anything secret that will not become known
              and come to light.

"For" ties Lk 8:17 closely to Lk 8:16, but the exact relationship between these two verses is debated. This verse
is associated with the preceding by similar contrasts (light/
darkness; disclosed/hidden; brought out into the open/con-
cealed) so that Luke probably used it as a commentary on
Lk 8:16 (Stein, 1992: 249). Light not only illumines, it
exposes. The standards in Jesus' proclamation also examine
how people are responding to God. God's truth is preached
publicly, and it is the function of truth to illumine, to expose reality (Lk 8:16). It will expose the various responses
that the soils give and make clear to the disciples that God
will evaluate how each person responds to the word (Bock,
1994: 745-746).

The words in verse 17 further explain the point made
in verse 10. It may be Luke's intention to stress that Jesus
had no secret communication (see Lk 22:53). He has taught
openly, and there is nothing subversive in his activity. But
it is more probable that the words originally echoed Deut
29:29: "The secret things belong to the Lord our God, but
the revealed things belong to us and to our children for-
ever, to observe all the words of this law." With the advent
of the Messiah, God reveals the mysteries, that is, the plans
for the end time, expressed in Jesus (see Lk 1:78-79; Danker,
1988; 1178).

Verse 18:   Then pay attention to how you listen;
              for to those who have, more will be given;
              and from those who do not have,
              even what they seem to have will be taken away."

Verse 18 should probably be taken as the closing statement of Lk 8:4-18. It takes up a proverbial sounding statement that the rich become richer and the poor become poorer
(Stein, 1992: 249), which is also applied to stewardship of

blessings given by God in Lk 19:26 (C.F. Evans, 1990: 376), and applies it to the way in which the disciples hear the word of God. Those who pay heed to it will receive further insight, while those who fail to pay attention will be deprived even of the little they seem to have (Marshall, 1978: 327-328; Stein, 1992: 249). In the context of receiving the word of God which is to be shared, Jesus' statement makes eminent sense. The word of God is not given as a private possession; it is not given to keep under lock and key. Those people who try to keep the word of God as their private possession will discover that they have lost even what they thought they had. The word thrives in being shared, and when it is shared with others the one who shares will be given more (McBride, 1982: 107-108). We should note the additional word "seem to" in Luke: "even what they seem to have" [RSV: "even what he thinks that he has"; Mk 4:25; Mt 13:12, "even what he has"].

When Jesus speaks to his *narrative* audiences (e.g., disciples, crowds, Pharisees) about seeing and hearing, the authorial audience [the general readers that the author had in mind as he wrote] infers a direct analogy to the reading/ listening process in which they are currently involved, their own seeing/hearing of the story. In other words, Jesus' references to perception guide and condition reading itself. When, for example, Jesus warns his followers to "pay attention to how you listen," the reader/listener realizes that he or she also must carefully attend to what is happening in the story world. The emphasis of Lk 8:18 is clearly on "how you listen," whose intention is at the center of Luke's presentation in Lk 8:11-17. The quality of the reception of the word is under discussion (Rauscher, 1994: 228).

"The reader" should probably be envisaged not as an isolated individual reading the narrative silently to him or herself, but rather as part of a group taking in an oral performance of the Gospel narrative. The fact that ancient readers were usually listeners buttresses our contention about the rhetorical function of Jesus' references to perception. The group literally hears Jesus' words, even as his narrative audiences hear them, and so is sensitive to instruction about how to listen (Darr, 1994: 88). Luke repeatedly refers to the seed/word being "taken away" from people who are not prepared to retain it (see Lk 8:12; Darr, 1994: 102 note 17).

Since the revelation brought by Jesus is so open, hearers have all the more responsibility to take heed how they hear. The mysteries of the kingdom have been given to the disciples. These mysteries become even more meaningful to them as they ponder their responsibility in the light of the message. The words in verse 18b express the opposite experience and restate the thought of verse 10b. The statement means: People who are complacent, resist further instruction, and do not review themselves in the light of Jesus' message will experience collapse of the foundations on which they built their false lives (Danker, 1988: 178).

The parable, its interpretation, and the accompanying sayings convey the promise and joy of God's reign, the hundredfold yield. But the promise and joy are wrapped in stern warnings. The "theological education" that these disciples (and especially the chosen Twelve) are receiving in the company of Jesus is no academic exercise or ecclesiastical requirement. Instead, everything is hanging in the balance in it: "To those who have, more will be given; and from those who do not have, even what they seem to have will be taken away" (Ringe, 1995: 116). The disciples must be very careful to hear so that through them others might hear. Discipleship is thus apostolic. Should the disciples fail to assume their apostolic mission, their own hearing as disciples would be dulled, and they themselves would no longer understand the word (Lk 18:18; LaVerdiere, 1980: 115).

When we approach this text, we tend to present it as a one-moment response: "as you hear this message today, which soil are you?" But the question is more comprehensive: "as you look at the direction your life has taken up to today, which soil are you?" The parable looks at a career of response. A plant does not sprout forth overnight, nor does the harvest of the heart (Bock, 1996: 232).

e. Jesus' Mother and Brothers: The Real Hearers (Lk 8:19-21)

Mark and Matthew continue with parabolic teaching at this point (Mk 4:26ff.; Mt 13:24ff.), but Luke turns to an incident Mark and Matthew locate at the conclusion of the Beelzebul controversy. When he comes to this controversy (Lk 11:14-28), Luke inserts something different, though on the same theme of obedience to God's word. Here the theme of obedience appropriately continues Lk 8:5-15 (Liefeld, 1995: 116).

Luke returns to Mk 3:31-35 for this account about the family of Jesus. He omits entirely one of Jesus' parables (Mk 4:26-29, the Parable of the Seed Growing Secretly) and postpones another (Mk 4:30-32, the Parable of the Mustard Seed; see Lk 13:18-19). Nothing is permitted at this point to detract from the main theme: responsive hearing. The thought of this passage is in harmony with Luke's frequent emphasis on the precedence of the kingdom of God over tribal loyalties (see Lk 9:59-62; 12:51-53; 14:25-26). One must be able to break out of that constricting cocoon. Jesus' own practice serves as an example to the community to be open to new relationships (Danker, 1988: 179). In this pericope Luke informs his readers that belonging to Jesus' family is not a matter of physical kinship, but of hearing and doing God's word (Stein, 1992: 250). But Luke does not present members of Jesus' family in any way that would mark them as "outsiders" to his mission (pace Schneider, 1977: 188). Neither does he at this point present his mother and brothers as exemplary disciples (pace Fitzmyer, 1981: 222-225,723, who is also opposed by Tannehill, 1986: 212-

213; Bauckham, 1990: 51), though he will count them within the group of Jesus' followers after Jesus' ascension (Acts 1:14). Jesus neither rejects nor praises his physical family; rather he uses their arrival as a catalyst to redefine in the hearing of his disciples and the crowds the basis of kinship (Green, 1997: 330).

This passage spells out a basic theme of Luke, who sees the good news centering in the "household" of believers rather than the Temple or the biological family. Moreover, this tendency to form "family" groups across the normal boundaries that separated people plays a key role in Luke's story of the spreading Church in the Acts of the Apostles.

Religion in the first century was embedded in either politics or kinship. There was political religion and domestic religion. Domestic religion took its social clues from the household or family system then in vogue. Thus extant household or family forms and norms provided the early Christian movement with one of its basic images of social identity and cohesion.

In antiquity, the extended family meant everything. It not only was the source of one's honor status in the community but also functioned as the primary economic, religious, educational, and social network. Loss of connection to the family meant the loss of these vital networks as well as loss of connection to the land. But a surrogate family, what anthropologists call a fictive kin group, could serve many of the same functions as a biological family. The Christian group acting as a surrogate family is for Luke the locus of the good news. It transcends the normal categories of birth, class, race, gender, education, wealth, and power—hence is inclusive in a startling new way. For those already detached from their biological families (e.g., non-inheriting sons who go to the city), the surrogate family becomes a place of refuge. For the well-connected, however, particularly the city elite, giving up one's biological family for the surrogate family, as Luke portrays Jesus demanding here, was a decision that could cost one dearly (see Lk 9:57-62; 12:51-53; 14:26; 18:28-30). It meant an irrevocable break with the networks on which the elite life-style depended. And it seems that Luke is concerned largely with the problems of such elite persons (Malina-Rohrbaugh, 1992: 335-336).

Verses 19-21: (19) Then his mother and his brothers came to him,
                    but they could not reach him because of the
                    crowd.
               (20) And he was told,
                    "Your mother and your brothers
                    are standing outside, wanting to see you."
               (21) But he said to them,
                    "My mother and my brothers
                    are those who hear the word of God and do it."

Lk 8:19 sets the stage for Jesus' remark in Lk 8:21. No mention is made of the reason for coming (different in Mk 3:31-35). Luke simply notes that the crowd prevented Mary and the brothers from getting to Jesus. In the history of the Church there have been three main explanations about who the "brothers" of Jesus were. (1) The Helvidian view argues that they were the subsequent sons (and daughters; cf. Mk 6:3) of Joseph and Mary. (2) The Epiphanian view argued that they were the sons (and daughters) of Joseph via an earlier marriage in which the wife died, that is, Jesus' older stepbrothers and stepsisters. (3) The Hieronymian view (the view of Jerome) argues that they were cousins of Jesus, that is, the term "brothers" is being used figuratively (Stein, 1992: 250-251).

EXCURSUS ON A RECENT DISCUSSION REGARDING JESUS AND HIS BROTHERS AND SISTERS

Recently the question has again been the subject of a number of publications by John P. Meier and Richard Bauckham. The latter, a Protestant writer, while rejecting Jerome's solution, is willing to give serious consideration to the Epiphanian as well as the Helvidian solution. His openness to the Epiphanian solution rests on his positive evaluation of certain patristic statements that many other critics would consider dubious as historical sources (Bauckham, 1990: 19-32). This "accepting" attitude reaches a remarkable high point in the treatment of the names of the sisters of Jesus (Bauckham, 1990: 37-44).

The New Testament evidence has been given extensive attention by John P. Meier (1991: 316-332; 1992: 1-28). He starts from the observation that ordinary Christians today, if they know anything about the problem of the brothers and sisters of Jesus, have a vague notion that Catholics hold that Jesus' "brothers" and "sisters" were really cousins, while Protestants maintain that they were true siblings having the same two parents. Actually, the theological battle-lines down through the centuries have been much more complex. In the first four centuries of the Church, different views on this question were held by various Christians, who were not formally excommunicated by the Church of their day for their differing positions. What is often considered the common teaching of the Roman Catholic Church, namely, that the brothers and sisters of Jesus were really cousins, and that not only Mary but also Joseph was a perpetual virgin, was first championed by Jerome in his tract *Against Helvidius* (ca. 383). This became the predominant position in the West during the Middle Ages, while the view that the brothers and sisters were children of Jospeph by a previous marriage remained predominant in the East (mentioned for the first time in the *Protoevangelium of James*).

A startling fact that many present-day Catholics and Protestants do not know is that the great figures of the Protestant Reformation, notably Martin Luther and John Calvin, held to Mary's perpetual virginity and therefore did not consider the brothers and sisters of Jesus as true siblings. It was only with the rise of the Enlightenment that the idea that the brothers and sisters were biological children of Mary and Joseph gained acceptance among "mainline" Protestants. With the exception of a few "high-church" Protestants, this is the common view in Protestant churches today.

That the brothers and sisters were really cousins or some other distant relatives is still the common teaching of the Roman Catholic Church, although, in recent decades, some Catholic theologians and exegetes have espoused the view that the brothers and sisters were true siblings. Prominent among Catholic exegetes is the German scholar Rudolf Pesch, who championed the "true siblings" position in his massive two-volume commentary of Mark (Pesch, 1976-1977: 322-325). Although his claims raised much controversy among German Catholics, he has never been officially censured or condemned by Rome for his views (Meier, 1992: 5-7).

In the following we ask simply and solely what can reasonably be deduced from the data of the New Testament viewed purely as potential historical sources (Meier, 1991: 318-332). A study of the major New Testament texts leads to the conclusion that "the immediate, natural, 'surface' sense of the passages favors the idea of bloodbrothers" (Meier, 1992: 8-15 [15]). To be honest, the so-called "Epiphanian solution" (sponsored by bishop Epiphanius of Salamis on Cyprus, A.D. 315-402), whereby these brothers are seen as sons of Joseph by a previous marriage, strikes one from the start as arbitrary and gratuitous. The infancy narratives of Matthew and Luke lend no positive support to such an idea. The solution of Jerome, who seems to be the first Father of the Church to have suggested that the brothers of Jesus were actually cousins and that both Joseph and Mary were perpetual virgins seems to be a solution thought up to defend the perpetual virginity of Mary. The idea that Joseph was a perpetual virgin was a novelty in the fourth century and has no basis in Scripture. But what about the heart of Jerome's claim, namely, that the Greek word for "brother," *adelphos*, actually means "cousin" in the Gospel texts that speak of the brothers of Jesus? A number of philological arguments can be brought forward to support Jerome's theory; but close examination shows that they are not as probative as might first appear (McHugh, 1975: 223-233). Depending on the immediate context, the Hebrew word *'ah* or the Greek *adelphos* can mean cousin, nephew, or some other relative. No such clarification is given in the New Trestament texts concerning the brothers of Jesus. Rather, the regularity with which they are yoked with Jesus' mother gives the exact opposite impression.

In the New Testament, if we prescind from the disputed case of "the brothers of the Lord" (1 Cor 9:5), there is no clear use of the Greek word *adelphos* ("brother") to mean precisely "cousin." The various meanings of *adelphos* in the New Testament can be boiled down to two basic senses, literal and metaphorical.

(1) First and foremost, *adelphos* is used literally to mean a bloodbrother, either a full brother or a half-brother (i.e., with one common biological parent). (a) The clear cases of "full brother" are so manifest that there is no need to belabor the point. When Mark introduces to us "James, his brother (*adelphon*) John..." (Mk 1:29-30), nobody takes this to mean that James and John are really cousins. Why an exegete, operating purely on philological and historical grounds should judge differently in Mk 6:3, where we hear that Jesus is the son of Mary and the brother (*adelphos*) of James, Joses, Jude, and Simon, is not clear. (b) Interestingly, Mark also knows the use of *adelphos* to mean "half-brother," as seen in Mk 6:17, where Philip is called the "brother" of Herod Antipas. (c) With "full brother" and "half-brother" we exhaust the literal mean-

ing of *adelphos* found in the New Testament—all the more surprising when we realize that the "literal" sense of "brother" could be fairly broad in the extended families of the ancient world. When we consider that *adelphos* (in either the literal or the metaphorical sense) is used a total of 343 times in the New Testament, the consistency of this "literal" usage is amazing.

(2) Every other use of *adelphos* in the New Testament falls under the general rubric of a figurative or metaphorical sense. This covers all those cases where "brother" refers to some broad relationship that cannot be equated with the bond forged by direct blood relationship or marriage. Under this metaphorical sense come all those texts referring to followers of Jesus (e.g., Mk 3:35), fellow Christians in the early Church (e.g., 1 Cor 1:1; 5:11), fellow Jews (Acts 2:29 [more in a religious sense]; Rom 9:3 [more in an ethnic or national sense]), any neighbor (without a particular stress on a common religious or racial bond; e.g., Mt 7:3-5), and potentially any human being (Heb 2:11,17). Obviously, the Gospel references to the brothers of Jesus do not fall into this category of metaphorical use. In short, the "cousin" approach of Jerome, like the "stepbrother" approach of Epiphanius, simply lacks sufficient philological basis in the usage of the New Testament. "Jerome thought that *adelphos* could mean 'cousin,' but this is almost certainly to be ruled out as the New Testament meaning..." (Fitzmyer, 1981: 723-724).

But what if we move beyond the New Testament into the early patristic period? Those who wish to sustain the cousin approach must face the further difficulty that it is a relatively late, post-Nicene solution. By contrast, both the Epiphanian solution and the view that the "brothers of Jesus" were real brothers can find supporters in the second and third centuries. The antiquity and spread of the opinion that the brothers of Jesus were real brothers are often overlooked by the supporters of the cousin approach. It is interesting to note here that in a text preserved in Eusebius' *Ecclesiastical History*, 2.23 #4, Hegesippus (second century) carefully distinguishes between the brother, the uncle, and the cousin (*anepsion*). Therefore, when he calls James the brother of Jesus there is no valid reason for not taking him at his word. And Hegesippus was not the only pre-Nicene Father to lean towards a "real brother" approach. The only pre-Nicene Father of the (Latin-speaking) Church to take up the issue, Tertullian (ca. A.D. 160-220), considered the brothers of Jesus true brothers. Interestingly, he argues especially from Mk 3:31-35 (paralleled in Lk 8:19-21), where the mother and brothers of Jesus are yoked together in an uncomplimentary light. This interpretation of Jesus' brothers as real brothers is all the more remarkable because Tertullian tended toward rigorist, ascetic views and had a high esteem for virginity.

Needless to say, all of these arguments, even when taken together, cannot produce absolute certitude in a matter for which there is so little evidence. Nevertheless, if—prescinding from faith and later Church teaching—the historian or exegete is asked to render a judgment on the New Testament and patristic texts, viewed simply as historical sources, the most probable opinion is that the brothers and sisters of Jesus were true siblings. This interpretation of the New Testament texts was kept alive by at least some Church writers up until the late fourth century (Meier, 1992: 8-27).

In his response, Bauckham contests what he considers Meier's opinion that the same arguments may serve to refute both the Epiphanian and Hieronymian view. While he considers the Hieronymian view very improbable, he believes that the Epiphanian view is a serious alternative to the Helvidian. He understands Meier's argument to mean that in the New Testament *adelphos* and *adelphē* cannot mean "stepbrother" and "stepsister," and disputes especially Meier's assertion that the general New Testament usage of a word exclusively determines its meaning in particular instances in the New Testament, excluding meanings which are attested in literature outside the New Testament. The range of use from which the meaning of a word in the New Testament must be chosen is the range of use in the language, not the range of use in the New Testament. Meier seems to treat the New Testament as though it were written in some kind of linguistic ghetto. The fact that the New Testament writers generally used *adelphos* in its most common sense of full brother cannot exclude the possibility of their using it in less common senses on particular occasions (Bauckham, 1994: 690-693).

Bauckham then presents some more specific comments on Meier's claim that the Epiphanian view is disproved because there is no clear instance of the meaning "stepbrother" for *adelphos* in the New Testament (Bauckham, 1994: 693-694). Then he faces Meier's redaction-critical argument (Bauckham, 1994: 694-695). The second-century evidence leaves the question open, but nothing in first- or second-century Christian literature contradicts this tradition of the Epiphanian view in early second-century Syria (Bauckham, 1994: 695-698). In the end Bauckham states that the issue between the Epiphanian and Helvidian views must remain more open than Meier concluded it should (Bauckham, 1994: 700).

In a recent article, Meier has outlined the points of agreement and disagreement.

1. St. Jerome's solution, namely, that the brothers and sisters of Jesus were really his cousins, is considered by both Bauckham and Meier to be highly improbable.

2. Both authors admit that one cannot entirely exclude the possi-

bility of either the Epiphanian solution or the Helvidian solution (that the brothers and sisters were the offspring of Joseph and Mary after Jesus' birth. In his book, Bauckman held that the historical evidence is not decisively in favor of either solution. In both of his works, Meier held that the evidence favors the Helvidian view, although he stressed in his article that absolute proof of the Helvidian view is impossible and that the Epipanian view could be upheld with intellectual integrity (Meier, 1992: 27). This seemed to leave a very narrow range of disagreement.

3. Bauckham sharpened the differences by suggesting in his article that an additional argument might tip the balance of probability slightly in favor of the Epiphanian view (Bauckham, 1994: 687). However, this sharpening of differences seems somewhat blunted by the last sentence of his article, "I should be content to have demonstrated at least that the issue between Epiphanian and Helvidian views must remain more open than Meier concluded it should" (Bauckham, 1994: 700).

Meier focuses on two areas of disagreement, namely Bauckham's use of second-century apocryphal gospels as sources for history, and his representation of Meier's use about the New Testament use of *adelphos*.

First, he considers three apocryphal gospels: (1) the *Gospel of Peter* (Meier, 1997: 515), (2) the *Protoevangelium of James* (Meier, 1997: 516-522), and (3) the *Infancy Gospel of Thomas* (Meier, 1997: 522-524). According to Meier, the three second-century apocryphal gospels to which Bauckham appeals cannot carry the weight of his thesis. In addition, the theological approach to the brothers and sisters of Jesus in second-century Christianity was not as simple as Bauckham would have it (Meier, 1997: 524-525).

Second, Meier shows that Bauckham misrepresents his position on *adelphos* in the New Testament (Meier, 1997: 525-527), and concludes his article by saying: "Bauckham's claims that the second-century gospels give united witness to the Epiphanian solution and that they are reliable sources of historical information about the exact relation of Jesus to his brothers have, upon examination, not been verified. Failing the vindication of these claims, any retrojection of the Epiphanian solution into first-century Christian gospels, or further into the actual family relationships of the historical Jesus, must be judged gratuitous" (Meier, 1997: 527).

In Mk 3:33-35 the response of Jesus is in three stages: (1) a rhetorical question, "Who are my mother and my brothers?" which could be dismissive of the physical family; (2) an indicative statement, "Here are...," pointing to his hearers as his family (in the view of some this is where the pericope originally ended); (3) a generalizing statement defining his family as whoever does the will of God. Luke omits (1) and (2), and concludes with a revised version of (3) (C.F. Evans, 1990: 378).

Lk 8:19-21 is a fitting conclusion to the section on the word of God. "Those who hear the word of God and do it" refers back to the Interpretation of the Sower: Lk 8:14, "these are the ones who hear" and 8:15, "these are the ones who, when they hear the word, hold it fast" (see Lk 6:47). Although some scholars have said that a contrast between Lk 8:19-21 (Jesus' family) and Lk 8:1-3 (Jesus' followers) is intended, and others found strong anti-family polemic and election theology in Lk 8:19-21 (Conzelmann, 1960: 48-49), Luke has elsewhere lessened Mark's harshness toward Jesus' family and here seems to have used the section for the positive purpose of giving an attractive designation for those who accept the word of God (Robinson, 1966: 133). At Qumran, the family of God replaced one's human family (1QH 9.34-36). Jesus' remarks are not that strong; but in terms of priority, his remarks reflect the importance that God's message has for him (Bock, 1994: 752).

Not simply hearing the word of God (presumably not even listening with understanding), but hearing and *doing* is what makes people Jesus' family. Whether the members of his biological family meet those criteria is not the issue. Rather, with those criteria the boundaries of that most intimate community are opened up. The implicit question posed to the people who have been accompanying Jesus (Lk 8:1-3) is whether they are ready to make the move from followers to family (Ringe, 1995: 116-117).

But how are we to understand Lk 8:19-21 in the Asian context of filial pietism? To many Asians, Christianity seems to rob them of their loyalty to their natural family since they think that it demands nothing less than an exclusive loyalty to God and Christ even to the extent of leaving their family. Many scholars agree that Luke is gentler than Mark. They assert that the redactional purpose of the former here is to omit the negative remark of Jesus found in the latter, and to remove possible strife between Jesus and his family. Thus, Luke's account does not imply denial of family ties but implies a relationship to himself that can be as close or even transcend that of natural family ties. Jesus' reply in Luke is not a denial of family ties but an extending of his family ties to the faith dimension. The absence of definite articles in Lk 8:21 probably means that those who do the work of God are not really his blood brothers or mother but just like his mother and brothers.

To avoid a possible misunderstanding of Mark, Luke does two things in his redaction. First, he does not portray any conflict between Jesus and his family. The arrival of Jesus' family becomes the right occasion (place) and *kairos* (time) for Jesus to say the right word. To be a Christian then is not to contrast one's relationship with God to that with one's family members, but to extend God's love and grace to all through the metaphor we are most familiar with, that is, the family. Second, Luke gives the challenge to being loyal to God not in contrast with being loyal to one's family (i.e., God's family), but in a broader discipleship challenges to hear and do the word of God. The word is the good news preached and lived by Christ. It is the word of accepting more people into the realm of God, extending to more people the love of God, energizing more people in the power of the grace of God. It is God's desire that we love our family, respect our elders and ancestors. To be mothers and brothers and sisters of Jesus therefore is not to abandon our natural parents and relations but to extend our natural family relations to outsiders as we all share the familial relationship through the person and work of Christ. Jesus' words in Lk 8:19-21 exhort us to have relationship with God as close as or even transcending the family ties we have. We who have heard and responded to God's message and God's love are therefore mothers, brothers, and sisters of Jesus (Khiok-Khng, 1992: 311-317).

Concluding our observations on Lk 8:4-21, we may say that the central lesson of Lk 8:4-21 is that fecund reception of the sacred depends on the condition of one's eyes and ears, which, in turn, depends on one's heart. Readers are thus encouraged toward introspection, to identify their own values, to compare them with those being promoted in the narrative, and, ultimately, to align themselves with the norms of the story (Johnson, 1991: 134). The values foregrounded in the Interpretation of the Parable of the Sower (Lk 8:11-15) are attention to, retention of, and (re)production of the divine revelation. Emphasis falls on perseverance (Lk 8:15) in the face of life's contrary pressures. The audience realizes, of course, that a good heart exhibits many other qualities, some of which may be inferred by contrast with the anti-values raised by the Lukan Jesus in his commentary: resistance to temptation (Lk 8:12-13); serenity or singleness of mind; willingness to live simply; and an orientation toward higher aspects of human life instead of toward physical pleasures or fiscal concern (Lk 8:14). The process of establishing the fundamental values (the good heart), however, continues throughout the entire narrative by means of a myriad of rhetorical strategies. Moving forward through Luke and Acts, the reader builds an image of the ideal heart— one that characterizes the ideal reader. This reader loves God and neighbor, has faith; is humble, repentant and loyal; shows compassion and mercy and practices economic justice (among other virtues; Darr, 1992: 91-92; 1994: 103).

PROGRESSIVE REVELATION OF JESUS' POWER
(LK 8:22–9:6)

A new section of Luke's description of Jesus' Galilean ministry now begins. It concentrates on manifestations of Jesus' power, beginning with several miracle stories (Lk 8:22-25; 8:26-39; 8:40-48; 8:49-56) and ending with the sending of the Twelve (Lk 9:1-6). The introductory verse in this section (Lk 8:22) clearly breaks with what immediately precedes. While the previous section (Lk 8:4-21) called for obedience in hearing and doing the word of God, this section provides a demonstration of the character and power of the word in the Messiah's confrontation with powers of nature, evil, sickness, and death. None of the stories in this section is original to Luke. Even Mark's sequence is maintained throughout Mk 4:35-5:43//Lk 8:22-56, and Luke follows Mark's content and phrasing relatively more closely than in many other places and with fewer alterations than Matthew (Mt 8:23-34; 9:18-26). Still Luke has shaped the narrative so that the portrait of Jesus' authority is highlighted in his giving commands and bringing salvation. The efficacy of his declaration of the word of God is demonstrated so that saving faith and obedience to Jesus' command are encouraged (Tiede, 1988: 170).

a. The Stilling of the Storm (Lk 8:22-25)

This story is the first in a series of four episodes in which Jesus performs wonders: the Stilling of the Storm, the Healing of a Demoniac, the Healing of a Sick Woman, and the Raising of a Dead Girl. The order is Mark's, but there seems to be

163

little if any connection with what precedes. Since these episodes will be followed immediately by the commissioning of the Twelve, it may be appropriate to view these four sections as examples of Jesus' ministry during the period of their preparation.

Of the four episodes before us, the Stilling of the Storm is in a class by itself. This is not a reference to this being the first demonstration of Jesus' power over nature. It is no more an exercise of power over "nature" than were the healings or the raising of the son of the widow of Nain. The Stilling of the Storm is, like the story that immediately follows, an exorcism: "He rebuked the wind and the raging waves" (Lk 8:24; recall Lk 4:35,39,41). From ancient times and in many cultures large bodies of water were believed to be the abode of evil spirits that sometimes stirred up storms against sailors. The belief was as old as Near Eastern flood stories in which the water tried to take over and destroy the land.

To say this episode is in a class by itself is to say that Jesus is with his disciples alone, away from the crowds or the critics, and Jesus ministers to them. It is rare in the Gospels for the disciples to be beneficiaries of Jesus' power; usually they are present as he ministers to others or they join him in that ministry (Craddock, 1990: 114-115).

Lk 8:22-25 has been classified among the rescue miracles which comprise not only stories of rescue at sea, but also the freeing of prisoners (Acts 12:1ff.; 16:16ff.). Both groups of miracle stories are concerned with the overcoming of hostile forces, defeating the power of nature or the state. The fact that the two groups present similar images and themes shows how little justification there is for a division of miracles into a natural and human domain. Rescue miracles include both object domains. They differ from exorcisms in that the miracles are performed on material objects, wind, waves, ships, chains, prison doors. The closeness of the two genres is shown by the command to be silent—typical of exorcisms—given to the raging sea (Mk 4:39), though this does not justify assuming that hostile demonic forces are at work everywhere. What appeals to us in rescue miracles is in fact that they give us some notion of victory over dull, "mindless," purely physical violence. We single out three motifs for discussion. The first is common to all rescue miracles, and the second and third appear alternatively, irrespective of whether the miracle is a sea rescue or a release miracle.

First, *the situation of distress and the petition*. Descriptions of distress at sea occur in other genres, especially in the ancient novel. Typical features include the following: the storm makes it impossible to see the sky, water crashes into the ship, the crew tries to jettison the cargo. The situation appears hopeless; there are cries for help (in Lk 8:22-25, the disciples turn to the sleeping Jesus). In Jewish rescue miracles in particular, prayer in distress at sea was given significant theological form. Second, *the epiphany that brings rescue*. Rescue from distress at sea may take place (especially in Greek and Hellenistic accounts) through an epiphany of the god. The visual basis for this idea is probably the sudden appearance of the stars when the clouds and storm have cleared: their light is taken as the appearance of the gods. Rescue from the sea and epiphany are also associated in the New Testament in Mk 6:45-52 and parallels: Jesus appears, walking across the sea, in a form that creates consternation. As with rescue at sea, so in the release of prisoners epiphanies occur. In Acts there are two instances of the release of prisoners with angelophanies (Acts 5:17-25; 12:3-9). Third, *the passenger or prisoner who rescues his companions*. Rescue through an epiphany of a god comes from outside. In many rescue miracles, however, there is no such intervention: in these cases the rescue depends on the numinous power of a person present in the ship or prison. The two variants of the motif are combined when the passenger who performs the rescue is also a prisoner (like Paul in Acts 27). Just as the walking on the lake in the New

Testament was one of the miracles in which rescue took place through an epiphany, the Stilling of the Storm belongs to the motif of the passenger who saves and protects. Jesus is asleep. The disciples fight without him against wind and waves. The threatening situation may once have been portrayed by the sinking of the "other boats" (Mk 4:36), which now have no function in the narrative. Be that as it may, the message of the story is that the mere presence of Jesus is reason enough to feel safe from danger (Theissen, 1983: 99-102). Because of his particular redactional activity Luke's version of the Stilling of the Storm has been called an "instructive rescue miracle" (Kirchschläger, 1981: 89). One has also noted the close parallels between the Stilling of the Storm (especially in the Markan version) and the thanksgiving song of the liberated in Ps 107:23-32 (Glöckner, 1983: 63-67).

Lk 8:22-25 is loosely linked with the preceding pericope about Jesus' relatives (Lk 8:19-21), which follows Luke's version of the parable discourse (Lk 8:4-18). With the emphatic stress on hearing and doing the word of God (Lk 8:21b, different in Mk 3:35), the brief pericope (Lk 8:19-21) is an additional instruction on the significance of Jesus' proclamation of the word (Schürmann, 1970: 29-41). Lk 8:22-25, then, begins a tripartite sequence of miracles of Jesus, which Luke narrates in the same order as Mark (Busse, 1977: 196; Drury, 1976: 94-96).

Lk 8:22-25 can be divided into four sections: Verse 22 contains the introductory depiction of the scene; verses 23-24b describe the threatening situation and the despair of the disciples contrasted by Jesus' initiative and its effect in verse 24cd (Busse, 1977: 201). Jesus' reproachful question and the disciples' reaction conclude the pericope in verse 25 (Kirchschläger, 1981: 71-72).

Verse 22:   One day he got into a boat with his disciples,
                 and he said to them,
                 "Let us go across to the other side of the lake."
                 So they put out,

Verse 22 is clearly redactional. It not only severs the new episode from the immediately preceding, but immediately introduces the mention of the boat. The reason for this modification is that, in Mark's Gospel, Mk 4:35-41 presupposes the beginning of the parable discourse (Mk 4:1-34), where Jesus was "beside the sea" and got into a boat because of the great crowd. Mk 4:35 recalls that boat. Luke, having omitted the introduction in Lk 8:4 (because of Lk 5:1), now has to change the setting of the miracles that follow. So we find Jesus getting into the boat and making for the other side of the lake. In the Lukan form of the story "his disciples" would mean the Twelve and the women of Lk 8:1-3 (Fitzmyer, 1981: 727, 729).

By the introductory *egeneto de* [not translated in English], he clearly indicates that a new section begins. By the temporal indication "one day" (Lk 8:22a; literally: "on one of those days") Luke links the story of the Stilling of the Storm loosely to Lk 8:19-21 (Kratz, 1979: 248-249). Jesus' summons addressed to the disciples is stated in direct speech, and the author briefly indicates that they execute Jesus' command (Kirchschläger, 1981: 75).

Verse 23:   and while they were sailing he fell asleep.
             A windstorm swept down on the lake,
             and the boat was filling with water,
             and they were in danger.

Luke continues his account by narrating Jesus' sleep. He has simplified some of Mark's details, such as not mentioning that other boats were sailing along (Mk 4:36) and reporting that Jesus "fell asleep" before the "windstorm" arose (Ernst, 1977: 274; Tiede, 1988: 170): Luke's better sense of storytelling depicts Jesus falling asleep before the mention of the windstorm coming up (Fitzmyer, 1981: 729). In graphic manner the author describes the "descent" (*katebē*) of the storm on the lake. The effect of the storm for the boat is described by two imperfect tenses, literally: "they took in much water and they were in danger" (Kirchschlager, 1981: 77-78). Luke speaks of the persons in the boat rather than of the boat itself (Fitzmyer, 1981: 730).

Verse 24:   They went to him and woke him up, shouting,
              "Master, Master, we are perishing!"
              And he woke up
              and rebuked the wind and the raging waves;
              they ceased, and there was a calm.

The reaction of the disciples is described as "they woke him up." They awake him with the cry, "Master! Master! We are perishing!" not "Teacher, do you not care if we perish?" as in Mk 4:38. There is no reproach in the disciples' cry, only terror. Calling Jesus "Master" (Greek: *epistata*) may not be to use the most lofty christological title, but it belongs in contexts where Jesus is being addressed as a person of significant authority (see Lk 5:5; 8:45; 9:33,49; 17:13). This is the same title that Peter used once before to address Jesus in a boat (Lk 5:5) when he certainly did not know what was coming. The disciples may not have known that Jesus could bring such a miraculous calm, but they must be credited with calling on the right "Master!" (Tiede, 1988: 170-171).

With the adversatively constructed relative connection (*ho de*, "but he") verse 24c leads to Jesus' intervention. "He woke" links up with the previously described action of the disciples, "they woke him up." Jesus' order is addressed to the storm and to the waves and thus counters the previously described danger: the windstorm descended on the lake and the boat was filling with water because of the waves. The wind and the waves ceased and consequently there was calm (Kirchschläger, 1981: 78-79).

Verse 25:   He said to them, "Where is your faith?"
              They were afraid and amazed,
              and said to one another,
              "Who then is this,
              that he commands even the winds and the water,
                  and they obey him?"

Two striking features of this story are the two questions with which it concludes. Jesus asks his disciples, "Where is your faith?" This is certainly less strong than the Markan rebuke, "Why are you afraid? Have you still no faith?" (Mk 4:40; Fitzmyer, 1981: 730). But what is Jesus asking them? He certainly is not saying that if they had had faith, there would not have been a storm; after all, Jesus was in the boat too. And most likely he is not saying that, with faith, they could have stilled the storm themselves. They have not yet been given power and authority to exorcise and heal (Lk 9:1-2). Jesus seems by his question to be addressing their faith during the storm—fear, not doubt, being the opposite of faith. They had been with Jesus long enough to have adequate ground for trust in God and in Jesus' access to God's power. Notice that with Jesus' stilling of the storm they are said to be afraid, perhaps even more so. They have just witnessed a power greater than the storm; why would they not be afraid? It is sheer sentimentalism to suppose that being in the presence of Jesus is total comfort. The question, "Where is your faith?" has the additional force of signaling a new level of expectation from Jesus. They have not been asked anything like that previously, but they are soon to be sent out to preach, to heal, to overpower demons. And it will not be too long before they are asked a variation on this same question: *What* is your faith? Who do you say I am? (Lk 9:18-22).

This leads us to the second question, the one the disciples asked one another: "Who then is this?" The disciples' question is not so much one of "identity" as a modern reader would assume, but rather one of status and honor. It asks about Jesus in the hierarchy of powers (Malina-Rohrbaugh, 1992: 336). Surely the question has been forming itself in their minds during their time with him, but now the question is clear, and it is out in the open: Who is Jesus? Of course, Luke has the reader in mind as well, not only in the asking, but in the anticipation of an answer. It will have to be asked, but who will ask and who will answer? Will they ask Jesus, Who are you? or will Jesus ask them, Who do you say that I am? If they ask him, as John did from prison, we can imagine his answer would be much the same (Lk 7:22). But if Jesus asks them, what will they say? (Craddock, 1990: 115-116). The fear and unbelief of the disciples is in contrast not only to the calm of their Master but also to the endurance they themselves should have had in "a time of testing" (Lk 8:13; Liefeld, 1995: 117).

The reaction of the disciples is caused by what they experienced and is detached from Jesus' question by an adversative *de* [not translated by NRSV]. Fear and amazement as well as talking to each other express their inner unrest and insecurity and are clarified in their question, "Who then is this?" (Kratz, 1979: 264-265). The disciples' question is intended to reveal to the reader the beginning of a sense of awareness in them, which may not yet be "faith," but which is leading in that direction (Fitzmyer, 1981: 730). The verb "obey" (*hupakouein*) is rare in the Gospels (Mk 1:27; 4:41; Mt 8:27; Lk 8:25) and expresses the complete submission of the forces of nature to Jesus. This brief reflection on Jesus' effective intervention concludes the Lukan version of the pericope (Kirchschläger, 1981: 81-82).

b. *The Gerasene Demoniac* (Lk 8:26-39)

The calming of the storm on the Lake of Gennesaret is followed by the exorcism of the Gerasene demoniac. Evil threatening human beings in the form of natural cataclysms now has a counterpart in evil afflicting the psychic being of a man. The latter story is a thematic complement to the preceding account (C.F. Evans, 1990: 383). This narrative provides the strongest expression yet of the power of Jesus against the forces of evil (Liefeld, 1995: 118).

Every age and culture has various ways of speaking of the experience of encountering awesome forces of death, disease, and destruction. The "naming" of such forces, even in modern scientific terms, is an effort to understand or differentiate conditions and circumstances over which humans have no real control (Tiede, 1988; 172). The story is derived from Mk 5:1-20, and the differences between the Lukan and Markan form are specifically Lukan redactions (Schramm, 1971: 126; Annen, 1976: 22-29). Luke has shortened the form of the story but still presents it with one demoniac. Mt 8:28-34 curtails it even more, but recounts it as the story of two demoniacs.

The account defies normal form-critical analysis. Scholars have rightly identified features from an exorcism narrative form and a miracle story form, as well as elements of exorcism ritual not elsewhere attested in the New Testament (Pesch, 1971: 354-355; 1972: 21-40). Even though Luke has eliminated some of the grotesque and fantastic details found in Mark, enough remain to identify the story as a symbolic statement of the power of Jesus, and not a report of a medical case needing only interpretation into clinical categories (Ringe, 1995: 120). Miracles are audiovisuals of spiritual activity (Bock, 1996: 242). Some commentators have seen an allusion to and even a midrash on Isa 65:1-7 in this episode (Schürmann, 1969: 480; Pesch, 1971: 361).

What we are dealing with in this pericope is not a simple miracle story of an exorcism (compare this one with Lk 4:33-37). For the basic miracle story has in this instance been enshrouded with elements of the fantastic and the grotesque. It has always raised questions and problems that strain the imagination: How could Jesus have caused the owners of the pigs such a financial loss? Did Jesus really go along with the popular superstitions of his time about demons and possession? Obviously, such questions miss the point of the Gospel story itself, being recounted for a symbolic and religious purpose. The details of this story—especially in its Markan version—reveal the tendency that was beginning to be associated with basic miracle stories in the gospel tradition, a tendency that comes to full bloom in the apocryphal gospel tradition. That such a folkloric, popular tradition should make its way into the canon might be surprising; but who can say that biblical inspiration, rightly understood, could not accommodate itself even to such a tradition with flamboyant and grotesque details? (Fitzmyer, 1981: 733-735).

Lk 8:26-39 includes details that are specifically reversed by Jesus' actions. The Gerasene demoniac is described as a man from the city who wore no clothes and "who did not live in a house but in the tombs" (Lk 8:27). Having often been driven into the desert by demon possession (Lk 8:29), he was "healed" (Lk 8:36: "saved") and "clothed and in his right mind," able to return to his home in the city and declare what God had done for him (Lk 8:39; York, 1991: 169).

Verse 26:   Then they arrived at the country of the Gerasenes,
             which is opposite Galilee.

"They arrived at the country...," literally, "they sailed to," relates this story to the stormy sea voyage and concludes it. "They arrived" expresses the opposite of "they set out" in Lk 8:22 (Kirchschläger, 1981: 97; Fitzmyer, 1981: 726; Nolland, 1989: 406; Liefeld, 1995: 118-119). The site of this episode is not uniformly stated in the three Gospels, and the difference among them is compounded by the variant readings in manuscripts of the three. In the manuscripts of the Lukan Gospel there are three variants: (1) Gerasa, in Transjordan, about thirty-three miles southeast of Lake Gennesaret, a city of the Decapolis in the mountains of Gilead near the edge of the desert to the east. (2) Gadara, another city of the Decapolis, about six miles southeast of Lake Gennesaret. (3) Gergesa, identified by Origen as "an old city in the neighborhood of the Lake now called Tiberias." This fluctuation in the manuscripts about the locality of the episode, when taken together with other details in the story, cautions us against trying too hard to reconstruct what actually happened (Fitzmyer, 1981: 736-737; Nolland, 1989: 406-407; Craddock, 1990: 116).

Whereas it seems important for Luke to stress that Jesus leaves Galilee and that Jesus enters Gentile territory (Kirchschläger, 1981: 98; Nolland, 1989: 406), the Lukan redactional addition, "which is opposite Galilee," nevertheless keeps the episode within the broad scope of Jesus' Galilean ministry (Fitzmyer, 1981: 735, 737).

Verse 27: As he stepped out on land,
a man of the city who had demons met him.
For a long time he had worn no clothes,
and he did not live in a house but in the tombs.

In verses 27 and 29 we have a classic description of demon possession (Liefeld, 1995: 119). Luke totally reformulates Mk 5:3-5. Leaving the boat ("stepped out") Jesus went ashore and was met by "a man who had demons." Luke introduces the plural, "demons" (compare Mk 5:2, "a man with an unclean spirit"), in light of verse 30 ("legion"); but beacuse of the demands of the dialogue, borrowed from Mark, Luke retains the singular in verse 29 (Danker, 1988: 181). Many demons possessing one person occur again in Lk 11:26.

One has drawn attention to the phrase repeated so often and in such variegated yet similar ways that it seems to constitute the melody of this pericope. This is the description of "a man...who had demons" and later, "the man from whom the demons had gone" (verses 27,35; also verses 29,33,36,38). The one who shares center stage with Jesus has no name in the narrative; his foremost characteristic is his bondage to and release from demonic power. If these variations on a theme help us to identify the melody, then the countermelody is recognized in the assorted clues that this is the first time Jesus has crossed over into predominantly Gentile territory. In this sense, the expression "opposite Galilee" is more than a geographical designation, even if it is significant at this level for the way it signals Jesus' crossing of geographical boundaries characteristic of this section of the Third Gospel, that is, the Galilean section, Lk 4:14-9:50. At the fundamental level this text concerns the crossing of boundaries in Jesus' mission, and more particularly the offer of salvation in the Gentile world (Green, 1997: 335-336).

At the beginning of the story the man is living outside the boundaries of human society. He lived among the tombs, presumably pagan tombs, which would be a source of uncleanness for a Jew. As in Acts 19:16, nakedness is one of the conditions into which people were forced by demons (Danker, 1988: 181). The loitering of the man among the tombs may be a sign of his alienation, but it may also signify the relation of the demoniac to the realm of the death (Fitzmyer, 1981: 737-738).

The demoniac's behavior matches that of what the rabbis regarded characteristic of the insane: "Our rabbis taught: 'Who is considered to be an imbecile? He who goes out alone at night, and he who spends the night in a cemetery, and he that tears his garments" (Lachs, 1987: 164).

Verse 28:   When he saw Jesus,
              he fell down before him and shouted at the top of
                 his voice,
              "What have you to do with me,
              Jesus, Son of the Most High God?
              I beg you, do not torment me"—

Luke changes Mark's "bowed down" (*proskunesen*, "worshiped"/"bowed the knee") into "he fell down before him," because *proskunesen* for Luke would indicate religious reverence; the demons are submissive but hardly reverent. So totally has the demonic taken control of this person that identifies are blurred (Danker, 1988: 182). Jesus is addressed as "Son of the Most High" (see Lk 1:32,35,76). According to Josephus, *Antiquities* 16.6.2 #163, this was the Gentile way to refer to the God of the Jews (Plummer, 1901/1977: 229-230; Bovon, 1991: 418-419 note 4).

Luke follows Mark closely for the rest of the verse except for softening the demons' adjuration by God ("I adjure you by God," Mk 5:7) into a simple request. We are not told what the "torment" consisted of until verse 31. "Torment" probably carries here something of its literal sense of torture in juridical examination, which Matthew effectively glosses with his "before the time," that is, before the time of the eschatological judgment. The request is, then, that they should not be brought (yet) to judgment. The request in verse 31 is essentially the same (Nolland, 1989: 408).

Verse 29:   for Jesus had commanded the unclean spirit
             to come out of the man.
             (For many times it had seized him;
             he was kept under guard and bound with chains
                and shackles,
             but he would break the bonds
             and be driven by the demon into the wilds.)

The imperfect tense *parangeilen* may be better translated Jesus "was about to command the unclean spirit," thereby avoiding the possible implication that Jesus' word could be ineffectual (Fitzmyer, 1981: 738; Danker, 1988: 182; Stein, 1992: 256; Bock, 1994: 784 and note 33)). By shifting Mark's description of the unsuccessful efforts to bind the man (Mk 5:4), Luke is able to account for the delay in the demon's departure and prepare the ground for the subsequent dialogue.

Luke keeps here Mark's "unclean spirit," but he changes the grammar to make it clear that Jesus addresses the demon and not the demoniac. Luke grounds Jesus' verbal intervention in the fact of the man's sorry plight. He here makes use of material passed over from Mk 5:3-5, but with almost none of the Markan language. The vocabulary is reasonably Lukan (Annen, 1976: 24-25). The demoniac's strength, indicated by the failure of the constraining efforts, prepares us for the plurality of possession and perhaps even for the military might reflected in the term "legion." The demons drove the man out from his place in human society. The being driven into the wilderness has its antithesis in Jesus' later sending the man back to his home (Nolland, 1989: 408-409).

The narrator breaks into the interaction between the demoniac and Jesus to explain the demoniac's condition and his reaction to Jesus. The reader is given a rather graphic description of the demoniac's affliction, as the narrator speaks of a man whose demonic seizures happened so often that "he was kept under guard and bound with chains and shackles" (Lk 8:29). Even this restriction was not sufficient, since the demoniac often broke the chains and shackles and was "driven by the demon into the wilds" (Lk 8:29).

This aside functions on two levels in the narrative. On the first level the information contained in the aside is necessary for the reader to understand not only the magnitude of the demoniac's affliction but the magnitude of Jesus' miraculous exorcism. The information provided in the aside is also necessary for the reader to understand the response of the people in Lk 8:36-39. The case was so dramatic that the sight of this man quiet and clothed was too great a shock for the people in the area. The reader, however, is not surprised at the ability of Jesus to calm the demoniac in the same fashion in which he had calmed the storm. The aside merely reinforces the natural parallel between the storm and the forces of evil which had been drawn in the reader's mind.

On the other hand, this aside suspends the action of the narrative. While the aside contains necessary information for the reader's understanding of the narrative, Luke's narrator could have begun the narrative with such information, as did Mark's. The presence of the aside in such an interrupting position forces the reader to pause in the midst of the dialogue between Jesus and the demoniac in order to focus on the condition of the demoniac. The parenthetical remark belies the words of the demons in Lk 8:28 as they beseech Jesus not to "torment" them. Once the reader is in possession of the true information regarding the demoniac's condition there can be no question that the demons are the ones providing the torment, while Jesus' action will provide release. The interruption forces the reader to stop and consider the situation before the narrative continues; it suspends the story in such a way as to create interest in the rest of the story (Sheeley, 1992: 100-101, 141, 166).

Verse 30:   Jesus then asked him, "What is your name?"
              He said, "Legion"; for many demons had entered
              him.

Only here in the Gospel materials does Jesus engage in a dialogue with a demon (Stein, 1992: 257). In the Lukan account there is no trace of any idea that possession of the name is the key to exorcism (contrast Hellenistic belief of the period in the power of possessing somebody's name [Annen, 1976: 152-153; Marshall, 1978: 338; Bock, 1994: 774; *pace* Fitzmyer, 1981: 738; Green, 1997: 339]). The possessing power is already at the mercy of Jesus. He can do no other than answer the question and would gain nothing from frantic attempts to conceal his name. The name is to be part of the information upon which Jesus will base his response to the demons' entreaty.

Although the demons themselves know Jesus' identity, they have no real name, but only a number, a statistic: A legion was a unit of the Roman army containing normally five to six thousand men. If the use of the word "Legion" brings the Roman military to *our* minds, it must have brought the Roman military presence to the minds of those who heard this account during the first century when the Roman military presence was a reality that constantly confronted the Jews and early Christians in the area of the Sea of Galilee and of the entire eastern Mediterranean area.

Comparison with somewhat similar exorcism miracle stories in the New Testament Apocrypha, *Acts of Peter* (Hennecke et alii, 1964: 293-294), and in Philostratus, *Life of Apollonius* iv.20 (Barrett, 1961: 293-294), together with attention given to the social, political, and religious situation of those involved in the development of the gospel tradition, raises the possibility that at least one portion of the account, Mk 5:9-17//Lk 8:30-37a, may have functioned at one time as a somewhat elaborate cryptogram, one of the few forms of protest available to oppressed people. Mk 8:9-17//Lk 8:30-37a may have been for the storyteller and for the hearers at certain stages in the early development of the story, a relatively safe way to assert the lordship of Christ over the Roman legion of unclean "pigs" who had crucified the Jesus of history and who continued to threaten the lives of followers of Jesus in the lands in which they lived. In this story followers of Jesus may have been able to use the quite common vehicle of an exorcism miracle account within which to include their cryptogram. In this way the storyteller may have been able to say that Jesus had proletically and would soon actually cause those unclean Roman "pigs" to rush headlong westward over a cliff to be drowned in that great Western Sea over which they had come (Beck, 1997: 107-108).

To residents of the Roman Empire, the presence of the Roman legions meant the loss of control over every dimension of their own society. What better name for the demons that were wreaking such havoc on this man's life? (Ringe, 1995: 120). This man was much more severely disturbed than Mary with her seven demons (Lk 8:2; Haenchen, 1968: 193). The brutalized state of the man, especially in the Markan account, may reflect via the name "Legion" the harshness of the Roman occupation. At a literary level, the multiplicity of the possession prepares for the role of the herd of swine (Schurmann, 1969: 483; Nolland, 1989: 409). Some scholars refer here to the Qumran *War Scroll* which describes legions of troops (Bovon, 1991: 425).

Verse 31:   They begged him not to order them to go back into the abyss.

Luke has alerted us to the plurality of the possession already in verse 27, but only now as this emerges in the action of the story does he begin to use plural forms to refer to the demons. From now on he will regularly use plural forms. Mark's demons do not want to be displaced from the region (Mk 5:10); Luke's do not want to be directed to depart into the abyss. The abyss may be viewed as the place of origin or permanent home of the demons; it may be seen as the place of containment of the rebellious spirits; or it may be conceived of as the place of ultimate judgment of the demonic powers (see Rev 9:1-2,11, etc.; Nolland, 1989: 409-410). This is the torment the demons were seeking to avoid in verse 28 (Stein, 1992: 257). Luke shows that the conclusion of the end time will be but the consummation of what has already been experienced (Danker, 1988: 183). Water, into which the swine plunged (Lk 8:33), was often associated with the abyss (Ellis, 1966: 128-129; C.A. Evans, 1990: 137).

Verse 32:   Now there on the hillside a large herd of swine was feeding;
and the demons begged Jesus to let them enter these.
So he gave them permission.

The uncleanness of the swine (Lev 11:7; Deut 14:8) would make them in Jewish perspective a totally appropriate residence for unclean spirits. The sending of demons into animals is well attested in Hellenistic demonology (Annen, 1976: 152). The agreement of Jesus to the arrangement proposed by the unclean spirits has puzzled many critics and has lead to a series of conjectures, none of which is fully convincing. The perspective of the pericope is that though Jesus is actively engaged in rescuing those who have become the victims of the devil's minions (see Lk 11:5-22), for whatever reason the time is not yet ripe for bringing to ultimate judgment and destruction these forces of evil. Only in an anticipatory way do the demons come up against Jesus, the one who means their ultimate demise (Nolland, 1989: 410-411).

Verse 33:   Then the demons came out of the man and
                       entered the swine;
                   and the herd rushed down the steep bank
                   into the lake and was drowned.

The effect of the exorcism is immediate and visible (Schürmann, 1969: 484; Bock, 1994: 776). The demons depart from the man and enter the swine. This part of the story has been understood in three main ways. (1) The pigs go to the abyss after all, because they go into the sea: Jesus has got the better of them (Lamarche, 1968: 586). In what may be ridicule of the legions' military exploits, the pigs are said to rush (in formation?) down the steep bank into the lake to their own destruction (Ringe, 1995: 120). (2) The demons take their revenge on Jesus by ensuring that he will be unpopular with the residents of Gerasa (Bauernfeind). (3) The demons unleash the same destructive powers upon the pigs that have up to that point brought misery to the possessed man. Beyond the destruction of the pigs we lose sight of the demons.

The first suggestion works best for a conflation of Mark and Luke: Mark does not mention the abyss; Luke does not have "the sea" but "the lake," which usually has no mythological role and certainly has no such role in Lukan usage. The second suggestion may be defensible in Mark but is quite impossible in Luke. Even for Mark, the structuring of the account with its shift of interest from the fate of the pigs to the fate of the man tells against this view. The third view is to be preferred. The dramatic turn of events also marks visibly the departure of the demons, but this does not at all appear to be the focus of concern (Nolland, 1989: 411).

Verses 34-35: (34) When the swineherds saw what had happened,
they ran off and told it in the city and in the
country.
(35) Then people came out to see what had happened,
and when they came to Jesus,
they found the man from whom the demons
had gone
sitting at the feet of Jesus,
clothed and in his right mind.
And they were afraid.

The presence of the swineherds at the scene guaranteed
testimony regarding the crazed behavior and demise of the
pigs. Their return to the city (from whence the man hailed,
Lk 8:27) provides for the additional witnesses of what Jesus
had done to this man. Hence, the repeated phrase "what
had happened" must be taken to mean both the drowning
of the pigs and the healing of the former demoniac (Green,
1997: 340). Through the flight of the swineherds knowledge of the event is extended to the city and region, and
eventually to the whole population (Lk 8:37; C.F. Evans,
1990: 387). The herdsmen flee in fear and tell what they
have seen to those who were out and about in the town
and to those they see working in the fields. In this way a
group forms. No doubt we are meant to think of a frightened but curious group, who have gathered just enough
courage from their group solidarity tentatively to make their
way back to the scene of these strange events (Nolland,
1989: 411-412).

The rather full description of the demoniac's behavior
before and after the exorcism emphasizes the great change
that Jesus has made in his existence (Talbert, 1986: 90).
The man was "sitting at the feet of Jesus" as a sign of discipleship (Lk 10:39; Acts 22:3). Luke thus prepares for the
man's request in verse 38 (Fitzmyer, 1981: 739). The man
is clothed as a sign of restoration (Schweizer, 1984: 159).

Verse 36:   Those who had seen it told them
                 how the one who had been possessed by demons
                 had been healed.

Luke rewords what it is that the witnesses report and
makes use of his favorite language of salvation that Jesus
brings (esōthē). He has no place for Mark's separate item,
"and to the swine": the "how" of the man's salvation includes the fate of the pigs (Nolland, 1989: 412; Danker,
1988: 183; Stein, 1992: 258). The demoniac is seen as completely recovered as indicated by the repeated designations
of the man as "from whom the demons had gone" (Lk 8:35),
"who had been possessed by demons" (Lk 8:36), and "from
whom the demons had gone" (Lk 8:38; C.F. Evans, 1990:
387).

Verse 37:   Then all the people of the surrounding country of
                     the Gerasenes
                 asked Jesus to leave them;
                 For they were seized with great fear.
                 So he got into the boat and returned.

Luke involves the whole population of the district of
the Gerasenes in the request that Jesus depart. Similarly
Acts 16:16-39 records Paul's experience in Philippi: he casts
out a spirit from a girl, and the conclusion of the matter is
that Paul is asked to leave the city (Craddock, 1990: 117).
Luke reiterates the note of fear from verse 35 and makes
this the basis for the request. But the basis for their fear is
not identified and it is of little value to speculate about
what caused this fear. Given the play on words present in
the name "Legion," one may be inclined to ask if Luke is
not also engaging in political allegory when he speaks about
the people's fear. Would not any power that could order
the legions' destruction inspire as much fear as the legions
themselves? But above all the fear seems to have been caused
by the numinous power implied in the exorcism (Schürmann,
1969: 486).

The story says nothing about the people's reaction to the economic loss represented in the destruction of the herd of pigs, as is the case in a parallel situation in Acts (see Acts 16:16,19; C.A. Evans, 1990: 138; Green, 1997: 341; *pace* Plummer, 1901/1977: 232; Talbert, 1982: 98); there is no demand for restitution for the swine; nor does the story address the issue of the morality of destroying the animals. Instead, the focus shifts to the man who has been "healed" (or "saved") and is now "clothed and in his right mind" (Lk 8:35-36) and to the response of the townspeople (Ringe, 1995: 120-121).

Rather curiously, Luke rounds the verse off by saying that Jesus "returned" (a favorite Lukan word [see Annen, 1976: 28]). The sentence anticipates verse 40, but leaves verses 38-39 oddly detached. We seem to have here the same technique that led his having John the Baptist arrested before the baptism of Jesus. The visit to the territory of Gerasa has run its course: Jesus had come and now he has gone. The man's desire to go with Jesus is another episode in its own right (Nolland, 1989: 412). (The departure here also prepares for a parallel between Jesus' return to Jewish Palestine and the man's return to his own people [verse 39]).

Verses 38-39: (38) The man from whom the demons had gone
begged that he might be with him;
but Jesus sent him away, saying,
(39) "Return to your home, and declare
how much God has done for you."
So he went away, proclaiming throughout the city
how much Jesus had done for him.

Owing an honor debt to Jesus, the man who had the demons wishes to stay with Jesus as client. But Jesus directs his attention to the proper place where honor is due (God, the patron) and sends him home. The man does not follow the instructions, however, giving honor to Jesus rather than to God (Malina-Rohrbaugh, 1992: 337).

Why does Luke record a conversation between Jesus and the man after Jesus has already departed? Luke's dramatic technique is familiar to us from his account of Jesus' baptism (Lk 3:18-22). There as here he is able to clear the stage of all distractions by introducing a minor anachrony into the narrative. The camera lens is focused narrowly on the concluding dialogue between Jesus and the former demoniac. Asking to be "with him," he is requesting the same relationship with Jesus enjoyed by the Twelve and the women who make up Jesus' company (Lk 8:1-3). Surprisingly, his request is denied—surprising, that is, because others rescued from demons have been included (Lk 8:2) and because of the nature of the unprecedented task Jesus sets before this man. Luke's introduction of this man had marked him as displaced, alienated from home and city (Lk 8:27). Now Jesus returns him to his home and gives him an assignment within his city. His healing, then, is not only physical and cerebral, but religious and psychosocial; and vocational. He is restored to his community and given a commission (Green, 1997: 341).

Luke speaks not of a refusal but of a dismissal: the man is not turned down but redirected. Jesus sends the man on a missionary errand that is not yet that of Christian discipleship, since the time for Gentile disciples has not yet come in the Lukan story (Fitzmyer, 1981: 740). The man's positive response stands in contrast to the people's negative response, thus ending the account on a positive note (Marshall, 1978: 341).

Luke's use of "return" establishes a parallel between Jesus' return to Jewish Palestine (Lk 8:37) and what this man is to do. Mark's mention of the man's family is trimmed away. This has the effect of leaving quite general the directive to tell people what has happened. The man who returns now to his home is the man unable to stay in a house in verse 27. Luke speaks simply of "how much God has done for you," whereas Mark has "how much the Lord has done for you, and what mercy he has shown you" (Mk 5:19). Luke abbreviates also the rest of the verse. He omits Mark's account of the amazement of all: for Luke the people's response to these events has already been given earlier and culminates in verse 37 (Nolland, 1989: 413). Luke's alteration of Mark's "the Lord" is not accidental. The man "declares" what Jesus had done for him. Luke emphasizes through his change of wording that *God* is at work in Jesus (Danker, 1988: 184). The emphatic position of "God" and "Jesus" is not to be missed (Fitzmyer, 1981: 740). The fact that he proceeds to proclaim to the whole town "how much *Jesus* had done for him" may not be a literal fulfillment of his charge to tell how much *God* had done, but it is still correct. Jesus has brought the salvation of God into the region, defeating the powers of evil with his command and leaving a witness to his saving reign among people who are afraid of such authority (Tiede, 1988: 174). All are called to evangelize, but not all believers are to serve Jesus in the same way (Bock, 1994: 780).

For this man, who is described as having lived outside the human community during the time of his illness, the opportunity to tell his story and communicate with his neighbors and family members might be seen as the completion of his healing and his restoration to full humanity (Ringe, 1995: 121).

EXCURSUS ON JESUS' EXORCISMS

At this stage the question may be raised which role exorcism played in the whole of Jesus' developing career as a public figure. Were exorcisms on the fringes or at the center of his career? Were they peripheral or at the core of his proclamation of the Kingdom of God? Were they incidental or central to the course that led him finally to execution in Jerusalem? It is only by attending to Jesus' exorcisms as actions in a total social setting, that is, it is only through using the methods and theories of the social sciences that we can answer such contemporary questions as the following: Can we find out how exorcisms figured in

Jesus' own vocational and intellectual development? Can we discover the significance of exorcisms in Jesus' own personal development as the leader of a social movement? Can we find significant social and political as well as personal dimensions of exorcisms that help us understand their significance in Jesus' career as a whole? (Hollenbach, 1981: 567,568).

When one begins by taking the evidence of the Gospels at face value, it is to be noted in the first place that, *quantitatively*, exorcisms played a rather large role in Jesus' career. In the Gospels there are more stories (five in all) of Jesus performing exorcisms than any other specific kind of healing. In addition, in the summaries of Jesus' activities exorcisms also figure very prominently (e.g., Mk 1:32-34; Lk 4:40-41). Moreover, *qualitatively* and much more importantly, exorcisms figure prominently in Jesus' own understanding of his career (Lk 11:20). Finally, Jesus practiced exorcism from the beginning to the end of his public life and it was directly in connection with this particular activity that he drew upon himself the wrath of all the important public authorities of his time (Mk 3:22-27; Lk 11:15-22; Hollenbach, 1981: 568-569). The central place of exorcism in the ministry of the historical Jesus is beyond dispute (Nolland, 1989: 405).

A perusal of some recent social-scientific literature on possession and exorcism yields five categories relevant to the study of those phenomena: (1) criteria for identifying demoniacs, (2) causes of demon possession, (3) demoniacs' living conditions, (4) their treatment, and (5) the consequences of their healing among interested persons, especially positive or negative reactions to the healer (Hollenbach, 1981: 570-572).

Social-psychological theories of mental illness as a way of trying to understand more fully the phenomena mentioned above, particularly the hostility that could develop between an exorcist such as Jesus and the establishment over his exorcising activity understand mental illness as both personal and social (e.g., Kiev, 1964: 230-232,260-263).

(1) Mental illness is caused, or at least exacerbated by, social tensions: it seems commonly accepted that social tensions of various sorts are at the core of the phenomena of mental derangement: class antagonism rooted in economic exploitation, conflicts between gradations where revered traditions are eroded, colonial domination and revolution (Kiev, 1964: passim). Most relevant is a study of mental illness during the Algerian revolutionary war (Fanon, 1963: 44-58), with its situation of oppressive colonialism, just as in the Palestine of Jesus' day (Theissen, 1985). The main point made is that the colonial situation of domination and revolution nourishes mental illness in extraordinary numbers of the population (Hollenbach, 1981: 573-575).

(2) Mental illness can be seen as a socially acceptable form of oblique protest against, or escape from, oppressions. At least in some people, some types of mental disorders become escapes from, "cures" for, as well as symptoms of, social conflict (Fanon, 1963: 290; Lewis, 1971: 72; Kiev, 1964: 218-219). In a rigid social structure, where individuals have little opportunity for acknowledgment and little control over their daily activities possession is more likely to occur (Bourguignon, 1976: 31). There is a distinct possibility that Palestinian possession performed a similar function and occurred within a similar social and political pattern. It may have functioned as a "fix" for people who saw no other way to cope with the horrendous social and political conditions in which they found their lot cast. From what little we know of such conditions in first-century Palestine such a possibility seems very likely (Hollenbach, 1981: 575-577).

(3) Accusations of madness and witchcraft can be used by socially dominant classes as a means of social control. The dominant class(es) of a society will define mental illness and view healers in such a way as to effect the neutralization, if not the actual ostracism, of undesirable members of society, that is, people who challenge the status quo. It almost goes without saying that accusations of madness and witchcraft, like possession, also increase in times of social unrest (Rosen, 1968: 5-17). Social control may be accomplished not only through accusations of witchcraft and sorcery, but also by accusations of madness (Hollenbach, 1981: 577-578).

In view of the above it is important to emphasize how thoroughly social the phenomenon of mental illness and its treatment is. Now it may be that at this point we have some help in understanding the tensions that develop between Jesus and public authorities such as the Pharisees and Herod over his exorcising activity. It may be that in various ways Jesus disrupted the dominant pattern of accommodation in society, particularly accommodation that held between the stronger and weaker members of society in relation to demoniacs and their treatment. If this were so, it could help to account for Jesus' ostracism and eventual execution.

What were the social implications and consequences of Jesus' healing demoniacs? Demon possession and its ideology were integral parts of the social accommodation of first-century Palestinian Jews to the conditions of the time. These conditions are those typical of the Hellenistic period, particularly those associated with the period of Roman domination. It may be that demon symbolism served not only as a means for the oppressed to express their degradation, but also as a means for the nervous dominant classes to subdue those who protested against their oppressors. They could do this by accusing their opponents of demon possession. The social-scientific theories delineated above indicate that demon possession flourishes in its various dynamics precisely in such conditions as we know prevailed in Jesus' day (Hollenbach, 1981: 579-581).

Lk 8:26-39 is a revealing and rare example of the complex dynamics of demon possession indicated by social scientists. In the first place, the Gerasene demoniac represents demon possession as an "oblique aggressive strategy" (Lewis, 1971: 32), as "a regression in the service of the self" (Bourguignon, 1976: 34), that is, as at once both a disease and a cure (Fanon, 1963: 290). For this demoniac is able to "give the Romans the devil" by identifying their legions, probably the most visible Roman presence to him, with demons (Brown, 1976: 78-79). However, he is able to do that only obliquely, through madness. It is likely that the tension between his hatred for his oppressors and the necessity to repress his hatred in order to avoid dire recrimination drove him mad. But his very madness permitted him to do in a socially acceptable manner what he could not do as sane, namely, express his total hostility to the Romans; he did this by identifying the Roman legions with demons. His possession was thus at once both the result of oppression and an expression of his resistance to it. He retreated to an inner world where he could symbolically resist Roman domination.

In the next place, his accommodation was accepted by his community, within certain limits, of course. His violence, reflecting perhaps the militaristic context of his illness, had to be dealt with. Thus, he was at first bound, but when that failed he was ostracized to the inhospitable cemetery. In all respects the status quo was preserved by the demoniac's community authorities—until Jesus came along and disturbed it by healing the man.

Jesus' disruption of the prevailing accommodation is indicated especially by one of the more puzzling aspects of the story, namely, the fear of some of the townspeople, which is manifested in their request to Jesus that he get out of their neighborhood. Perhaps we can account for this response, which seems not to be directly connected to the loss of 2,000 swine (or is this another slur on the legions? "They are swine!"), by suggesting that Jesus' healing of the demoniac brought the man's and the neighorhood's hatred of the Romans out into the open, where the result could be disaster for the community. The man eventually was a loudmouth (see Mk 5:20), which made his healing doubly dangerous. Jesus appears as an outside troublemaker whom the locals wish would get out of town and never show up again.

All of the accommodations surrounding the Gerasene demoniac were part of the accepted order of things in a manner similar to the socially approved protest cults described by anthropologists. The story of the Gerasene demoniac, as well as other descriptions of demoniacs in the Gospels, suggest that there were regularized and approved ways of handling demoniacs. Demoniacs and exorcists had their place in the social system as much as Sadducees, Pharisees, and the like. Only when one overstepped the limits set by the ruling powers did conflicts occur and the ruling person or group act to reinstitute an acceptable order of things, either by persuasion (as in the case of the Gerasene demoniac) or by force. Herod's action vis-à-vis John the Baptist is a perfect example of this pattern of behavior (*Antiquitates* XVIII:116-119). Just as soon as John's movement becomes threatening Herod takes action.

Now, is it possible that Jesus' exorcising activity as a whole can be understood in terms of this pattern? This appears to be the case, since he is said to come into conflict with the two most important Galilean authorities (the Pharisees and Herod) in connection with his exorcising activity. That the Pharisees take particular notice of Jesus as an exorciser is indicated by their accusation that as an exorciser he practices witchcraft and is himself a demoniac (Mk 3:22; Mt 12:24; Lk 11:15). In Matthew's report of this encounter there is a hint that Jesus is competing with the exorcising activity of the Pharisees (Mt 12:27: "sons of Pharisees" = Pharisees). In any case, the fact that they also regularly exorcise indicates that exorcising could be and was a regular part of the medical establishment's practice. Why is it then that Jesus' exorcisms go beyond the acceptable limits? How do they exceed the limits?

If we exclude jealousy, two factors remain as possibilities: Jesus *interpreted* exorcisms and *practiced* exorcisms differently from the Pharisees and was thus regarded as a deviant. Jesus not only explicitly stated that exorcisms are the central act of God in the world (Lk 11:20), but he also sent out his followers on an exorcising mission (Mk 3:14-15), which indicates the central importance he attached to exorcisms. Jesus' interpretation constituted a transformation of the values held by the Pharisees. They themselves originally had been a radical and revolutionary party within Palestinian Judaism, but for the most part they now were (to be sure, still relatively vibrant) conservatives who focused fairly narrowly on doing God's will in everyday life. This permitted them to escape confronting directly the terrifying social conditions and issues of their day. They were willing, naturally, to practice a kind of genteel medicine that included intermittent exorcising. But to focus on exorcising (and other kinds of healing) as a major form of action was not within their purview, probably because they understood, even if they refused to face up to, the connection between the illnesses of their time and the unjust colonial system of which many of them were an integral, privileged part. Thus, Jesus' exorcising activity must have appeared to them as an independent countercultural move that would ultimately be a threat to their social position.

The other important Galilean authority with whom Jesus came into conflict in connection with exorcising was Herod Antipas (Lk 13:31-33). Jesus' response to the news that Herod wanted to kill him ("Listen, I am casting out demons and performing cures today and tomorrow") shows both that at that time exorcising was still Jesus' central activity and that it was because of that specific kind of activity that Herod moved against Jesus. It is significant too that some Pharisees were the ones who informed (warned?) Jesus about Herod's threat. The preceding argument has shown that they were vitally concerned with Jesus as an exorcist. On the part of those hostile to Jesus, that concern could very well have spilled over to Herod. The involvement of Herod was probably stimulated by the expansion of Jesus' movement, known as the "mission of the Twelve" (Mk 3:13-15). The disciples spread out through Galilee, doing and preaching the same things as Jesus. This activity appeared to Herod and others to be similar to John the Baptist's movement and to be, similarly, a threat to Herod's position and security (Mk 6:14-16; Lk 9:7-9).

Thus, once again we find a public authority responding hostilely to Jesus specifically in connection with his exorcising activity because that activity threatened to upset the social and political status quo in relation to demoniacs. It was alright to have numerous demoniacs of various kinds filling various niches of the social system, and it was alright for professional exorcists to ply their art; but it was not alright for an unauthorized exorcist to make so much over demon possession and demoniacs that he identified their healing with God's saving presence and led a widespread exorcising mission that attracted a large following, thereby challenging the prevailing social system and its underlying value system. If Josephus' description of Palestine during Jesus' time is correct—that it was relatively free of public disturbances—this condition would make Jesus' movement all the more exceptional, visible, and threatening. Such a challenge had to be met head on and its leader liquidated. Thus it was that Jesus as an exorcist struck out directly into the vortex of the social turmoil of his day and before long became a public figure of sufficient stature that at first local, but finally national, authorities had to take account of his movement. Jesus' movement would threaten to effect the release of the smoldering discontent which appeared more and more until its final explosion in A.D. 66-70. In this way, then, Jesus' exorcisms led inevitably to his crucifixion.

Because demon possession and exorcism were integral parts of the social structure and manifested in important ways its dominant value of *social stability*, when Jesus disrupted this structure by countering it in his exorcisms with his own dominant value of *social healing,* conflict between Jesus and the public authorities was inevitable. Through his exorcising activity Jesus became a militant exorcist, or in Old Testament terms, an activist prophetic disturber of the peace (Rosen, 1968: 59-64; Hollenbach, 1981: 581-584).

Some people see a demon behind every bush, while others often make the opposite error of dismissing such talk as reflecting merely a primitive worldview. Both approaches are a victory for the dark side. One never fights against what one does not believe is there. On the other hand, to be preoccupied with the demonic can produce a type of fixation that does not reflect spiritual balance and can deflect taking spiritual accountability (Bock, 1996: 244).

c. The Raising of the Daughter of Jairus and the Healing of the Woman with the Hemorrhages (Lk 8:40-56)

The most obvious and important structural feature of this unit is the intercalation of the two episodes: The narrative of the Healing of the Woman Suffering from Hemorrhages (Lk 8:42b-48) has been embedded into the narrative of the Raising of Jairus' Daughter (Lk 8:40-42a, 49-56). The relationship between these two episodes transcends concerns of structure. They are also tied together by numerous commonalities at the linguistic and topical levels. Through the technique of intercalation, Luke presents the simultaneous unfolding of these two narrative events. Moreover, the interruption of the one healing by the other heightens the drama of the first (Green, 1997: 343).

The Lukan form of the stories is dependent on Mark, and the specific differences have to be attributed to Lukan redaction (Fitzmyer, 1981: 743; Nolland, 1989: 416; Bovon, 1991: 431), although a rather high number of minor agreements of Luke and Matthew against Mark has made some scholars question this opinion (Fuchs, 1992: 5-53). But, except for *kraspedou,* "fringe" in Mt 9:20 and Lk 8:44, these agreements are considered coincidences (Schramm, 1971: 126).

Luke's narrative moves forward by means of a geographical observation: Jesus has returned to the side of the lake where the earlier incidents were set (Craddock, 1990: 118). Luke suggests a rapidly moving story, for there is no indication of any delay between Jesus' arrival welcomed by the crowd (Lk 8:40, which points us back to Lk 8:4,19), and the approach of Jairus (Lk 8:41), whose plea to Jesus sets in motion the two healing stories that follow. The stories of the Raising of Jairus' Daughter and the Healing of the Woman with the Hemorrhages are unusual on several counts. First, they both focus on Jesus' ministry to women (Genest, 1987: 107). Second, whereas originally they existed as two independent accounts, they are now presented as a "sandwich" (Nolland, 1989: 417,418), in which the first story is begun (Lk 8:41-42), the second interrupts it (Lk 8:43-48), then the first is completed (Lk 8:49-56). The sandwiching of one unit in the middle of another like this is regularly called "intercalation" (Robbins, 1987: 502). Third, the middle story presents an ambiguous picture of Jesus' role in healing.

The Synoptic Gospels contain a number of collections of healing stories, where one leads into the next in rapid succession. But the present pattern of the interweaving of two healing stories—the "sandwich" design—is unique to this passage (Bock, 1994: 785; 1996: 247).

Some interpreters point to its uniqueness as a basis for concluding that the story therefore reports an actual incident in Jesus' life, when he was interrupted on the way to complete one task, took care of the interruption, then continued on his way.

Others suggest that the early Church might have interwoven the two accounts. They point out that the interruption serves the dramatic need for a delay during which the condition of Jairus' daughter deteriorates (Craddock, 1990: 118). They note also the number of parallels between the two stories (Genest, 1987: 105)—the use of "daughter" in both stories (Fitzmyer, 1981: 743); twelve years as the girl's age and the duration of the woman's illness (Fitzmyer, 1981: 745-746); the girl's being just at the threshold of puberty,

and the woman's illness that would have made her unable
to bear children; the stark contrast between the solicitous
family and the community caring for the girl, and the woman
who appears without companion or advocate; and the contrast between the woman's speech following her healing and
the command of silence at the end of the other story. Such
echoing back and forth between the stories suggests the work
of storytellers accenting the stories to make them work together into a coherent whole. However, we have no way of
judging whether this (or any other) specific incident actually happened as it is described. A more productive line of
questioning to pursue is how this passage in its current form
functions in Luke's Gospel (Ringe, 1995: 122-123).

Even though in all three Synoptic Gospels the two healing
stories are interwoven, each of them deserves to be looked
at on its own as well as in conjunction with the other. In
fact, the question may be raised whether the redactor(s)
inserted the story of the healing of the woman into that of
the raising of Jairus' daughter, or framed the healing of the
woman by the story of the raising of Jairus' daughter? (Genest,
1987: 105-106). We first discuss the framing story (Lk 8:40-
42,49-56) and then the healing of the woman (Lk 8:
43-48).

(1) The Raising of the Daughter of Jairus (Lk 8:40-42a,49-56)

Verses 40-42a: (40)   Now when Jesus returned, the crowd (*ochlos*)
            welcomed him,
            for they were all waiting for him.
      (41)   Just then there came a man named Jairus,
            a leader of the synagogue.
            He fell at Jesus' feet and begged him to
              come to his house,
      (42)   for he had an only daughter, about twelve
            years old,
            who was dying.

According to Lk 7:2, a centurion's slave was terminally ill but did not die. The youth at Nain had died before Jesus came to the city (Lk 7:12). In the present account the request for Jesus' benevolence is made before death occurs, but the patient will be dead when Jesus arrives (Danker, 1988: 185).

The framing story begins with abundant detail introducing the situation and its characters. The words "Now when Jesus returned" establish a continuity with the preceding episodes and alert the reader to the sequence of Jesus' mighty works (Liefeld, 1995: 122). We learn Jairus' name—itself an unusual detail. Apparently, at some point in the telling of the story, that name would have been recognized by the community who told it. Jairus is described as the leader (*archōn*, "ruler") of a synagogue, that is, one who had general supervision of the order and arrangements of the synagogue worship in a place (Schürmann, 1969: 489 note 127; Marshall, 1978: 343; C.F. Evans, 1990: 389). He is a Jewish "establishment" figure (Nolland, 1989: 423). Being a leader in the religious establishment does not exempt him from personal tragedy, but neither does it place him outside Jesus' compassion (Craddock, 1990: 120). This man falls at Jesus' feet and begs Jesus' help for his only daughter, who is dying. In the economics of health care delivery in the ancient world, a man of Jairus' station would normally go to one of the established medical centers or to a physician for help. Itinerant healers like Jesus represented the primary health care system for the destitute—those who did not have the money, or the leisure, or the confidence in the system to take advantage of more established resources (Ringe, 1995: 123-124).

Luke formulates Jairus' request in indirect, not in direct speech (Mk 5:23) and places the request for Jesus' coming in front, thereby drawing special attention to the house by way of the expression "to his house." This may serve as contrast to the centurion who said he was not worthy to receive Jesus in his house (Lk 7:6; Fischbach, 1992: 215). At Lk 7:19-20 the question was asked, "Are you the one who is to come, or are we to wait for another?" Here the word "waiting" (Lk 8:40) is the same word (*prosdokaō*), and the succeeding series of miracles is a further answer to the question (Danker, 1988: 185).

The resuscitation of Jairus' "only" daughter parallels the resuscitation of the widow of Nain's "only" son in Lk 7:11-17. In both instances Luke emphasizes the tragedy of the situation by his comment (Stein, 1992: 260,261), although the death of a twelve-year-old girl would have been a rather common occurrence in antiquity. Through much of the first century sixty percent of the persons born alive had died by the mid-teens (Malina- Rohrbaugh, 1992: 338). Verse 42b, "as he went, the crowd pressed in on him," marks the transition to the second healing story (see verse 45: "Master, the crowds surround you and press in on you" (Tiede, 1988: 175). At this stage occurs the encounter with the Woman with the Hemorrhages (Lk 8:43-48; see below). We continue here the story of the Raising of the Daughter of Jairus.

Verse 49:   While he was still speaking,
             someone came from the leader's house to say,
             "Your daughter is dead;
             do not trouble the teacher any longer."

Luke returns to the pericope with which he had opened this narrative unit, with the initial clause, "while he was still speaking" serving as the seam at the intersection of these two stories of healing. Because of the heightened drama of the encounter between Jesus and the hemorrhaging woman, Jesus' original destination must be brought again into the foreground. This is achieved by the introduction of a messenger from the house of the leader of the synagogue (Green, 1997: 394).

The story of Jairus' daughter resumes. Again, as in Lk 8:42-43, there is a link between one account and the sec-

ond installment of the other. One daughter has been saved,
now Jairus' daughter has her turn (Danker, 1988: 187). Following the story with the woman in the crowd, and in fact,
"while Jesus was still speaking" to her, that is, right on the
heels of Jesus' declaration to that "daughter" that her "faith"
has made her well (Lk 8:48), Jairus receives the message
that his daughter has died. Even those who had been hope-
ful before are silent as the messenger advises Jairus "not to
trouble the teacher any longer" (Tiede, 1988: 176; Bock,
1994: 799). The messenger who brought word that the girl
had died assumed that death placed her beyond the reach
of Jesus' power and suggested they cease pleading with Jesus
(Craddock, 1990: 120). This sets the scene for what follows.

Verse 50:   When Jesus heard this, he replied,
                 "Do not fear. Only believe, and she will be saved."

Jesus takes charge and urges Jairus to have the faith
that the woman has exhibited. In words that echo Isa 41:13,
Jesus says, "Fear not." The program spoken of in Lk 7:22 is
still in movement. The mention of being "saved" is unique
in Luke's version (compare Mk 5:36; see Lk 8:12), again
elaborating Luke's favorite theme that all of Jesus' saving
words and works are expressions of God's reign (Tiede, 1988:
176). Salvation for Luke is rescue from all that separates
one human being from another, or humankind from God
(see Lk 2:11; 8:12,36; Acts 16:13; Danker, 1988: 187). The
addition of "and she will be saved" provides a juxtaposition
of faith and salvation parallel to that encountered in Lk
8:48: she will be saved just as the needy woman. Now with
the presence of Jesus, the eschatological abolition of the
death barrier begins to take effect. It is a view of Jesus which
is affirmed, not the resurrection of the dead as such (Kertelge,
1970: 160; Nolland, 1989: 421).

Verse 51:   When he came to the house,
             he did not allow anyone to enter with him,
             except Peter, John, and James,
             and the child's father and mother.

The inner group of disciples is mentioned here in Luke for the first time. Luke's reference to the three disciples, Peter, John, and James, prepares for the account of the Transfiguration (see Lk 9:28), and possibly also for the association of Peter and John in Acts 3 and 4 (Danker, 1988: 187; Bock, 1994: 800-801), which may explain the unusual order of names (Fitzmyer, 1981: 749; C.F. Evans, 1990: 392; Stein, 1992: 263 note 221). With the disciples as primary witnesses, Jesus has been about the same activities since Lk 8:22, culminating in this episode in which he will raise a young girl from the dead. This explains why he takes only the child's parents and representatives of the Twelve with him into the room—in order to assist their perception of him, in preparation for Jesus' question in Lk 9:20, "Who do you say that I am?" (Nolland, 1989: 421; Green, 1997: 350).

Verse 52:   They were all weeping and wailing for her;
             but he said, "Do not weep;
             for she is not dead but sleeping."

Through his briefer account Luke brings into sharper focus the picture of Jesus in full command of a most desperate situation (Danker, 1988: 187). "All," that is, Jairus and his wife and the inner core of the group of disciples, Peter, John, and James (Genest, 1987: 111; different C.F. Evans, 1990: 392), are not able to accept Jesus' reassurance. Like the widow whose son had died (Lk 7:13), the girl's family and the other mourners are told not to weep, but rather to "believe" (Lk 8:50). Jesus' statement that the child is not dead but sleeping "is prognosis, not diagnosis" (Nolland, 1989: 421). "To sleep," generally *koimasthai*, is common in Greek literature, the Septuagint, and the New Testament as synonym for death (e.g., 1 Cor 15:51), and occasionally the verb here, *katheudein*, is so used (Dan 12:2; 1 Thess 5:10; Schürmann, 1969: 494-495; Bock, 1994: 802). The words can hardly represent an alternative diagnosis of the child's condition as not death but in coma—Luke's addition, "knowing that she was dead," in verse 53, is substantiated by the return of her spirit mentioned in verse 55 (C.F. Evans, 1990: 392).

Verse 53:   And they laughed at him, knowing that she was
              dead.

They laughed the bitter laugh of disbelief (Ringe, 1995: 124). Indeed, the laughter of the mourners is more bitter than sarcastic in Luke, since they knew that the girl was dead (Tiede, 1988; 176). According to others the verb "laughed" (*kategelōn*) implies ridicule (Fitzmyer, 1981: 749; compare the reaction to Paul's teaching on the resurrection in Acts 17:32; Bovon, 1991: 439).

Verses 54-55: (54) But he took her by the hand and called out,
                    "Child, get up!"
               (55) Her spirit returned, and she got up at once.
                    Then he directed them to give her something
                    to eat.

Isaiah's God took Israel by the hand (Isa 41:13; 42:6; Fitzmyer, 1981: 749). Jesus takes the young girl "by the hand," perhaps to communicate compassion (Danker, 1988: 188; Bock, 1994: 803) and, as in Lk 7:14, calls out in personal address, "Child, get up!" Once again Jesus touches a corpse. Previously it was the only son of a mother (Lk 7:11-17). Now it is the only daughter of a father (Fitzmyer, 1981: 744; Tiede, 1988: 176; C.A. Evans, 1990: 135). The verb translated "called out" is *phonein*, which in Luke-Acts, when it does not mean "to summon," is "to shout" (C.F. Evans, 1990: 393). As Lk 8:55 makes clear, Jesus is summoning back her spirit (Acts 7:59 [of one dying]; 9:41; Schürmann, 1969: 495; Marshall, 1978: 348).

Luke marks the girl's healing by noting that "her spirit [or breath] returned" (Lk 8:55), suggesting that she had been no longer the integrated, enlivened body that is the basis for human life: In other words she was dead (Tiede, 1988: 176). As evidence that she is now not only alive, but also fully restored, Jesus tells her family to give her some food (Ringe, 1995: 124). The motive of this latter clause is also to demonstrate the reality of the girl's resuscitation to earthly existence. Indeed, the girl returned to her former earthly life, not to the final resurrection state (Fitzmyer, 1981: 749; Stein, 1992: 263).

Verse 56:   Her parents were astounded;
              but he ordered them to tell no one what had
              happened.

The miracle is but a small part of a much larger message—the proclamation of the good news (*parengeilen*; Danker, 1988: 188). The story does not tell us directly, but the daughter's age clearly implies that now that she is well she will soon be ready to be given in marriage. Thus she is not only restored to her life in her present family, but she will soon take her new place in another household as someone's wife and subsequently as mother. This story thus has implications beyond the specifics of the girl's individual life. Implicitly, the story also holds out a social promise of well-being for the family and the household structures that are the heart of the social and economic system of the Roman Empire. For the moment, however, the family and the disciples who have witnessed the event are told to tell no one what has taken place (Ringe, 1995: 124), in contrast to the preceding order to "declare how much God has done for you" (Lk 8:39; Fitzmyer, 1981: 750; Stein, 1992: 264; Bock, 1994: 804-805). The injunction to silence imposed by Mark's theme of secrecy is reproduced. It is more than usually artificial in Mark, for how could the parents possibly conceal what had happened? It is even more so in the more public scene which Luke depicts, when all knew that the girl was dead (C.F. Evans, 1990: 393).

(2) The Healing of the Woman with the Hemorrhages (Lk 8:42b-48)

The story in the middle of the "sandwich" has a different feeling about it. The woman who is ill moves onto the stage by herself. The reader is struck by her independence and initiative. On the other hand, however, one notes the contrast with the surrounding story, where a beloved daughter of a prominent family is surrounded in her illness by a family ready to do anything to get help for her. The story provides no basis for drawing any conclusions about whether the woman actually has a family at home (Ringe, 1995: 124-125).

Of the three versions of the story (Mk 5:25-34; Mt 9:20-22; Lk 8:43-48), Mark's is the most elaborate, of which Matthew presents a radical abbreviation (Theissen, 1983: 134), while Luke remains closer to Mark, although he also omits a number of Markan elements (Ringe, 1995: 123; Fischbach, 1992: 213). All three start out with the fact that the woman had a flow of blood for twelve years. According to Mark [and some manuscripts of Luke] she had spent all she had on doctors and yet none of them could heal her. According to all three she comes to Jesus from behind to touch his garment, for—according to Mark and Matthew—she tells herself that if she can only touch his garment she will be made well. She is instantly healed [Matthew puts the healing at the end of the story, after Jesus' pronouncement to the woman]. According to Mark and Luke, Jesus asks who touched him, because he feels that something has happened to him, that power has gone out from him. The disciples disqualify the question, since in the midst of the crowd around them anybody might have touched him. But Jesus glances upon the crowd. According to Mark and Luke the woman comes forward on her own, whereas according to Matthew he sees her. Both the former Gospel writers emphasize her fear and trembling while she comes forward to tell her need. Jesus' answer is the same in all the gospels: "Daughter, your faith has made you well" (Mk 5:43; Mt 9:22; Lk 8:48; Fonrobert, 1997: 122-123).

The narrative has been dealt with in two recent monographs (Selvidge, 1990; Trummer, 1991), in numerous articles, and, of course, in all the major New Testament commentaries. Most of this literature discusses the Jewish milieu of the narrative. The story of the Woman with the Hemorrhages becomes for New Testament scholars the occasion to reflect not just on this particular incident in which Jesus is said to heal a woman from her sickness, but on what some call "Jewish blood-rites" or "Jewish fear of blood," others "Jewish precautionary anxieties about the blood of menstruation," and again others women's "restrictive cultic roles in society" (Selvidge, 1990: 83), and most often the "menstrual taboo." Such terms indicate, at best, the persisting lack of understanding with which New Testament scholars reconstruct the presumed Jewish milieu of the story.

Based on such reconstructions the narrative has become a "banner for equality of women within church and society" (Selvidge, 1990: 30) for many Christian feminists. Selvidge herself claims that "this story was written to free early Christian women from the social bonds of *niddah*, 'banishment' [a rather inadequate rendering of a term that means 'the physiological process of the flow of blood' (Levine)] during a woman's menstrual period" (Selvidge, 1990: 30). However, this approach seems to fall right under what has been called "Jesus-was-a-feminist strategy" (von Kellenbach, 1994: 30). Such an hermeneutic strategy and the implied anti-Judaism often running alongside it, has been extensively criticized from a feminist critical perspective (von Kellenbach, 1994).

The interpretation of Lk 8:43-48 and parallels by both feminist and non-feminist Christian New Testament scholars more often than not proves to be part of what has been described as "the unself-conscious, small, seemingly innocent distortions of Judaism which add up and sustain more pernicious forms of prejudice" (von Kellenbach, 1994: 13). For by passing a judgment on the suffering and oppression of the woman not only in this particular narrative, but by implication on Jewish traditions surrounding menstruation in general, and by making her the emblematic Jewish woman whom Jesus comes not only to heal but presumably also to liberate from the oppressive rituals of her culture, such hermenutic approaches in New Testament scholarship also pass a judgment on Jewish women today who choose to observe menstrual separation as a part of living their Jewishly-defined lives (Fonrobert, 1997: 123-125).

The challenge then is to determine or at least to speculate how the story would be read from the position of a woman who is committed to the observation of menstrual separation as a meaningful part of her tradition, who regards this observation as part of what it means to live her life in relation to the biblical God. Such a perspective would refuse to regard the traditions surrounding menstruation exclusively as a patriarchal tool, invented by men in the service of patriarchy in order to keep women in a subordinate position, from which they need to be liberated. What, then, does the miracle as part of the canonical literature for Christians really achieve for Christian attitudes toward menstruation, and regulation of menstruation?

The story is one among the many in which Jesus appears as a miraculous healer. It underlines the contrast between Jesus' power to heal and that of regular doctors. As far as the remarks on the extent of the suffering and the failure of doctors are concerned, these are typical characteristics of miraculous healing stories in and outside the New Testament. Similarly, the instantaneous healing at the end of the story represents a characteristic typical of miraculous healings. The narrative element of touch as a means of healing does not appear only in this story, but also in others in the Synoptic Gospels. In these other incidents, it is mostly people with undefined illnesses who are healed by touch. Hence the semantic weight of the woman's touching of Jesus' garment lies in the healing power of this touch: after the doctors have tried whatever medical treatments, a mere touch of Jesus suffices to heal her (Hengel, 1980: 346-347; Fonrobert, 1997: 126-127).

Verses 42b-43: (42b) As he went, the crowds pressed in on him.
(43) Now there was a woman
who had been suffering from hemorrhages for twelve years;
and though she spent all she had on physicians, no one could cure her.

The crowds are "pressing in on him"; in the words of Jesus' Parable of the Sower, they threaten to "choke" him. That Lk 8:14 and 42 are the only two places where the term "to choke" (*sumpnigō*) is used in Luke-Acts, and that this account is calculated as a vignette illustrating Jesus' earlier tale, makes it altogether conceivable that we should read the smothering action of the crowds as integral to the setting Luke is working to establish. According to Jesus' teaching in Lk 8:4-21, faith on its own is not enough, for it must prove itself in testing. In Lk 8:42b-48, the evangelist will portray such a test—not of Jesus, as will become clear, but of the faith of the woman who comes to Jesus on a quest for healing. The woman whom Luke introduces provides him with yet another opportunity to define "the poor" to whom the good news is brought (Lk 4:18-19; 7:22). The simple fact that she is a woman in Palestinian society already marks her as one of relatively low status. In addition to this, she was sick, and her sickness, while apparently not physically debilitating, was socially devastating (Green, 1997: 346).

Luke abbreviates Mark's "she had endured much under

many physicians, and had spent all that she had; and she was no better, but rather grew worse" (Mk 5:26), and a number of manuscripts do not contain the clause "and she had spent all she had on physicians." Since Luke abbreviates elsewhere in the story, it cannot be ascertained whether he does so out of professional courtesy; especially since he declares the woman's case medically hopeless (compare Lk 8:27). The verse's point, with or without the textually disputed phrase in Luke about doctors, is that she had suffered in this condition for a long time and could not get help (Nolland, 1989: 419). If the phrase is included, then the tragic situation is painted more graphically (Bock, 1994: 794). In any case, Luke's stress on the seriousness of the malady focuses attention on the greater power of Jesus (Danker, 1988: 185-186). The phrase "all she had" renders the Greek word *bios* (see also Lk 15:12,30; 21:4), which really means "life," therefore, not just money, but property, all she had to live on. The Greek word used for "to cure" from which our word "therapy" is derived is used more often in Luke than that which describes the specific activity of a physician (*iaomai*; *iatros*, "physician"; Trummer, 1991: 103-104).

Two details about the woman's circumstances are clearly implied by her condition. First, for twelve years she would have been unable to become pregnant and thus to participate in what her society (and probably Luke's as well) would have seen as her principal role in the family and the economy, bearing children. That fact might have had an effect on a woman's marriage, particularly if she had not already borne children, but this story itself says nothing about any such circumstances. Apparently Luke would have his readers assume that she lived in normal circumstances—that is, within a family and a household. Secondly, after twelve years of even mild but constant bleeding, she would have been physically weakened.

The story itself tells us further that the formal system for medical care—the "physicians"—had "bled" her economically as well. She may have shared Jairus' sense of desperation in coming to Jesus for help, but she also had become part of the population whose lack of financial resources made them dependent on itinerant healers when the techniques of folk medicine routinely practiced in the family were not effective (Ringe, 1995: 125).

Verse 44:   She came up behind him and touched the fringe of his clothes,
     and immediately her hemorrhage stopped.

Luke omits the woman's conversation with herself (Mk 5:28; Mt 9:21); for him the essential point is that "no one could cure her" (Lk 8:43). The term "stopped" here refers to the stoppage of blood (corresponding to "hemorrhages," literally "flow [*rhusis*] of blood" in verse 43)" and has medical overtones (Marshall, 1978: 345; Bock, 1994: 794).

In the rabbinic tradition of the Misnah anyone with bodily discharge was considered to be in a state of ritual impurity. Seven days without the discharge must pass before the person could even begin the rituals of purification. Luke, like Matthew (Mt 9:18-22), uses the word "fringe" in describing the place that the woman touched. Which garment worn by a Jewish man had a fringe? The answer is the *tallit*. The *tallit*, or prayer shawl, was worn by all religious men in the first century A.D. Jewish men were (and are) required to wear one to help them remember the law (Num 15:37-39). In the first century A.D. the *tallit* symbolized three things about the owner.

First it was a symbol of the wearer's status. The Law required the tassels in the corners to be blue in color. The more blue that was found in one's prayer shawl, the higher status one had in the community. These blue tassels became such a symbol of status that eldest sons would inherit their father's prayer shawl and incorporate their father's blue threads into their own *tallit*.

Second, the *tallit* also symbolized a person's authority.

It was the custom for a wealthy peron to wear a family signet ring. When finalizing a business transaction, the person
would make an impression of this signet ring in a clay tablet. For the poor, who had no rings, the tassels of the *tallit*
would serve the same purpose. When a transaction was being completed the people involved would wrap the tassels
around their fingers and press them into the clay tablet,
thus authorizing the transaction's completion. The Mari tablets
report that when a prophet offered a prophecy and an interpretation to a king in ancient times, the prophet would
be required to give the king a piece of his tassel and a lock
of his hair as a guarantee that the prophecy and interpretation were true.

Third, the *tallit* was a symbol of the covenant, of covenant election and holiness. The Torah says that the *tallit*
would be worn to help the men of Israel remember the Law.
To demonstrate the holiness required from the covenant
people (Ex 19:5-6) and their belonging to it, the men of
Israel would wear the prayer shawl dyed God's color, blue.

One last comment, before returning to Jesus' encounter
with the woman with the hemorrhage: there was an oral
tradition that prohibited a person from touching the *tallit*
of someone who was not a member of one's own family. In
other words, it was against the tradition for the woman to
touch Jesus not so much because she was defiled, but because she was not of his family.

When the woman heard that Jesus was coming she decided to try just to touch the fringe of his garment; if only
she could touch his holiness, authority, or status, she might
be made well (Mk 5:28; Mt 9:21). Yet, after she was caught
violating the Law, instead of admonishing her, Jesus called
her "daughter," thereby telling her that she was indeed in
his family and invited to touch him.

Jesus would certainly have worn a *tallit*. Knowing how
the *tallit* was used helps us to have a clearer understanding
of what happened between Jesus and this woman (Page II,
1995: 91-95).

In spite of the context in the Gospels and the later wide reception of the story as a narrative that enhanced Jesus' powers in folkloric imagination, the story comes to be read on the background of biblical impurity regulations and by extension also on the "background" of the mishnaic discourse of impurity. Indeed, the woman's sickness is identified mostly as what could be called specifically a "Jewish sickness." It is not only a physical ailment from which she suffers, but she also suffers from the *mastix* (the term Mk 5:29 uses to describe the woman's affliction; it can be used both in a physical and a spiritual sense, and is best translated as "affliction") of her Jewish culture. Jesus then comes to heal her from both.

First of all, she is identified by almost every commentator as a Jewish woman. By "Jewish" woman then the commentators mean a woman whose life is unquestionably defined and circumscribed by the biblical text, on the one hand, and the mishnaic text, on the other. But even if the narrators indeed imagined her as a Jewish woman, one would still have to ask what kind of Jewish woman, since the Jewish community in first-century Palestine turns out to be so vastly diverse. The biblical text on menstrual regulations, which is prescriptive and not descriptive, requires interpretation in order to be applied to the regulation of daily life. Hence, would she be a woman in whose community purity laws were more strictly observed or more leniently interpreted and observed? Be that as it may, the fact remains that the Gospel narrators leave her ethnic identity unspecified. This keeps the possibility open that the woman's status of impurity according to the priestly regulation in Leviticus is of no interest to them, since they are primarily concerned about the healing miracle.

Secondly, her sickness is identified as a "Jewish sickness" by choosing Leviticus 15 as Mark's intertext. Hence the woman is identified as a *zavah*, or a woman with an irregular and extended blood-flow. The connection with

Leviticus 15 is established primarily linguistically. The linguistic similarity between the description of the woman's sickness in the Gospels and the Septuagint appears to identify Leviticus 15 as an intertext which the narrators, and if not the narrators of the pre-literary story, so at least writers of the Gospels, had in mind. Commentators point out the suffering of the woman from her "Jewish sickness" (Guelich, 1989: 296). But even here it is important to keep in mind that this linguistic connection is not a necessary one, for, as it has been pointed out, the verb *aimorein*, "suffer a chronic bleeding," exists as a component of medical vocabulary (Hengel, 1980: 346 note 35).

However, most important in this reading of the story as a repudiation of Jewish traditions surrounding menstruation, is the narrative moment of the woman's touching of Jesus. Identified as a *zavah*, she is bracketed between Leviticus 15, on the one hand, and mishnaic law, on the other. At the one end of the spectrum stands Leviticus 15, according to which supposedly the *zavah* transfers the status of impurity by touch. Surprisingly enough, however, none of the New Testament commentators take note of the fact that as far as the *zavah* is concerned, the masoretic text does not include an explication that she communicates impurity by *being touched*, as does the menstruous woman (Lev 15:19). Nor is there any mention that either she or the menstruant woman communicate impurity by *touching anyone*. The difference between *being touched* and *touching* is more significant than it seems. The menstruant woman does transfer impurity by being touched (Lev 15:19). However, Leviticus does not mention that she communicates impurity by touching. This can only mean that in fact her hands do not transmit impurity. The consequence is that she is not banished but remains at home. Neither is she isolated from her family. She is free to prepare their meals and perform household chores. They, in turn, merely have to avoid lying in her bed, sitting in her chair, and touching her (Milgrom, 1991:

936). This could all the more apply to the *zavah*, who could even be touched, according to the masoretic text. The *zavah*, then, communicates impurity only indirectly: if somebody touches her bedding or anything on which she sat, "whoever touches *them* shall be impure; he shall launder his clothes, bathe in water, and remain impure until the evening" (Lev 15:27). Nonetheless, two manuscripts and the Septuagint translation of Lev 15:27 read: "whoever touches *her*, shall launder his clothes..." Only if we accept the latter reading, the *zavah*—similar to the *zav*, that is, the man with an irregular discharge—communicates impurity by being touched (Milgrom, 1991: 943).

However, at the other end of the spectrum stands the mishnaic ruling in m. Zab. 5:1: "He who touches a *zav*, or he whom a *zav* touches, transfers a status of impurity to food, drink and vessels that (can be purified by immersion)." M. Zab 5:1 extends Leviticus 15, for according to the biblical text, as we have just seen, only the person who touches (somebody in the status of impurity) becomes impure, but presumably not the one who is touched (by somebody in the status of impurity). As a mishnaic *zavah* the woman in our story is then compared to the status of a leprous person (Schottroff, 1990: 113; Schmithals, 1979: 293). Some go as far as to write that "the woman in the miracle story was beaten because of her physical ailment. She was taboo to all. She could have no intimate relations with men, nor could she, as responsible Jewess, with a good conscience, be milling about among the masses" (Selvidge, 1990: 88; compare Trummer, 1991: 84).

Consequently, the presumption is often that the woman, deliberately or not, would have rendered Jesus impure (Selvidge, 1990: 92; Luz, 1989: 52; Mann, 1986: 286). Or she touched Jesus only secretly, because she knew that she really should not touch Jesus, since a status of impurity would be transferred to him: "Coming from the rear of the crowd, the appropriate place for the defiled, she risked defiling others by approaching and deliberately touching Jesus' clothes" (Guelich, 1989: 297; compare Trummer, 1991: 121). Further, her fear and trembling at the end of the story is often explained as being caused by her guilt-complex about having rendered Jesus deliberately impure (Kertelge, 1994: 59) or revealing "her awareness of having violated a taboo" (Ruether, 1975: 65). Finally, and perhaps most importantly, Jesus is regarded as having abolished the levitical impurity regulations concerning women by not only disregarding the fact that she committed the dreadful act of touching him, but by even praising her for her faith (Sand, 1985: 201).

However, even if we accept Leviticus 15 and by extension its mishnaic elaboration as the intertexts of the story, and even if we assume that the woman is Jewish, what is disregarded in all these speculations is the fact that the woman does not commit a transgression by touching Jesus, neither according to the priestly writings nor according to mishnaic law. Thus it is pointed out that in Leviticus 15 "there is no prohibition barring the menstruant from touching anyone" (Milgrom, 1991: 936). That is, neither Leviticus 15, nor the mishnaic expansion of biblical impurity regulations, ever prohibit to touch, and thus do not treat the event of touch as a transgression, as opposed to, for example, forbidden sexual relationships. The latter, including the sexual relationship with a menstruous woman, are indeed a matter of transgression, whereas the biblical and rabbinic discourse of impurity is not a punitive discourse. If it should so happen that someone touches, and that might even be quite often, then the person who touches the *zavah*, or the woman with a regular menstrual blood-flow (or is touched by such a person in the mishnaic view), is simply also rendered impure until the evening of that day.

One should not conclude on the basis of the levitical laws that the woman's presence in the crowd would have put her in jeopardy for "contaminating" those she touched. Luke's story does not suggest that she has taken any particular risk by moving about in public or by approaching Jesus (Ringe, 1995: 125).

The woman in our Gospel story, therefore, never commits a transgression when she touches Jesus' garment. Neither biblical nor mishnaic law consider the case of a person in a status of impurity who deliberately touches somebody else. Hence, rabbinically speaking, the woman of our narrative would only have committed a transgression had she done anything that might lead to or initiate sexual contact, which is clearly not the point of the story. But otherwise, she does not commit an act of transgression. Further, to the best of our knowledge, there is not a single *case story* in talmudic literature of someone in the status of impurity touching somebody else. Thus, in spite of the *halakhic theory* expressed in m. Zab. 5:1, the concern about touch remains at the very most subdued in rabbinic literature. The contention that "a responsible Jewess with a good conscience" would not have been milling around in the masses (Selvidge) is, therefore, unfounded aside from having slightly polemic overtones. For, again, there is no indication that rabbinic literature expresses any concern about milling around in the masses, for either those who are in the status of impurity because of a regular or irregular discharge, or those who are concerned about remaining in the status of purity. We might have expected such an indication had there been hermeneutic or practical concern about being touched by a person with such an invisible impurity.

The case for impurity according to either biblical or rabbinic law as a primary concern of Lk 8:40-48 and parallels cannot therefore be consistently argued. The attempt to read this story as abrogation of biblical traditions concerning menstruation and irregular discharges of blood remains unsuccessful. The Jesus of this narrative appears as someone who has the powers to heal a woman with a severe sickness, where others have failed. It is because of the open and unclear relationship of this narrative with the biblical text in Leviticus that Christian writers already in the early period can use the story for whatever purpose they want to use it. A feminist reading of the Gospels that is developed at the expense of women's life within the Jewish cultural context does not fulfill its promise of women's liberation (Fonrobert, 1997: 128-138).

Verses 45-46: (45) Then Jesus asked, "Who touched me?"
When all denied it, Peter said,
"Master, the crowds surround you and press in on you."
(46) But Jesus said, "Someone touched me;
for I noticed that power had gone out from me."

The significance of the woman's action is highlighted by the fourfold appearance of the verb "to touch" in verses 44-47. After the more specific "fringe of his clothes" in verse 44, Luke now in Jesus' words makes Mark's touching of the clothing into a touching of Jesus: it is contact with Jesus that is significant (Nolland, 1989: 420). Jesus' question, "Who touched me?," triggers of a reaction proper to Luke, "all denied it," upon which Peter [instead of "his disciples" in Mk 5:31; some manuscripts have "Peter and those with him"], the acknowledged spokesperson for the apostolic band, gets into action and enters alone into conversation with Jesus (Trummer, 1991: 106). Jesus displays his miraculous knowledge and power before all the people with his statement "Someone touched me" (Theissen, 1983: 135). Queries about why Jesus should have asked such a question—since he should have known who touched him—are out of place; they are born of later christological conceptions of him (Fitzmyer, 1981: 746).

Jesus' power may be tremendous, but as Luke (and Mark) tells the story, he has not controlled its use. The power has been tapped by a determined touch in the midst of a pressing crowd. Jesus is said to have felt something identified as "power" flowing out of him, but not to know who touched him in this special way (Ringe, 1995: 126).

Some have argued that Luke had a "magical" view of Jesus' "power" as if it were a reservoir of energy not directly connected with his saving word. But Luke's telling of the story only raises these possibilities in order to identify the unity of this "power" with the work of the Spirit of the Lord (Lk 4:14) which has anointed Jesus and endowed the mission with the saving authority of the kingdom of God (Tiede, 1988: 176).

Verse 47: When the woman saw that she could not remain
    hidden,
  she came trembling;
  and falling down before him,
  she declared in the presence of all the people
  why she had touched him,
  and how she had been immediately healed.

We have been told that Jesus did not know who had touched him, and presumably the woman could have slipped away (Trummer, 1991: 107), returned to her home, performed the appropriate rituals of purification required by law, then presented herself to the proper authorities who could certify her healing. Instead, she recognizes that she cannot remain hidden. Luke does not explain how she came to that conclusion. Likewise, no reason is given for her "trembling." To say that it indicates her reaction to Jesus' knowledge is mere speculation (*pace* Bock, 1994: 795). For Luke "fear" was an appropriate response to the experience of divine presence (Stein, 1992: 262). Like Jairus when he approached Jesus, she falls down before him. Instead of asking for help, she "declared" what she had done and what had happened to her.

Several details highlight the importance of her action. The word translated "declared" is one of a family of Greek words that convey the meaning of public announcement or "proclamation." The woman preached to the crowds. Luke tells us two things about the importance of her preaching. First, up to this point in the narrative, he has mentioned the "crowds" who were pressing around Jesus (Lk 8:40,42,45). Suddenly her preaching is in the presence of all the "people." It is clear that the cast of characters has not changed, but now they are referred to by a word Luke sometimes uses for Israel as the people of the promise (e.g., Lk 1:10,17,68,77; 7:16; 24:19) and for people to whom Jesus preaches or teaches (e.g., Lk 6:17; 7:1,29; 18:43; 20:1,9,45; 21:38). It is the Greek word *laos*, underlying the English word "laity." The formless "crowds" take shape as a "people" in response to the woman's proclamation. We know little of the proclamation itself. We read only that she said why she had touched him, and how she had been immediately healed (Ringe, 1995: 126). It has been noted that the woman's confession before all the people gives the impression of entering a cultic domain in which God's saving act is proclaimed before the whole community (Theissen, 1983: 40).

Verse 48:   He said to her, "Daughter, your faith has made you
               well;
               go in peace."

"Daughter" is a reminder that she is to be accepted in the family of Israel (Fitzmyer, 1981: 747; Bock, 1994: 798). Like the demoniac, the woman is rehabilitated socially. A similar word will be spoken at Lk 19:9 over Zacchaeus (Danker, 1988: 187). Jesus refers to her "faith." Furthermore, he says that faith "has made her well" (the same word that is often translated "save"). Faith is not the psychosomatic cause of healing, but only the subjective condition that opens one to the power of God (Schürmann, 1969: 492; Nolland, 1989: 420).

Luke clearly implies that more has happened than simply the cure of her physical illness. That cure itself would have enabled her to return to full participation in family life, including, presumably, again being able to bear children. But even the social dimension of the healing is eclipsed in importance for Luke by the importance of her telling

the story. By calling the articulation of her story "proclamation," Luke links it to the proclamation of the gospel (a
word with the same root in Greek) that is his principal
agenda. In the logic of the narrative itself, what is called
"faith" is not simply her enacted belief that Jesus could heal
her, nor is it any creed, or in particular a "christological"
confession that conveys a correct statement of Jesus' identity. Rather her faith is the proclamation—speaking "the
whole truth," as Mk 5:33 calls what she does—that reads
her life in terms of the gospel, and that does so out loud.

Having "faith" or "believing" (the verb has the same
root in Greek) and being "saved" are linked twice in Lk
8:40-56. In the case of Jairus' daughter, they are linked in
the form of a promise: "Do not fear. Only believe, and she
will be saved" (Lk 8:50). In Jesus' parting words to the woman,
having faith and being saved are linked as an accomplished
fact (Fitzmyer, 1981: 747), which is expressed in a benedic-
tion (Lk 8:48). In neither case, though, does that connection lead to a formula for achieving a personal or private
salvation, whether from immediate physical ills or in some
eternal hereafter. Rather, in these stories, whatever the human need or assumption about Jesus' power that may account for people's coming to Jesus, "faith" draws them beyond that moment. By their "faith" they participate in a
project whose effects stretch far beyond them (Ringe, 1995:
126-127).

The idea of "peace" associated with Jesus' ministry is
key to Luke (Lk 1:79; 2:14,29; 7:50; 10:5-6, etc.). Peace
here is not an internal, subjective feeling; it is a state that
exists between the woman and God because of her faith
(Bock, 1994: 799).

d. The Mission of the Twelve (Lk 9:1-6)

Four different reports of the Disciples' Missions have
come down to us (Mk 6:7-12,30; Mt 10:1-14; Lk 9:1-6;

10:1-11, 17-20), but it has been convincingly shown that this variety of traditions arose just from two sources. Mk 6:7-12 is one account followed by Luke 9, and the other is Luke 10, probably Q. Mt 10:1-14 is to be seen as a conflation of these two accounts. The question arises: Do these two traditions represent one common mission discourse or two? From the pattern of the two traditions that are roughly paralleled in Mark and in Luke it is probably best to see just one source behind these two traditions (Hahn, 1965: 41-46; Twelftree, 1993: 123). And when, in Lk 22:35, Luke refers back to instructions given to the Twelve, he alludes not to Lk 9:11-12 but to Lk 10:4, the mission of the Seventy (-Two) (Marshall, 1978: 412; Metzger, 1958-1959: 299-306).

It has been suggested that Luke 9 answers Herod's question about Jesus' identity (Lk 9:7-9). Ironically, as the narrator informs the reader about the identity of Jesus, the disciples seem to know and understand less and less about that identity (Fitzmyer, 1978: 139-152).

The miracle stories recounted by Luke in this section of his Gospel (Lk 8:22-9:6) have come to an end in Lk 8:56 and are immediately followed by an episode in which Jesus sends out the Twelve on a mission in Galilee. This episode comes from Mark, but since Luke has used Mk 6:1-6a in his Nazareth story (Lk 4:16-30), the collocation of this episode takes on a different significance in the Lukan Gospel, coming, as it does, on the heels of the miracle stories, and acting as a sort of conclusion to them. The witnesses from Galilee that Jesus has been in the act of training are now being sent to participate in his own mission, even during the ministry in the Period of Jesus (Fitzmyer, 1981: 751).

In Lk 9:1-6 the reader is introduced to Luke's understanding of prophetic succession. Jesus' ministry has been summarized in terms of being "mighty in word and deed" with particular reference to exorcism, healing, and preaching the kingdom of God (Lk 4:18-19,40-44; 6:17-18; 8:1-2). And now the Twelve are given "power and authority" to carry on the same ministry that Jesus has had. Just as Jesus' ministry was prophetic in character (Lk 4:24-27; 7:16), so also the apostles are now called to follow Jesus' prophetic ministry. And just as Jesus' ministry has met with rejection, the opposition that Jesus anticipates for his apostles is not unexpected: "If people do not welcome you, shake the dust off your feet when you leave their town, as a testimony against them." Jesus is rejected as prophet, and therefore those who carry on Jesus' prophetic ministry can also expect rejection. Just as the mission of the Twelve is an extension of Jesus' own ministry, so also the rejection of their ministry will be a continuation of the rejection of Jesus' mission. Thus Luke intends the passage as a foreview of the missionary activity and associated rejection in Acts (Nolland, 1989: 425-426).

In Lk 9:1-6, Jesus refers to first-century hospitality customs. During this period there were five traditional acts, or gifts, of hospitality people were required to offer to a guest in their home, once that person had crossed the threshold into the house. The five acts of hospitality were (1) offering a drink of water; (2) washing the feet of the guest; (3) greeting the guest with a kiss; (4) anointing or washing his head; and (5) offering their guest something to eat. Jesus knew that the disciples would be met with hospitality wherever they went. Therefore, they need not take anything with them on their journey. Should they happen upon a village where they were not received appropriately, they were to leave that place (Page III, 1995: 95-96).

The passage can be broken down into the following subdivisions: (1) the disciples were given power and authority over demons and sickness; (2) they were told to preach God's kingdom and to heal; (3) rules of travel were given that prohibit taking provisions; (4) rules of lodging were given requiring that they be satisfied with the first offer of hospi-

tality; (5) the disciples were instructed to sever symbolically all relations with those who rejected their message;
and (6) they are described as having fulfilled their commission (Fitzmyer, 1981: 752; Stein, 1992: 267).

By giving the Twelve power over demons and disease,
Jesus moves them up in the hierarchy of powers. He also
offers them the role of brokers in bringing God's benefits to
the people (Malina-Rohrbaugh, 1992: 338).

Verses 1-2:   (1) Then Jesus called the twelve together
                     and gave them power and authority over all
                        demons
                     and to cure diseases,
                (2) and he sent them out to proclaim the kingdom
                        of God
                     and to heal.

Lk 9:1-6 is to be read in close connection with the two
preceding accounts—the healing of the Gerasene demoniac
(Lk 8:26-39) and the double healing of the woman with
the flow of blood and Jairus' daughter (Lk 8:40-56)—but
also with the linked sections in Lk 8:1-21. The preceding
episodes exemplify the exorcising and healing which the
Twelve are now called to perform; the preaching of the
kingdom of God has been the dominant focus of the earlier
sections (Nolland, 1989: 425).

Luke omits Mark's "two by two" (but he has it at Lk
10:1), perhaps because, while apostolic practice sometimes
followed this practice (Acts 8:14; 13:2), it did not invari-
ably do so (Acts 9:32; C.F. Evans, 1990: 395). The omission of "two by two" may also give a greater sense of the
Twelve as a unified body (Stein, 1992: 267). Luke adds "power
and" to Mark's "authority" in Mk 6:7. The immediate link
here will be Lk 8:46 ("I noticed that power had gone out
from me"), but there may also be an anticipation of the
post-resurrection empowering (Acts 1:8; Nolland, 1989: 426).
Both terms are also found in Lk 4:36, where again Mark
has only "authority." Luke typically emphasized Jesus' power

(Stein, 1992: 267). Mk 6:7 makes no mention of the proclamation of the kingdom. Luke enlarges on this aspect. Lk 9:2 is not a repetition of Lk 9:1 but affirms that the authority given by Jesus coincides with God's interests. The kingdom proclamation is Jesus' responsibility and he administrates it through the Twelve. Luke's added "all [demons]" will highlight the failure of the disciples which Luke will later report in Lk 9:37-43 (Danker, 1988: 189).

The Twelve Jesus had chosen in Lk 6:13-16 to be apostles have now completed their time of preparation for the task (Lk 6:17-8:56). In a "commencement ceremony" they are vested with power and authority and are sent out to continue what they have learned in their time of apprenticeship to Jesus. In their general outline the Gospel accounts of the sending out of disciples on their journeys may reflect the experience of the early Church. Its missionaries too were prepared by being steeped in the accounts of Jesus' life and teachings. They were then sent out to continue Jesus' work of preaching and healing, with faith and confidence in God's accompaniment and providence on their way (Ringe, 1995: 129).

Jesus specifies the objective of the Twelve. They should proclaim "the kingdom of God," they should "bring the good news" (Lk 9:6). But the text insists first of all, not on the proclamation of the message, but on the power to return to people their health by expelling demons and curing them of their diseases. Evangelization is brought about not only by the word but also and primarily by a liberating action (Rolland, 1988: 361).

Today—although there is also a proliferation of healing ministries—many Christians do not think so much in terms of exorcisms and healings but are more sensitive to other forms of liberation. They have become aware of the tremendous possibilities of the human intellect, which is a gift of God, to alleviate and cure illness. The direct intervention of God in this domain is no longer considered the usual thing. But we have also become aware of the fact that humankind faces other terrible sufferings: endemic hunger, the disparity between North and South, the arms race, dictatures of various kinds. We know that "the kingdom of God is righteousness and peace and joy in the Holy Spirit" (Rom 14:17). We have a tremendous desire to manifest God's mercy by healing humankind of these forms of slavery, by contributing to the building of "a new earth, where righteousness is at home" (2 Pet 3:13; Rolland, 1988: 361-362).

Verse 3:   He said to them,
                "Take nothing for your journey,
                no staff, nor bag, nor bread, nor money—
                not even an extra tunic.

Luke softens Mark's "commanded" to "said," and moves the account into direct speech. The standard equipment for the traveler is not for the apostles. They are to rely completely on God's resources. Mk 6:8 permits them a staff. Whereas Mark has them sent out two by two, Luke reserves that detail for the mission of the Seventy (Lk 10:1; Danker, 1988: 189; Craddock, 1990: 121).

The staff could be used either as a walking stick or for protection against bandits or animals. It was also a characteristic trademark of the "wandering" Cynic preachers of that day. The bag was used for carrying provisions. The tunic was the garment worn under the outer cloak (see Lk 6:29). The idea is of carrying a spare tunic, not of wearing two (Stein, 1992: 268).

Several suggestions have been made as to the point of these restrictions. Is the matter so urgent that there is no time to get properly equipped (contrast the standard picture of the equipped traveler in Josh 9:3-6)? The prohibitions seem to be more positively intended than this would allow. More likely and still somewhat along the same lines is the possibility that we have here a deliberately staged prophetic sign of eschatological urgency (C.F. Evans, 1990:

396). Identification with the poor could also be involved: Good news to the poor must be so in the very way of announcing it. It is fitting that those who come with good news for the poor should be identified with the poor by being made vulnerable in this way (Nolland, 1989: 429). Or is the point to express in the conduct of the mission an utter dependence on God, so that the Twelve may discover the amazing providential care of God as they live out in this unique context the unique directive of Lk 12:31 (Schürmann, 1969: 502)? It has been pointed out that the Essenes often traveled without any provisions in anticipation of being received by fellow believers as one of the family (Fitzmyer, 1981: 753-754; C.A. Evans, 1990: 140-141). This would mean, then, that the Twelve went without the trappings of security, "just in case." Some of these external conditions of the journey will be modified later (Lk 22:35-38). (But how many of the Church's sermons are contradicted by budgets and programs of self-protection and security? [Craddock, 1990: 122]). Other suggestions based on rabbinic prohibitions are less likely (Nolland, 1989: 427). Jesus demands from his disciples a great personal poverty. The details vary from one Gospel text to another, indicating that what matters is not the letter of these prescriptions, but that it is essential to be a free, liberated person (Rolland, 1988: 362-363).

Verses 4-5:   (4) Whatever house you enter, stay there, and
                    leave from there.
               (5) Whenever they do not welcome you,
                    as you are leaving that town shake the dust off
                    your feet
                    as a testimony against them."

Verse 4 is very compressed, and is stated more fully in Lk 10:5-7. The disciples should receive hospitality graciously. Unlike itinerant philosophers who brought their philosophy into disrepute by begging from house to house (see the warning in Lk 10:7), the Church's missionaries are emissaries of God and from their hospitable bases they are to carry out the kingdom assignment (Danker, 1988: 190). This going from house to house to get provisions became such a problem later in the Church that Didache 11-12 gives detailed instructions about how to deal with traveling missionaries. It can still be a problem today to know if someone who consistently speaks of the need for money truly represents the Church (Bock, 1996: 252 note 3). When they are welcomed into someone's house for lodging, stability is recommended; they should not be seeking out better quarters (Fitzmyer, 1981: 754).

Luke envisages a whole town making a response corporately to the message. Acts provides various examples of corporate response to the missioners. Wherever they are not favorably received, they are to make the gesture of the prophets who declare themselves free of the judgment about to overtake those who reject God's message (see Lk 10:10-11; C.F. Evans, 1990: 396). Shaking of the dust is a fairly transparent image for separation. As emissaries of the kingdom of God, the apostles are to threaten unresponsive towns with exclusion from what God is now doing. The act is a final witness to the town of the seriousness of failing to respond to the message (Nolland, 1989: 428). They have merely left them with the declaration of God's reign, and now the matter is between that town and God. This is the meaning of the phrase "as a testimony against them" (Danker, 1988: 190; Tiede, 1988: 178).

Verse 6:   They departed and went through the villages,
              bringing the good news
              and curing diseases everywhere.

The summary account prepares for the introduction of Herod. "Villages" suggests outreach to the "poor" in Israel. Verse 6 ends on a pandemic note: evangelizing and healing were done "everywhere" (Danker, 1988: 190). "Everywhere" balances "through the villages." Significantly Luke avoids

Mark's "that people may repent" (Mk 6:12), a notion that is otherwise dear to him; instead he uses here "bringing the good news" (*euangelizesthai*; Fitzmyer, 1981: 754). Neither Luke nor the other evangelists have any idea of the location or territorial scope of the mission (C.F. Evans, 1990: 396).

WHO IS THIS? (LK 9:7-50)

The groundwork for the twin focus of Lk 9:1-50, Christology and discipleship, is laid in Luke 8, with its concerns with perceptiveness and active faith. This new section is distinguished from the previous one primarily by the explicitness of the portrayal of the disciples and by its heightened, even candid concern with Jesus' identity. Already in Luke 8, the presence of the disciples *with* Jesus had become more emphatic than at any other time since their being called in Luke 5-6. Now, however, they are active agents involved in the mission of Jesus, and they begin to be developed less as companions and more as characters in their own right within the larger narrative of Luke-Acts. The end of this new section is clearly marked, with Jesus departing from his divine mission in the region of Galilee (see Lk 4:14-15) in order to begin the meandering journey to Jerusalem (see Lk 9:51,53).

Luke 9 is for the evangelist a transitional chapter (O'Fearghail, 1991: 47; Green, 1997: 352), or maybe better the pivot or turning point of Luke's Gospel (Talbert, 1984: 102; Ravens, 1990: 119). In it we see the Galilean phase of Jesus' ministry draw to a close. We also see the inauguration of his Jerusalem ministry at his Transfiguration, where the heavenly voice speaks again (Lk 9:35) as it had at his baptism (Lk 3:22). The journey to Jerusalem is finally launched at Lk 9:51 (C.A. Evans, 1990: 140). Not only is Luke 9 rich in incident, it is also rich in the range of titles given to Jesus. The complexity of the Christology in Luke 9 stems not only from the variety of explicit titles but also from Luke's direct mention of, or allusions to, Old Testament prophets who are used as antetypes for the prophetic role of Jesus. Moses plays an important part in Luke 9, both explicitly and by allusion, but Luke is much wider ranging in his use of the Old Testament in his list of possible candidates as prophetic antetypes for the role of Jesus (Ravens, 1990: 119,120).

One of the most notable features of Luke 9 is the so-called great omission of Mk 6:45-8:26 (Noel, 1994: 183-242). The omission has the effect of removing any stories that have Gentile associations, thus ensuring that all that happens does so within Israel. It also serves to compress the remaining Markan material so that Luke is able to achieve a much tighter structure that brings the Feeding of the Five Thousand next to Peter's Confession as well as closer to the Transfiguration (Ravens, 1990: 121).

It has long been recognized that Luke's account of Jesus' Transfiguration (Lk 9:28-36) introduces the subsequent journey. But from a literary standpoint the whole of Lk 9:1-50 performs such a function through Luke's carefully carved continuity in audience and scenery (Moessner, 1983: 588).

Luke 9 reveals certain interests of the evangelist that ought to be more fully considered. It is not simply that this is the part of the Third Gospel in which the elaborate so-called Travel Narrative is introduced; but in his own way Luke has here woven into it a subsidiary treatment of Jesus of Nazareth to which one should perhaps more closely attend. It is an identification of him that gradually builds up, with titles and other elements, that makes it a crucial section in the Gospel as a whole, especially since this identification serves in its own way as an important prelude to the Travel Narrative and to the function that this part of the Gospel has (Fitzmyer, 1978: 139).

When we look at the episodes that follow Lk 9:7-9, we find that they either implicitly or explicitly answer Herod's question. This is the purpose of the Lukan presentation at this point in his Gospel. In looking at the episodes, however, it is important that we keep in mind the concatenation of them and the resultant series brought about by the modifications in the order of episodes that we have already mentioned. However, at the outset we admit that not everyone fits into this scheme as perfectly as the others; and yet, enough of them do to make this interpretation of the series plausible.

The episodes which follow that of Herod's perplexity are eight: (1) the Feeding of the Five Thousand (Lk 9:10-17); (2) the Confession of Peter and the First Announcement of the Passion (Lk 9:18-22); (3) Sayings of Jesus about the Conditions of Discipleship (Lk 9:23-27); (4) the Transfiguration (Lk 9:28-36); (5) the Cure of the Possessed Boy (Lk 9:37-43a); (6) the Second Announcement of the Passion (Lk 9:43b-45); (7) the Dispute of the Disciples about Greatness (Lk 9:46-48); (8) the Saying of Jesus about the Strange Exorcist (Lk 9:49-50; Fitzmyer, 1978: 143-144, who adds a ninth episode, Lk 9:51-56).

When one considers the distinctive form of the Herod episode and reflects on the episodes that Luke has retained from the Markan source (with modifications) and has strung together between that question of Herod and the Travel Narrative, it seems clear that they are mainly intended to answer Herod's question and to serve as a christological climax of what has preceded as well as a prelude of the Travel Narrative itself. The answers in these episodes are not all presented in equal fashion; in some instances, it is a matter of titles being used of Jesus that may already have been present in the pre-Lukan tradition; in others, there are titles only found in Luke; and in still others, the answer to the question is implicit in the narrative and derived from the Lukan retention and re-use of the narrative-forms (Fitzmyer, 1978: 144).

A survey of the episodes of Luke 9 between that of Herod's perplexity and the beginning of the Travel Narrative (Lk 9:51) produces in a broad outline the picture of Jesus that Luke seeks to present at this point in his Gospel. It aims at an identification of him in terms of answers given to the question dramatically posed by Herod (Lk 9:9): "Who is this about whom I hear such things?" Luke's answer, achieved by various modifications of the Markan source, has produced what has been called "a series of christological statements which Luke harmonizes one with the other by altering his sources and introducing variations of Markan motifs" (Conzelmann, 1960: 56). Thus chapter 9 is crucial in the Lukan Gospel, as a sort of climax of all that has preceded, but also transitional to the Travel Narrative and all that it means in the Lukan writings. This series of christological statements about Jesus made through the literary device of a question and various implicit or explicit answers to it, precedes the Travel Narrative proper that also begins in Luke 9 (Fitzmyer, 1978: 149,150).

a. Herod Thinks Jesus Is John, Risen (Lk 9:7-9)

At Lk 7:18-35, John the Baptist is still alive. At Lk 9:7, the audience learns that John is dead. At Lk 9:9, the audience learns, from Herod's own words, that Herod has executed him. Herod was first introduced in neutral terms (Lk 1:5; 3:1). Then Herod turned his attention to John, to John's peril (Lk 3:19-20). Now the audience learns that Jesus has caught Herod's attention (Lk 9:7), that Herod has beheaded John (Lk 9:9), and that Herod is attempting to see Jesus (Lk 9:9). Audience sympathy moves toward the dead John and against Herod. But the vignette's overriding effect is what this scene portends for Jesus (Roth 1997: 177-178).

The significant aspect of Lk 9:7-9 is not its mere retention despite the omission of the following Markan story, Herod's imprisonment and beheading of John, but rather the peculiarly Lukan reformulation of the episode (Schramm, 1971: 128). This indicates that Luke's composition here is noteworthy. Whereas Mark had simply recorded Herod's impression of Jesus as one of several reactions to him—in fact, it sounds there like a guilty conscience merely repeating a popular reaction—Luke dramatizes the Herodian involvement (Fitzmyer, 1978: 141). The story of the perplexity of Herod raises the christological question to which the rest of the chapter provides a wide variety of answers. But the popular opinions also mention Old Testament figures which Luke uses in presenting his view of Jesus' prophetic role (Ravens, 1990: 121).

The issue here is again status (honor, prominence) rather than the modern notion of identity. When Herod inquires where Jesus is to be placed in the hierarchy of powers, he is assessing the potential threat to himself (Malina-Rohrbaugh, 1992: 338).

Verses 7-8:   (7) Now Herod the ruler heard about all that had
                     taken place,
                 and he was perplexed,
                 because it was said by some
                 that John had been raised from the dead,
             (8) by some that Elijah had appeared,
                 and by others that one of the ancient prophets
                 had arisen.

Luke corrects Mark's "King Herod" to "Herod the ruler (tetrarch)": this Herod (Antipas) never had rights to the royal title (Nolland, 1989: 431). It was Herod Antipas' ambition to be recognized as king that led to his exile in A.D. 39 (C.A. Evans, 1990: 142). Only Luke among the Synoptics has introduced the mention of Herod's perplexity. In other instances of *diaporein*, "being perplexed" (Acts 2:12; 5:24; 10:17), it expresses reaction to the miraculous or supernatural, but Luke omits the reference in Mk 6:14 to Jesus' "powers," and makes Herod's perplexity a reaction to popular opinion (C.F. Evans, 1990: 397). It has been suggested that the similarity between Jesus' message and John's call to repent is what produced the association with a resurrected John. Herod may have meant "John is Jesus" in a loose sense of "this is like John all over again" (Creed, 1957: 127) or "Jesus has the spirit of John" (Schweizer, 1984: 153; Bock, 1994: 822).

Herod's perplexity or anxiety is ominous: Anxious rulers always bode ill for those in their power (Ringe, 1995: 131). In fact, Herod appears in the narrative almost as a bad omen (Moxnes, 1988: 59). An astute politician would know that such stories as told by the people were not merely religious talk of negligible importance. Among the people already restless under foreign rule and heavy taxes, stories that joined Jesus to ancient prophecies about God's future for Israel could become socially and politically inflammatory (Craddock: 1990: 123). Even the rumor that a prophet or a righteous martyr had been raised from the dead could be dangerous when people believed that God had intervened against a despot (Tiede, 1988: 179). Herod's question is a reformulation of the Markan bland statement, "some were saying..." But the Lukan reformulation, highlighting Herod's perplexity, foreshadows the question that Herod is made to ask at the end of the episode (Lk 9:9c). It is difficult to see Herod's intrusion into the present scene as anything but menacing, portending the possibility that the apostles will share fully not only in Jesus' ministry but also in his fate. That his chief quality in this report is his "perplexity" only intensifies his presentation as one who opposes God and those agents who serve the divine purpose, for he is thus aligned with those who hear but do not perceive the word of God (see Lk 8:4-21; Crump, 1992: 29; Green, 1997: 361).

For some reason Luke omits here all reference of Jesus' miraculous power (*dunameis*), which in the Markan account eventually specifies in detail what Herod had been hearing, and the omission of this detail heightens the vagueness of the initial "all that had taken place." In dependence upon Mark, Luke introduces the popular reaction that Jesus might be Elijah, "that Elijah had appeared," and rephrases the saying "that one of the ancient prophets had arisen." He thus achieves an elegant threefold parallel subject-clause, introduced by "that" which functions as the subject of the passive infinitive "it was said" (Fitzmyer, 1978: 142).

Verse 9:   Herod said, "John I beheaded;
                but who is this about whom I hear such things?"
                And he tried to see him.

"John I beheaded" serves for the whole of the account of the Baptist's fate in Mk 6:17-29, and also dismisses the popular view that Jesus is John redivivus as out of the question (C.F. Evans, 1990: 398-399).

After the borrowed and modified Markan phrase about the beheading of John, we come to the significant Lukan reformulation of the episode. Luke puts on the lips of Herod the dramatic question, "Who is this about whom I hear such things?" The question is distinctly Lukan, being found neither in the Markan nor the Matthean parallels. It sums up Herod's perplexity in verse 7. But it also serves to pinpoint the function of the following episodes in Luke 9. Herod is made to ask the crucial question, and the answer to it is provided in many ways in the episodes to follow; the question and the answers act as a prelude to the Travel Narrative itself and to its function in the Lukan Gospel. Thus the transposition of the story of the Baptist's imprisonment (see Lk 3:19-20) has produced, along with various Lukan modifications, a form of the Herodian episode that has its own peculiar function in the Third Gospel. Finally, verse 9d, "and he tried to see him," is a Lukan foreshadowing of Lk 13:31 and 23:8 (Fitzmyer, 1978: 142-143). Before turning to the answers that Luke 9 provides to Herod's question, we may note that the question itself has been foreshadowed earlier in the Gospel. It is similar to that posed by the disciples in Lk 8:25, after Jesus rebuked the wind and the waves, "Who then is this, that he commands even the wind and the water, and they obey him?" There Luke's formula for the question in the main clause was derived directly from Mark; here in the Herod episode its phrasing is slightly different and is, indeed, closer to other Lukan questions (Lk 5:21; 7:49; Fitzmyer, 1978: 143).

b. The Feeding of the Five Thousand *(Lk 9:10-17)*

In Luke's story of meals with Jesus, this is the first of five described as hospitality meals (Koenig, 1985: 85-123). Part of the purpose of the breaking of the bread is to answer the question of Jesus' identity. But unlike the various opinions circulating, it *shows* who Jesus is instead of merely *saying* who he is or associating him with a biblical figure (LaVerdiere, 1994: 59,62). The Feeding of the Five Thousand, which is the only miracle story found in all four Gospels, is set firmly within the prophetic tradition of miracles (Ravens, 1990: 122). The traditional story may also have been an implicit answer to the questions of Ps 78:19-20, "Can God spread a table in the wilderness? ...can he also give bread, or provide meat for his people?" Of course this psalm was itself a commentary on the stories in Exodus 16 of God feeding the whole people of Israel in the wilderness. Was Jesus fulfilling the Exodus? (Lk 9:31; Tiede, 1988: 180).

Whereas Mark and Matthew have two multiplications (Mk 6:30-44; 8:1-10; Mt 14:13-21; 15:32-39; C.A. Evans, 1990: 144-145), Luke reports only one. Derived from the Markan source (Mk 6:30-44), the Feeding of the Five Thousand is retained by Luke, but used very creatively (Fitzmyer, 1981: 762-763; Schenke, 1983: 25-29), as an implicit miraculous answer to Herod's question. As a sequel to the Herod episode, this story is an answer to the tetrarch's question: "Who is this about whom I hear such things?" (Tiede, 1988: 181). In fact, because of Lukan omissions of Markan material, the pericope occurs in between the question, "who is this?" (Lk 9:7-9) and the Confession of Peter, "The Messiah of God!" (Lk 9:18-22). Therefore, it serves a christological function (Stein, 1992: 274), and is intended by Luke to make a special contribution to the disciples' insight into the identity of Jesus (Nolland, 1989: 445). Obviously, the multiplication helps to prepare and illustrate the Confession of Peter, just like the Transfiguration (Lk 9:28-36) afterwards underlines and confirms it (Schürmann, 1969: 510; Wanke, 1973: 46).

The retention of traditional pre-Lukan material here does not include a specific title; but Jesus' preaching of "the kingdom of God" (Lk 9:11) and the miracle story, telling of an act of Jesus described in formulas with eucharistic overtones of a later vintage and with symbolic nuances (e.g., "he looked up to heaven, blessed, broke, gave" [eucharistic formulation]; "twelve baskets of fragments" [symbolic nuance]), clearly identifies Jesus as a person in whom God's message, activity, and creative presence are revealed (Wilkens, 1976: 194). The Lukan explanation of the episode is not formulated here; in fact, it is striking that the first episode after Herod's question should be one related to the *dunameis*, "powerful deeds," of Jesus, whereas Luke has omitted precisely all reference to them in the Herod episode itself. But the mentality that is behind the retention of this episode and its concatenation with the others is manifested in an explanation of Jesus' identity that Luke has penned elsewhere. In Peter's speech in Acts there is a Lukan interpretation of Jesus' miracles: "Jesus of Nazareth, a man attested to you by God with deeds of power, wonders, and signs that God did through him among you" (Acts 2:22). Such an explanation underlies the use of the miracle story of the Feeding of the Five Thousand as an implicit answer to Herod's question (Fitzmyer, 1978: 144-145).

That the story has been influenced by liturgical practice related to the Last Supper can hardly be demonstrated, since the words for the ritual acts—"taking, blessed, broke, gave"—are customary words for the host at any Jewish meal; but it is unlikely that a Christian would have thought of the former without the latter (C.F. Evans, 1990: 401).

Verse 10:   On their return the apostles told Jesus all they had
             done.
             He took them with him
             and withdrew privately to a city called Bethsaida.

Verse 10 takes up where Lk 9:1-6 left off; it wraps up
the mission report on the Twelve. Luke is particularly partial to the verb "return" which he uses in place of Mark's
"to gather around." The phrase "the apostles" is taken over
by Luke from Mk 6:39 and suits the Lukan designation of
"the Twelve," who were sent out (Lk 9:1-6), because of Luke's
earlier understanding of them in Lk 6:13. "The Twelve"
reappear in Lk 9:12, where Luke has changed the Markan
"disciples" to this expression. Luke mentions no details other
than to speak of "all they had done."

Then Luke sets up the circumstances of the miracle.
After such an experience it is natural to seek some rest
(Bock, 1994: 828). The phrase "privately" expresses Jesus'
intention to get away from the crowd, not to avoid an "encounter" with Herod (*pace* Ellis, 1966: 138). Luke alone
mentions a city/town as the site of the miracle (Fitzmyer,
1981: 764, 765). Luke has obviously derived the name
Bethsaida from Mk 6:46, the first verse of the first Markan
episode that Luke drops in his great omission (Creed, 1957:
128). This miracle in the neighborhood of Bethsaida will
be alluded to in Lk 10:13-14 (Stein, 1992: 272).

Verse 11:   When the crowds found out about it,
             they followed him;
             and he welcomed them,
             and spoke to them about the kingdom of God,
             and healed those who needed to be cured.

Whatever the purpose of Jesus' and the apostles' with-
drawal, a gathering crowd cuts short the interlude. Presumably, the presence of the crowds must be regarded as unexpected and, therefore, intrusive (Crump, 1992: 26-27). That
the crowd interrupts its movement is reflected in the brev-

ity of the account of the apostles' report. Luke also impresses us with the interruptive nature of the crowd's presence by immediately resuming the story of Jesus' privacy with the Twelve at verse 18. One could read the account from verse 10 to verse 18, omitting verses 11-17, and the continuity would be smooth. What are the Twelve to learn from the interruption? That those who come with pressing needs do not interrupt; that ministry continues, and often is as effective in the break as in the plan. The feeding of the crowds takes place during a planned retreat which becomes a full ministry of preaching and healing (Craddock, 1990: 125).

Despite his desire to be in private with the apostles, Jesus welcomed the crowds. The verb "to welcome" or "to receive" is a favorite with Luke (fifteen times in Luke-Acts). For some reason Luke omits mention of the compassion of Jesus and does not liken the crowd to sheep without a shepherd (see Mk 6:34); he also loses a series of possible allusions in the continuing Markan text to Psalm 23, "The Lord is my Shepherd..." (Nolland, 1989: 440-441). The image of the shepherd in the parallels (Mk 6:34; Mt 14:14) is here replaced by that of the Savior who "welcomed" all who came to him (Liefeld, 1995: 127). Jesus continued to speak, or kept speaking (imperfect tense) about the kingdom. Mk 6:34 merely ends with "and he began to teach them many things." Luke clearly wants to relate the coming miracle to Jesus' kingdom-preaching. "And healed those who needed to be cured" is another Lukan redactional addition (Fitzmyer, 1981: 766).

Verse 12:   The day was drawing to a close,
              and the twelve came to him and said,
              "Send the crowd away, so that they may go
              into the surrounding villages and countryside,
              to lodge and get provisions;
              for we are here in a deserted place."

In Lk 9:12b the "disciples" are replaced by the "Twelve." As a college, the Twelve receive the commission to take care of the table service (see Acts 6:2). This service of the Twelve will be once more underlined in Lk 9:17 where the term "twelve" is repeated—in fact, in Greek it is found in the emphatic final position: "of fragments baskets twelve"—so that Luke begins and ends his account with the same word. Thereby Luke refers to the future of the Church in which the disciples will not only celebrate the Eucharist but will also feed the poor (Schürmann, 1969: 514; Wanke, 1973: 48). In Lk 12:41 Peter responds to the preceding Parable of the Waiting Servants (Lk 12:35-40) by asking, "Lord, are you telling this parable for us or for everyone?" Jesus responds with further comment, relating the parable to a steward who has been placed in charge of household servants while the master is away (Lk 12:42-46). That is, the parable is applied to leaders who are given responsibility for others. This responsibility is pictured in terms of feeding the servants; the steward is to give to them at the proper time "the allowance of food (*sitometrion*)" and will be judged by whether he has done this faithfully (Tannehill, 1986: 217).

The mention of "a deserted place," which Luke takes over from Mk 6:35, does not seem to agree very well with the reference to "Bethsaida" in verse 10. But "deserted place" need not imply a vast desert region like Sinai; here it may refer to an uninhabited area in the vicinity of Bethsaida (Stein, 1992: 273). The suggestion made by the Twelve creates a problem: Where would five thousand people find food and lodging in villages? In reality, it is a literary suggestion, designed to advance the story (Fitzmyer, 1981: 766).

Verse 13:   But he said to them:
"You give them something to eat."
They said, "We have no more than five loaves and two fish—
unless we are to go and buy food for all these people."

The Greek second person plural pronoun *humeis* placed emphatically at the end of the sentence adds a special note of stress to the command given to the disciples: "You *your-selves* give them something to eat." This command appears to have been literally understood by the early Church as something the disciples not only *had* to do—impossible as it might seem—but something they *could* do as well. Jesus' multiplication of loaves for the hungry and the poor was considered a *repeatable* phenomenon in the early Church as the Christian community listened to the command of Jesus and began to share their food with the hungry (Wanke, 1973: 50). Response to this command of Jesus was thus placed on the level of a direct response to the word of God rather than as a corollary of social implication of the gospel. Luke is especially concerned to show that whenever the command of Jesus is obeyed—"You yourselves give them to eat"— the presence and the power of the risen Lord is experienced in a special way. Luke shows this by drawing a dramatic parallel between the multiplication of the loaves and the meeting of the risen Christ by the two disciples on the road to Emmaus (Lk 24:13-35; Wanke, 1973: 34-40,45; Tannehill, 1986: 219). In both cases the time is the same: "the day was drawing to a close" (Lk 9:12) and "it is almost evening, and the day is now nearly over" (Lk 24:29). Luke's account adds the detail that the Twelve wanted to send the crowd to a village not only to find food but also lodging (Lk 9:12; compare Mk 6:36; Mt 14:15). The disciples on the way to Emmaus reach the town to which they are going (where they will presumably find food and lodging). Both stories also have the same sequence: "he took bread, blessed it, broke it, and gave it to them" (Lk 9:16; 24:30). Then fol-lows the recognition of the power and the presence of the Lord: "Then their eyes were opened, and they recognized him; and he vanished from their sight" (Lk 24:31). It par-allels the climactic ending of the multiplication of the loaves, where the leftover loaves, on the model of the miracle of

Elisha, are according to the word of the Lord (2 Kgs 4:43; Ravens, 1990: 122). Luke, in the Acts of the Apostles, gives special attention to Jesus' commands and their fulfillment. When it comes to the distribution of food to the needy and hungry in the early Church, Luke describes it in a manner that makes it appear like an extension of the miracle of the loaves. The social message of the Gospel has often been relegated to an addendum or by-product. However, when we see the centrality and importance of Jesus' command to feed the hungry, it can be more easily understood that the *Gospel itself is a social message* directly connected to the command and the example of Jesus himself (Grassi, 1978: 1704,1706,1709). The fact that in Lk 9:13b the disciples refer to their own provisions ("We have...") and not to those of the crowd is another indication that the post-Easter meal praxis of the early Church influenced the formulation of the tradition of the multiplication (van Iersel, 1964-1965: 180ff.; Wanke, 1973: 48).

Most scholars rightly reject any symbolic force given to the numbers five and two (Bovon, 1991: 460; Bock, 1994: 831). Jewish exegesis sometimes interprets the quails from the sea (Num 11:31) as flying fish and may thus explain the presence here of two fish (Bovon, 1993: 28; van Cangh, 1975: 105-109). But a connection with this or other traditions is rather tenuous (Nolland, 1989: 442).

Verses 14-15: (14) For there were about five thousand men.
And he said to his disciples,
"Make them sit down in groups of about fifty each."
(15) They did so and made them all sit down.

The narrator breaks into the narrative to explain the dismay of the disciples at Jesus' command to feed the multitude that has been with Jesus all day. As the disciples bemoan the fact that they have no more than a few loaves and fish and probably do not have the money or the ability

to buy more food, the narrator interrupts the story to in-
form the reader that "there were about five thousand men"
present. Without entering into the discussion of the actual
number of people present—considering the terminology of
the time and whether or not the women and children were
to be counted in that number—the fact remains that the
narrator intended the reader to understand that far too many
people were present for the limited amount of food available. Once again the "narrative aside" places the miraculous behavior of Jesus in its proper perspective. Only a miracle
could have fed this many people, and Luke's narrator is careful
to tell the story in such a way that there can be no doubt
that a miracle has taken place. The numbers involved admit no other explanation (Sheeley, 1992: 101-102). "About"
is common in Luke with numbers (C.F. Evans, 1990: 402).

In Lk 9:14b the "disciples" are again introduced (different in Mk 6:39) and in Lk 9:16 (same in Mk 6:41) he
maintains the word. Luke knows that the hands of the Twelve
will not suffice to execute Jesus' command and that more
disciples will be needed (Schürmann, 1969: 518; Wanke,
1973: 48; Ringe, 1995: 133).

Whereas in Mark's "by hundreds and by fifties" (Mk
6:40) some see a allusion to Ex 18:25, in Luke, "in compa-
nies of about fifty" refers possibly to the group of people
who could be accommodated in the house churches (Acts
2:46; Wanke, 1973: 49). Acts 4:4 repeats the numeral five
thousand: "But many of them who heard the word believed,
and they numbered about five thousand" (Danker, 1988:
192).

Verse 15 briefly states that the disciples follow through
on Jesus' instruction. With the crowd clustered in groups,
Jesus turns to meet the crowd's need (Bock, 1994: 832).
The question of how the food was made available has been
greatly debated. We are not told exactly how the food grew
to feed so many, but it is clear that Jesus was miraculously
responsible for it (Van der Loos, 1965: 627-631; Bock, 1994:
833-834; 1996: 257).

Verse 16:   And taking the five loaves and the two fish,
              he looked up to heaven,
              and blessed and broke them,
              and gave them to the disciples to set before the
              crowd.

As is the case in the Gospels of Mark and Matthew, the disciples are associated with nourishing the multitudes. There is an important difference in detail, however. While in both Mark and Matthew they are called "the disciples" (Mk 6:35; Mt 14:15), in Luke they are called "the Twelve" (Lk 9:12). The mediating role of the apostles attracts considerably more attention in Luke than in Mark (Nolland, 1989: 444). The Twelve ask Jesus to send the people away, but he commands them: "You give them something to eat" (Lk 9:13). However, it is Jesus who takes from their poverty (five loaves and two fish), looks up to heaven, blesses, breaks, "and gave them to the disciples to set them before the crowd" (Moloney, 1991: 26; Grassi, 1978: 1707).

It has been pointed out that the correspondences between Mark and Luke are concentrated in Mk 6:41 and Lk 9:16. The differences are minimal. Here is the heart of the matter (Nolland, 1989: 443). We should already reckon with a eucharistic interpretation in the Markan version. Luke did not introduce the eucharistic allusions in Mk 6:32-44, but has only developed them (van Iersel, 1964-1965: 170-171; Wanke, 1973: 51-52).

Verse 17:   And all ate and were filled.
              What was left over was gathered up,
              twelve baskets of broken pieces.

In accordance with Lk 6:21, where the same phrase, "were filled," is used, "all" are satisfied. Luke's Greco-Roman audience, well acquainted with distributions by generous patrons, would note this emphasis on the inclusiveness of the Great Benefactor's bounty (Danker, 1988: 192). Luke moves the "all" to a more emphatic position that puts stress on all being satisfied (Nolland, 1989: 444). Verse 17 contains a clear parallel to the miracle of the barley loaves by Elisha in 2 Kgs 4:42-44. "So he repeated, 'Give it to the people and let them eat, for thus says the Lord, They shall eat and have some left.' He set it before them, they ate, and had some left, according to the word of the Lord" (2 Kgs 4:43b-44; Grassi, 1978: 1705).

After the feeding, with its obvious eucharistic overtones, twelve baskets remain. The twelve baskets have obviously a symbolic reference to the Twelve in verse 12; they each bring back a basketful and now have enough to feed still others (Fitzmyer, 1981: 769; Seethaler, 1990: 111). Luke's vision of founding apostles is very important in his re-telling of the traditional story of the feeding of the multitudes. The association of the Twelve in the story of Jesus "then," makes sense of a Church looking back to trace its own roots in the life of Jesus to make sense of its "now" (van Cangh, 1975: 148-155; Moloney, 1993: 26-27). In this connection it has been pointed out that in the multiplication already occur all motifs which, in the Acts of the Apostles, Luke presents as characteristic for the life of the early Church: "They devoted themselves to the apostles' teaching and fellowship, to the breaking of the bread and the prayers" (Acts 2:42; Seethaler, 1990: 111).

The multiplication of the loaves in the present Lukan context prepares for the admission that Peter is to make about Jesus. The disciples have been taken by him away from the crowd; but the crowd follows. When the feeding is over no reaction of the crowd is recorded. Whereas what the disciples had, five loaves of bread and two fish, was inadequate to feed the crowd, what Jesus had feeds them abundantly, and with leftovers. On the heels of this largesse comes a reaction from the spokesman of the disciples (Fitzmyer, 1981: 764).

c. The Confession of Peter/First Prediction of the Passion (Lk 9:18-22)

Luke's presentation of the inseparability of Christology and discipleship reaches its acme in the tightly woven sequence of the Confession of Peter followed by the First Prediction of the Passion (Lk 9:22) and Instructions on Discipleship (Lk 9:23-27; Green, 1997: 366). The Confession of Peter provides an explicit answer to Herod's question, but in a formulation that is Lukan. Between the preceding episode of the Feeding of the Five Thousand and the Confession of Peter intervenes what is usually referred to as the "great omission," the material of Mk 6:45-8:26 not used here. The Lukan account has nothing of the additional Matthean material (Mt 16:16b-19; Hendrickx, 1992: 61-69) or of the rebuke of Peter found in the earlier Markan source (Mk 8:32-33; Fitzmyer, 1978: 145).

The reasons for the omission of the Markan material are not nearly as important as the resultant shape of this part of the Lukan Gospel. It gives to chapter 9, along with the insertion of the Travel Narrative at Lk 9:51, a crucial form. Immediately, it brings the Confession of Peter into close proximity, not only with the Feeding of the Five Thousand, but also with the question posed by Herod in Lk 9:9 (Fitzmyer, 1981: 771).

This episode presents the reader with Jesus' perspective, the crowd's, then Peter's, then Jesus' again. At the beginning of the episode, Jesus is praying. This mention of Jesus' posture is more than the narrator's statement of fact. Coupled with other references to Jesus engaged in prayer, this statement communicates Jesus' high assessment of the value of prayer.

When his disciples interrupt him, Jesus asks, "Who do the crowds say that I am?" To this the disciples respond with the perspective of the crowds (seen, of course, through the eyes of the disciples), namely, the view that Jesus is

John the Baptist, Elijah, or some other prophet. Between the perspective of Jesus and the perspective of the crowd there is a disjunction, a gap. We recognize the gap's existence when we begin to consider basic exegetical questions: Is there a connection between Jesus' practice of prayer and the crowd's view of who Jesus is? If so, what is the connection? How is it made? The text suggests these questions and provides data on Jesus and the crowds that can be used to formulate answers to these questions. But the text is sufficiently silent so as to require readers to draw their own conclusions. We, the readers, make the connection between Jesus' practice of prayer and the crowd's views of who Jesus is by pulling together what we know of the narrative from the perspective of Jesus, the crowds, the narrator, and others as we have encountered them up to this point in the narrative (Roth, 1997: 63).

How does one explain the development in the disciples' understanding from Lk 8:25 to 9:20? Was their witnessing and participation in the feeding miracle sufficient to generate the enlightenment Peter manifests on behalf of Jesus' followers? This is often claimed. In fact, however, Luke records no response on the part of the disciples to the feeding miracle, and the current scene, in which Jesus is acclaimed by Peter as the Messiah, is not woven into the feeding account by any temporal, geographical, or explicitly causal connectives. Hence, even if causality is implicit in the narrative sequence, Luke provides no particular reason to think that the feeding miracle is more significant as an immediate cause of the enlightenment of the disciples than are the other miraculous events recounted in Lk 8:22-56. Luke simply does not ground Peter's enlightened perspective in the observation of Jesus' powerful deeds (Strauss, 1995: 252; Brawley, 1990: 27). Indeed, as repeated reference to the popular views of the crowds proves (Lk 9:7-9,18-19), even though miraculous acts may put forward the necessary evidence, these are insufficient in and of themselves to lead to a correct interpretation of Jesus' status. What is needed is a lens through which to grapple with the meaning of these phenomena, and this is what Luke provides in his staging of this account. He associates Peter's Confession with Jesus' praying, as if to declare that access to Jesus' identity is supernaturally mediated (Kingsbury, 1991: 50; Crump, 1992: 33-34; Green, 1997: 367-368).

Verse 18:   Once when Jesus was praying alone,
with only the disciples near him,
he asked them,
"Who do the crowds say that I am?"

The quality of Luke's narration shifts in a subtle way with the introduction of this pericope. From Lk 8:22 to 9:17 he has used temporal and geographical markers to indicate the association of each pericope with the next. Now, however, his presentation takes on a more episodic look, with the dialogue between Jesus and his followers only loosely connected to the preceding account of the feeding miracle. The report of Peter's Confession is therefore more closely related to the material that follows—the Transfiguration scene, the exorcism account, the passion prediction, and the argument concerning the relative greatness of the disciples (Lk 9:28-50)—than to the material that precedes it. As a consequence, this scene is determined above all by the picture of Jesus' praying apart from the crowds, with only the disciples present. Previously, when Jesus retreated for prayer, he did so alone (Lk 5:16; 6:12); with the heightened presence of his disciples characteristic of Luke 9, they now withdraw with him (see Lk 9:10; Green, 1997: 368 and note 44).

Lk 9:18a is a redactional introduction as can be seen from its formulation and the reference to Jesus' prayer in typically Lukan terms (Claudel, 1988: 182-186). Luke's omission of the geographical locality of the scene ("the villages/the district of Caesarea Philippi," Mk 8:27; Mt 16:13)

has often been explained in terms of his geographical perspective (Conzelmann, 1960: 55, etc.). This may still be a
valid reason, but it is just as likely that the location of Peter's
Confession in the present lineup of Luke 9 is also a reason
for the omission. There is no need for a geographical setting because the episode serves the purpose of answering a
larger literary question, that of Herod. One cannot help but
note the typically Lukan setting of Jesus at prayer "alone"
(Lk 9:18; see Lk 3:21; 5:16; 6:12; 9:28; 22:41; Flender, 1967:
53).

Luke does not want to begin an entirely new series of
pericopes with Lk 9:18, but he intends to present the preceding narrative complex at least as a background for the
prayer notice. A series of literary indications show that Lk
9:1-17 is a coherent unit that does not only precede the
prayer notice of Lk 9:18, but also stands in connection with
it (Feldkämper, 1978: 109-112). The mention of Jesus at
prayer enhances the occasion not only for Peter's Confession, but much more importantly for the declaration that
he himself will make in verse 22; for his prayer is usually
introduced when there is some significant episode to be
recounted (Fitzmyer, 1981: 773). The "christological question" (Lk 9:18b, 20a) is very closely related to the prayer
notice. Jesus poses the question in the context of prayer,
right after he prayed. Thereby, and by the fact that he himself
poses it, the "who-question" is here still more important
than in the other occurrences (Lk 5:21; 7:49; 8:25; 9:9).
Jesus is here both the one questioned and the questioner.
The question concerns the mystery of his person that comes
to light, or is at least suggested, by his actions. As before
(Lk 5:21; 7:49; 8:25) Jesus' or his apostles' activity gave
rise to this question, so also here Jesus' question must be
seen in the context of his immediately preceding activity,
that is, the Feeding of the Five Thousand. Indeed, Luke
has no intervening event between the feeding miracle and
the Confession of Peter (Danker, 1988: 193; Bock, 1994:

852). Luke refers explicitly to this when he lets Jesus ask the disciples what is the view of the *ochloi*, "people" (in Mark/Matthew: *anthrōpoi*), that is, of those who had followed him (Lk 9:11a) and to whom he had shown his authority in word and deed (Lk 9:11b; Feldkämper, 1978: 117-118). It seems clear that Luke intentionally places the feeding miracle between Herod's question about Jesus (Lk 9:7-9) and Peter's Confession (Lk 9:18-20) to partly answer Herod's question (Lk 9:9) and to serve as christological climax of the succeeding pericope (Fitzmyer, 1981: 763; Tiede, 1988: 181).

True, the episode does contain a pre-Lukan question, which is also answered: "Who do the crowds say that I am?" Though it is Lukan in its use of *hoi ochloi*, "the crowds," instead of the *hoi anthrōpoi* of Mk 8:27, "Who do people say I am?" (Flender, 1967: 47), the question is clearly derived from Mark. And yet, it is really secondary in the Lukan use of the episode. It introduces the popular answers, "John the Baptist," "Elijah," and "one of the ancient prophets has arisen" (Fitzmyer, 1978: 145).

Verse 19:   They answered,
             "John the Baptist; but others, Elijah;
             and still others, that one of the ancient prophets has
             arisen."

According to the "rule of three," the emphasis is on the third of the three opinions expressed in this verse. Luke suggests this by the fact that, after the mere mention of John the Baptist and Elijah, he expresses the last statement in a complete sentence: "one of the ancient prophets has arisen." Unlike Mark and Matthew, he does not call Jesus "one of the prophets" but one of the classical prophets. This lifts Jesus out of the company of contemporary prophets and places him alongside the classical prophets (Friedrich, 1968: 842). Since according to Jewish beliefs, the ancient prophets did not all die, but were taken up into heaven, the term *anestē*, "has risen," should not necessarily be understood as rising from the dead. In intransitive (Acts 5:36f.) as also in transitive sense (Acts 3:22,26; 7:37), Luke uses the verb *anistanai* also often of the public appearance of prophetic figures. The people's opinion that Jesus is a prophet is completely in line with the rest of Lukan Christology (Lk 3:22; 4:18f.; 7:16; 24:19). Whereas Luke simply ascribes the opinion that Jesus is John the Baptist or Elijah to the tradition, he appropriates the idea of Jesus as prophet, so much so that in Acts he speaks twice of Jesus as a prophet like Moses (Acts 3:22,26; 7:37; Feldkämper, 1978: 118-119).

Though these popular answers repeat the substance of the Markan formulas, the third one echoes precisely a phrase in the Herod episode "one of the ancient prophets has arisen." The connection between this Lukan form of Peter's Confession and the earlier Herod episode is thus established; the echo of the phrase is literal. It relates the questions posed here to that of Herod the ruler (Fitzmyer, 1978: 145).

Verse 20:	He said to them,
	"But who do you say that I am?"
	Peter answered, "The Messiah of God."

Jesus' second question, introduced with the adversative "but," indicates Jesus' dissatisfaction with popular hypotheses regarding his status that have been circulating. He calls upon all of his disciples ("you" is plural) to tender an alternative evaluation. As a result, for the first time within the narrative of Jesus' public ministry, a human being recognizes Jesus as God's Messiah (Green, 1997: 369).

The real answer to Herod's question is given through another pre-Lukan question asked of Peter, "But who do you say that I am?" In this case Luke borrows the phraseology word for word from Mark. But the answer differs slightly: "The Messiah of God." Peter's answer goes far beyond the answers of the "crowds" (Fitzmyer, 1978: 145).

Mark wrote simply: "You are the Messiah" (Mk 8:29). By the addition "of God," Luke achieves a clarification and emphasis on the relationship between the Messiah and God. Jesus and his mission are thought of together with God. Jesus is the Messiah of God insofar as he belongs entirely to God.

The expression "the Messiah of God" occurs only here (but see the similar "the Messiah of God, his chosen one" (Lk 23:35). It is unique to Luke. "Of God" is a genitive of authorship: Jesus is the Messiah sent from God (Bock, 1994: 841); it expresses a special relationship of Jesus as the Messiah to the Father (Fitzmyer, 1981: 774). The statement that God has anointed Jesus occurs in Acts 4:27 and 10:38. An explanation of the title "Messiah of God" based on this verbal expression (*chriein*, "to anoint") is valid since Luke himself takes "his anointed" (Acts 4:26) up again by "one you did anoint" (Acts 4:27; Feldkämper, 1978: 119).

Peter's confession has to be understood as an admission of what at that time he thought Jesus to be. *Christos* would have to be understood in the Jewish sense of an expected anointed agent sent by God in the Davidic, kingly, and political tradition. For Luke *Christos* is a title clearly related to this tradition, as Lk 2:11 has already shown: "in the city of David" is born one who is "Messiah, Savior, and Lord." In other words, Peter, having witnessed Jesus' kingdom-preaching, healing, and miracles, is depicted as acknowledging him as God's anointed agent sent "to restore the kingdom of Israel" (Acts 1:6; Fitzmyer, 1981: 775; Tiede, 1988: 184-185; Bock, 1994: 841-842).

In Luke's understanding, then, the Confession of Peter is, on the one hand, in the form of a title, a summary of Jesus' saving activity to date; and, on the other hand, the anticipation of his passion, his way through death to resurrection, again in the form of a title. Long before Easter, but nevertheless from an Easter perspective, the Lukan Peter gives here a confession of Christ, whose essential components are found in Jesus' God-determined further way, namely, cross and resurrection. The title "Messiah of God" thereby unites Jesus' saving-historical significance as the prophet sent by God and rejected by people (Feldkämper, 1978: 119).

Verses 21-22: (21) He sternly ordered and commanded them not
                    to tell anyone,
               (22) saying, "The Son of Man must undergo great
                    suffering,
                    and be rejected by the elders, chief priests,
                    and scribes,
                    and be killed, and on the third day be raised."

It is strange that Luke retains Jesus' charge to the disciples that they tell no one about Peter's answer—a detail that certainly suits the Markan theme of the messianic secret much better than the concern of Luke in his Gospel to make known the identity of Jesus. In any case, this truncated Lukan form of Peter's Confession seems better understood as an answer to Herod's question than as an episode concentrating on the role of Peter, an emphasis that seems more appropriate for the Markan and Matthean form. In the Lukan Gospel this passage is much less one that enhances Peter's role (Dietrich, 1972: 94-104; Fitzmyer, 1978: 145-146).

In Lk 4:40-41, Jesus had rebuked the demons and refused to allow them to speak "because they knew he was the Messiah." Superficially, Jesus' response here is similar. This correspondence does not mark the disciples as diabolic, however, because Jesus' warning to them is differently motivated than was his earlier directive to the unclean spirits. Nevertheless, the disciples' knowledge is thus designated as inappropriate, perhaps even dangerous, but this is due to the partiality of their information. Luke has coordinated the clauses of verses 21-22 so that verse 22 provides the basis for verse 21. The disciples must maintain silence because *the Son of Man must suffer and be vindicated*. This means, first, that Jesus' requisite suffering and vindication have not yet been integrated into the disciples' messianic conception, and, second, that the time for proclaiming openly the messiahship of Jesus will come following the events Jesus has predicted (Green, 1997: 37).

In Lk 9:22, which is not un-Lukan and can very well have been Luke's own re-working of Mk 8:31 (Neirynck and Friedrichsen, 1989: 390-394) and is not influenced by Mt 16:21 (Friedrichsen, 1996: 398-407), the narrative begins to turn a literary corner. Many of the loose strands that have previously foreshadowed the ultimate fate of Jesus now come together in an explicit prophecy of his violent destiny. The Galilean ministry will soon draw to a close and Jesus will begin the journey to Jerusalem in order ultimately to fulfill his prediction.

The First Announcement of the Passion is closely linked to Peter's Confession (Büchele, 1978: 126-127). Luke omitted the introductory Markan phrase, "and he began to teach them" (Mk 8:31) and thus joined the announcement more closely to the preceding than it was in his source (Fitzmyer, 1981: 777). This pre-Lukan element, retained in modified form in Mark (Schramm, 1971: 30), serves basically the same purpose in Luke that it has in Mark, as a corrective to the acknowledged messiahship of Jesus. The corrective, however, is far more closely linked to Peter's Confession in Luke and provides still a further answer to Herod's question. Put on the lips of Jesus, it says in effect that he may be the Messiah, but he is such as the suffering Son of Man: He will be recognized as Messiah insofar as he is seen as the one predestined for suffering and death as the Son of Man (Fitzmyer, 1978: 146).

Lk 9:22 is the first of a number of passages in which Jesus himself predicts his own coming death. Scholars often speak of the "three passion predictions," referring to those found in the Triple Tradition. However, if the Gospel of Luke is taken by itself, one can no longer speak of only

three such passion references. Rather, the narrator will re-
petitively direct the movement toward Jesus' death through
his sayings about his impending fate. At times the references are veiled; at others much more direct. But together
they serve to bring the persecution of Jesus to its literary
conclusion (Lk 5:35; 9:22; 9:43b-45; 11:29; 12:50; 13:31-
35; 17:25; 18:31-34; 20:9-18; 22:19-22). These passages can
be described as "literary prophecy," where statements made
by characters *within the narrative* are explicitly shown to
find fulfillment. Within the Gospel, Luke uniquely points
out how Jesus' prophecies of his own death are fulfilled (Lk
24:7,44; Johnson, 1991: 16).

Being the first explicit disclosure of Jesus' death, Lk 9:22
takes on a programmatic character. The remaining chapters
of Luke shift the concern through this prediction of Jesus'
death. Not only does this passage direct the course of the
narrative and inform the reader of what can be expected to
take place, it interprets those events in advance (Cunningham,
1997: 80-81).

The confession of Peter that Jesus is "the Messiah of
God" is followed by Jesus' warning to tell no one and his
announcement that "the Son of Man must undergo great
suffering, and be rejected by the elders, chief priests, and
scribes, and be killed, and on the third day be raised." The
phrase "Son of Man" is derived by Luke from Mk 8:31.

The verb *dei* ("must") fits into a larger pattern in Luke's
Gospel, where much is made of the necessity incumbent on
Jesus in the realization of the Father's plan of salvation
(Fitzmyer, 1981: 780). The word *dei* ("must") is a favorite
Lukan expression. Of the 101 occurrences in the New Testament, forty are in Luke's writings. Luke's use of the word
has some degree of variation, and therefore one is warned
against understanding it as a sort of *terminus technicus* that
always refers to divine necessity or fatalistic compulsion
(Cosgrove, 1984: 172-173). However, in a majority of passages the term is, in fact, used by Luke to refer to divine

design. This is supported by two observations. First, *dei* is frequently associated with the fulfillment of the divine will, as it is revealed in Scripture (e.g., Lk 22:37; 24:26,44,46). Second, *dei* is linked to Luke's wider vocabulary that demonstrably refers to divine providence. The best illustration of this is suffering, which not only must (*dei*) happen but is also placed into the divine design through the use of a number of other words. Therefore, while not always referring to the design of God, *dei* often has this connotation. In fact, the entire scope of God's plan of salvation in history invites divine necessity (Cunningham, 1997: 82-83; Stein, 1992: 278).

The word Luke uses (in common with Mk 8:31) for "be rejected" (*apodokimasthēnai*), echoes Ps 118:22: "The stone the builders rejected." In all but one occurrence in the New Testament, the verb appears in quotations of or allusions to Psalm 118 (Mk 8:31//Lk 9:22; Lk 17:25; 1 Pet 2:4,7). The sole exception is Heb 12:17, which describes the rejection of Esau after he forfeited his blessing. This evidence strongly suggests that the verb in Lk 9:22 should be understood as a reference to Ps 118:22. Although Luke has here adopted the wording from Mark, his repetition of *apodokimasthēnai* in the context of the passion prediction of Lk 17:25 suggests a recognition of a further exploitation of this intertextual echo of Psalm 118. In the context of Jesus' (and later the Church's) conflict with the leaders of Israel, this faint echo of Ps 118:22 will be amplified into a triumphant fanfare announcing that the words of the psalm find their fulfillment in Jesus' death and resurrection (Lk 20:17; Acts 4:11; Wagner, 1997: 162).

The Son of Man will be raised, that is, by God, as the theological passive of the verb suggests. He will be raised "on the third day" [Mk 8:31 has "after three days"; Büchele, 1978: 125]. A number of scholars see in this expression an allusion to Hos 6:2, "After two days he will revive us, on the third day he will raise us up" which is possible but not certain (Fitzmyer, 1981: 781; see Lehmann, 1968).

The prediction of Jesus' suffering, death, and resurrection clearly owes its form to the Church that has summarized details of the passion narrative itself (including the list of the religious leaders opposed to Jesus). Whether the prediction records a core formula from Jesus himself is harder to say. If one believes that Jesus knew everything that would befall him and thus could have predicted the exact manner of his death —but note that the Gospels never say that he predicted his *crucifixion*—there is no problem. Such an assumption, however, contradicts the Church's affirmation of Jesus' full humanity, as well as the picture of the human Jesus presented by the writers of the Synoptic Gospels. If one affirms Jesus' humanity, and therefore assumes that Jesus (like all other people) could not have known his fate or the precise cirumstances of his death, it is still possible that he might have been remembered to have predicted his premature death. He would not have needed special foreknowledge to recognize that if he persisted in his proclamation of God's reign and his ministry of liberation for persons pushed to the margins of society, and if he was acclaimed as a leader by many of them, representatives of public order (both political and religious) would soon be ranged against him. To continue on this road could well lead to death for him and even for his followers. Such a simple and general statement, remembered through the lens of the horrifying events of Jesus' final week, could easily be refined into a formal passion prediction like the one in Lk 9:22, the general predictions in Lk 9:44 and 17:25, or even the very detailed one in Lk 18:31-33 (Ringe, 1995: 135).

d. Conditions of Discipleship (Lk 9:23-27)

After the saying about Jesus' own way of the passion, Luke skips the objection of Peter to Jesus' suffering and Jesus' counter-rebuke of Peter (Mk 8:32-33). Luke presents, in close resemblance to Mark and Matthew, five sayings about following and discipleship (Lk 9:23-27), which he has obviously derived from Mk 8:34-9:1, and which address themselves (different from Mark/Matthew) to "all" (Danker, 1988: 194), so not only to the disciples but also to the *ochloi*, "people, crowds," who have followed Jesus since Lk 9:11, and to "all" (Lk 9:15,17) who have participated in his meal and were satisfied. The general homiletic character of the sayings as statements of the nature of Christian discipleship is indicated by the audience provided—in Mark a crowd specially summoned from nowhere, in Luke his favorite "all" (C.F. Evans, 1990: 409).

Except for the last one, all these sayings occur in Luke a second time in their Q-version (Lk 9:23 = 14:27; 9:24f. = 17:33; 9:26 = 12:9), which indicates that they are very important to Luke. Since we are dealing here with sayings that were originally independent from each other, one must pay attention to the logical connection in which they are found at this stage (parallel Mark). Luke has found them in this order, but together with their adoption he has shaped their train of thought even more purposefully.

In Lk 9:23 the demand of self-denial and readiness to carry the cross "daily" is in principle held up to all who decide to follow Jesus' way of salvation. The term "daily" suggests that occasional scintillating displays of courage or interest in notoriety are not under discussion here (Danker, 198: 195). The following verses 24-26 are designed to draw out the meaning of the summons to discipleship in verse 23, and they do so by focusing on the disposition of one's life, symbolized first in socio-economic terms, then in the language of honor and shame (Green, 1997: 374). They underscore this demand in that they develop it further (Lk 9:24), or point out the concrete dangers of the desire for gain (Lk 9:25) and the failure of the courage to witness (Lk 9:26), in the midst of which the decision in everyday life ("daily") has to be sustained. This indicates a life of struggle and witness, rather than a specific moment of truth (Tiede, 1988: 186). The last saying contains the promise of the kingdom to "some," that is, some among the "all" addressed in Lk 9:23; that means—in the present context—more specifically to those who decidedly go the way of Jesus (Feldkämper, 1978: 121). Most likely Luke refers to an understanding of the kingdom that will become apparent after the resurrection, when the disciples will be given a knowledge of the secrets of the kingdom (Lk 8:10) in a new sense (Fitzmyer, 1981: 789-790).

The five sayings intimate that discipleship means a daily share in the fate that eventually will be Jesus'. The way that Jesus must *go* (Lk 9:22) becomes the way that the disciple must *follow*. The conditions of discipleship that the sayings incorporate are expressed, first of all, in terms of "following," a notion that takes on a greater significance in the proximity of the Lukan travel account, that is, his foreordained journey to the city of destiny, Jerusalem. The following is further specified as a carrying of one's cross behind him, as a proper esteem for one's life that cannot be measured by worldly gain, as an attitude toward him that will falter in the face of public confrontation (shame before others because of him), and as an attitude that may expect a new and better understanding of the mysteries of the kingdom (Fitzmyer, 1981: 784). All these ideas are part of the question of who Jesus is (C.A. Evans, 1990: 149).

Verse 23:   Then he said to them all,
               "If any want to become my followers,
               let them deny themselves
               and take up their cross daily and follow me.

Immediately on the heels of the first prophecy of his passion Jesus utters a saying concerning the demands of discipleship that probably alludes to persecution for those who would follow Jesus.

In verse 23, the pattern is ABB'A': follow—self-denial—cross bearing—follow. Clearly self-denial is parallel to taking up the cross. Discipleship is summarized in three commands: deny one's self, take up, follow. The tense sequence (two aorist imperatives followed by a present imperative) shows that fundamental decisions made about the self and about day-by-day bearing of the cross emerge in a continual following of Jesus. In other words, the last act emerges from the others. The disciple's life consists of basic self-denial (Bock, 1994: 852; 1996: 265; Green, 1997: 373).

Now there is another tradition about taking up the cross that makes no reference to self-denial. Instead of reference to self-denial, there is the emphasis on family denial. This is the Q tradition (Lk 14:25-27//Mt 10:34-38), likewise cited in the *Gospel of Thomas*. Since renouncing one's kingroup is parallel to taking up the cross, it would seem from this saying that such renunciation is equally much like self-denial. Further, kin-denial and self-denial would both be equivalent to taking up the cross to follow Jesus (Malina, 1994: 107).

"Denying" one's self does not mean giving up pleasures or comforts (denying something to one's self), or to cultivate a weak, nonassertive personality (Liefeld, 1995: 129), but rather saying of one's self what Peter will say of Jesus, "I do not know him" (Lk 22:57). In any context where honor and prestige are primary values, status depends on a person's competing to be known and recognized. To set aside such goals for the sake of Jesus (and, by implication, for the sake of the program he represents) is to negate the competitive and hierarchical social order of the dominant society. The saying is aimed at those who want to be held—or who hold themselves—in high esteem, not at persons whose value and dignity as human beings is already threatened. Furthermore, the saying does not celebrate self-denial for its own sake, but rather, in the name and for the cause of Jesus. As the teachings and the stories of Luke's Gospel have already made

clear, persons on the margins of society, for whom honor
and dignity as well as material well-being are distant dreams,
find in that same cause an affirmation of life in its fullness
(Ringe, 1995: 138).

Luke modifies verse 23 to underscore the continuing
experience of discipleship for his audience. Just as the Spirit-
filled Jesus—the conqueror of this age—must suffer, so the
would-be followers must share the same experience of self-
denial, daily taking up a cross and following Jesus (York,
1991: 81). "If you wish to be my disciple, you must put
your head on the choppng block" (Nolland, 1993: 484).

Verse 23 is the basic saying, since the three that follow
are all introduced by "for," which is at times omitted in the
translation. Since it is only the joining of Jesus' own
messiahship with the cross on which he was crucified that
makes the metaphor have any sense, the saying as we now
have it must come from the early Christian community. But
this does not mean that it is fabricated out of whole cloth.
Ever since David F. Strauss commentators have compared
this saying with Mt 11:29, "Take my yoke upon you," where
Matthew uses the same verb *arate* ("take up"), it has been
suggested that Jesus more plausibly expressed the following
of himself as a bearing of his yoke.

The saying on taking up one's cross pointed to being
ready to be shamed, to face shame, to be shamed even to
death. The motivation for bearing such shame was allegiance
to Jesus and the gospel, professing the crucified Jesus. This
reference to the cross and the motivation specified have a
wider scope. Shame fits into all the nooks and crannies of
life. Taking up one's cross thus generalizes a more specific
injunction or directive. Yet it surely fills out the meaning
of Jesus' yoke by drawing the yoke's implications in terms
of Jesus' actual fate. In other words, while the yoke better
fits the house of Israel, the cross could be universally amplified by Mediterranean experience, wherever Romans crucified, yet still relate to Jesus' distinctive yoke (Malina, 1994:
108-109).

The reformulation of an original saying of Jesus about carrying his yoke stands the best chance of surviving as an explanation of the enigmatic demand for discipleship in terms of carrying/bearing one's cross (Fitzmyer, 1981: 783-787 passim).

The qualifier "daily" has been taken to mean that Luke does not have martyrdom in mind, and persecution only marginally so, for in what sense could one be martyred "daily"? But rather than softening the reference to persecution, the qualifier may actually strengthen the reference, so that the disciple must be willing each day to undergo persecution or even martyrdom (Schütz, 1969: 18). Luke has previously introduced the theme of perseverance in the midst of persecution (Lk 8:15), and it appears that "daily" is best understood in that light. The call of discipleship to bear one's cross daily should be understood as self-denial, but specifically includes the possibility of persecution and even martyrdom in which the disciple must daily renew his attitude of saying no even to one's very life (Fitzmyer, 1981: 787-788; C.A. Evans, 1990: 149; Cunningham, 1997: 86-88).

The degree to which verse 23 and the further explanations of discipleship in verses 24-26 serve as introduction to the Travel Narrative (Lk 9:51-19:44), and, thus, to Luke's understanding of discipleship, will become even more transparent. This is because the content of Jesus' "recruiting speech" (Derrett, 1986: 71-84) is repeated during the journey (see Lk 12:8-9; 14:27; 17:33; Green, 1997: 374).

Later, Luke will give his readers an illustration of a person who follows after Jesus bearing a cross: Simon of Cyrene (Lk 23:26; Jonhson, 1991: 372; Tannehill, 1986: 273). The only verbal parallel between Lk 9:23 (or 14:27) and Lk 23:26 is the use of *stauros*, "cross." However, this link is strengthened by the observation that the only three uses of *stauros* in all of Luke-Acts are these three passages: two describing discipleship, and then the third, that then concretely illustrates it. Luke "christianizes" Simon as a literary illustration of the disciple who follows after Jesus bearing a cross. Jesus is being persecuted unto death. His disciples, as metaphorically pictured by Simon, must be willing to endure that same fate (Cunningham, 1997: 88, 152).

Verse 24:   For those who want to save their life will lose it,
               and those who lose their life for my sake will save it.

By applying the criteria of dissimilarity and multiple attestation one can trace the saying about losing and finding one's life (Mk 8:35; Mt 16:25; Lk 9:24; 17:33; Jn 12:25) back to Jesus: "Those who wish to save their *psuchē* will lose it; those who lose their *psuchē* will find it." Whereas before Easter the saying referred to the kingdom of God, after Easter it was interpreted and expanded in a christological direction (Rebell, 1989: 202-218).

The aphorism "those who want to save their life will lose it, and those who lose their life for my sake will save it" is used twice in Luke (Lk 9:24; 17:33). The first occurrence follows the confession of Peter that Jesus is "the Messiah of God" (Lk 9:20) and the first passion prediction (Lk 9:21-22). The aphorism is part of a collection of five sayings that explain the manner and means of "following" Jesus (Lk 9:23-27). While the account follows the Markan order closely, there are distinctive differences that shape Luke's presentation. Rather than dividing the material into three different scenes, as both Mark and Matthew do, Luke combines verses 18-27, making a single scene. He does this primarily by omitting words and phrases that separate the scenes in Mark (York, 1991: 80 note 2). In so doing, the tension between Peter's confession of Jesus as the Messiah and Jesus' immediate prediction of suffering is heightened. The suffering Christ then becomes the background for the call to follow Jesus.

"Those who want to save their life" literally reads "those who want to save their *psuchē*." In the context of a saying originally uttered in Palestine, *psuchē* almost certainly does not denote "soul," as opposed to "body" in the understanding of the classical Greek dichotomy. Nor is one to think of it as expressive of the afterlife, in contrast to present life. The emphasis is to be put rather on what one does with one's concrete life or existence; it could mean in this way the self. The contrast in the two members of the saying is that of "life" in an earthly or earthbound sense, and in a transcendent sense, that is, not measured merely by material concerns (Dautzenberg, 1966: 51-82; Nolland, 1993: 483). What the saying demands is a readiness to give up even one's life for Jesus or the kingdom (Fitzmyer, 1981: 788).

The eschatological tension of the present versus the future, or now versus yet (Talbert, 1982: 105), dominates verses 24-25. They present the future that must be avoided by choosing self-denial in the present. "For those who want to save (*sōsai*) their life will lose (*apolesei*) it, and those who lose their life (*apolesei*) for my sake will save (*sōsei*) it." *Apollumi* and *sozo* are juxtaposed as opposites, and two types of people are placed in opposition. Wishing to save one's life will bring about the opposite, destruction or loss of life (Tannehill, 1975: 190 note 39). On the other hand, the one who loses his/her life "for my sake" will save it. The person who "wishes to save" (*thelei sōsai*) his/her life, in this context, is the opposite of the one who "wishes to come after me" (*thelei opisō mou erchesthai*, Lk 9:23) since the latter requires self-denial, not self-preservation. If you try to save yourself from the opposition of the world and/or to accommodate yourself to the world, what results is loss of real life (Bock, 1996: 266). Two opposite attitudes paradoxically bring about reversed conditions (York, 1991: 81-82).

The saying does not make death itself something good to be sought, nor is it an encouragement to seek martyrdom in the cause of the gospel. Rather, it addresses the likelihood that this particular discipleship will have death as a consequence, in a social, political, and economic context whose values the gospel contradicts (Ringe, 1995: 138).

Verse 25:   What does it profit them if they gain the whole
                      world,
                 but lose or forfeit themselves?

Verse 25 illumines the error one makes by choosing to
"save" rather than to "lose" one's life. The link between
verses 24a and 25 is made clear in Luke by the addition of
apolesas; there is no profit in gaining the whole world if
one loses or forfeits himself. The hyperbole "the whole world"
is used, without exact parallel in the New Testament, for
the sum of possessions (C.F. Evans, 1990: 419). Verse 25 is
tied to verse 24 by the common use of the verb "to lose,"
but the images with which Jesus is now working are financial. "To profit" and "to forfeit"—these words stem from
the world of commerce, and so constrain what Jesus means
by "the whole world": he is concerned with possessions, whose
potential for strangling faith he has already mentioned (Lk
8:14). Jesus thus uses the language of business dealings—at
one level to highlight again the threat of possessions, and
at another, more direct level as a symbol of the disposition
of the self (Green, 1997: 375).

Verse 26:   Those who are ashamed of me and of my words,
                 of them the Son of Man will be ashamed
                 when he comes in his glory
                 and the glory of the Father and of the holy angels.

Verse 26 then explains this reversal in terms of one
rejecting Jesus' call to discipleship ("those who are ashamed
of me and of my words") and makes explicit the relationship of the present to the future. Mk 8:37 is omitted by
Luke, tightening the structure of verses 24-26 with the three
sayings beginning in a similar way as better seen in the
RSV text: "For whoever"; "For what"; "For whoever." Negative
response in the present means negative reception by the
Son of Man in the future (York, 1991: 82 and note 2). The
implication is that the profit amounts to nothing; it is useless and senseless. Jesus' words bear on the earthly striving

for gain and success. The verb *kerdainein* ("to gain") is generally used of the pursuit of wealth, earthly riches, and business success (Fitzmyer, 1981: 788).

The importance of how one responds to Jesus' summons to discipleship is established in the vision Jesus presents in verses 26-27 (Green, 1997: 375). The key to the teachings on discipleship comes in their ultimate or "eschatological" consequences (Lk 9:26-27; Ringe, 1995: 138). Verse 26 affirms that Jesus' ministry words will be ratified upon his return as the glorified Son of Man. The emphasis on Jesus' "words" contrasts with the disciples interest in their performance (Lk 9:10; Danker, 1988: 195-196). The Son of Man does not appear here as a judge (in contrast to Mt 16:27), but rather as an advocate in the public setting of appearance before God. The contrast in the shame has to do with its public character in each part of the saying.

The notion of vindication is found in the threefold reference to "glory." "Glory" denotes heavenly effective majesty, divine radiance, and power. It belongs to God and can be almost a synonym for him. The composite triadic glory (his, of the Father, of the holy angels) here is Luke's creation (C.F. Evans, 1990: 411-412). The "glory" belongs not only to the Father, as in Mk 8:38, but also to the Son of Man [and the angels]. "Glory" denotes the status of the risen Christ (Lk 24:26); it is a quality associated with God himself (Lk 2:9; Acts 7:2,55). In the present context, in which a saying on the kingdom is juxtaposed, the coming with glory seems to be related to a phase of that kingdom (Fitzmyer, 1981: 788-789).

Verse 27:   But truly I tell you,
             there are some standing here who will not taste
                  death
             before they see the kingdom of God."

Luke omits Mark's linking "and he said to them" (Mk 9:1), and so makes the link to the preceding closer (Nolland,

1993: 485). The expression "taste death" is also found in John 8:52 and Heb 2:9, and in rabbinic texts, but there it refers to "death as a bitter experience" (Sabourin, 1984: 215; 1985: 206; C.F. Evans, 1990: 412; Stein, 1992: 280).

The assurance that a short time remains before they see God's reign adapts Mark's version of the saying in this same passage (Mk 9:1, "...until they see that the kingdom of God has come in power"). In Mark, Jesus assures his hearers that God's reign will have *come* before some who are present with Jesus die. Jesus' words in Luke contain, instead, the assurance that some will *see* that reign. The crucial question is what the "kingdom of God" refers to (Bock, 1994: 858-859 presents four major views).

Luke apparently recognizes that the coming of that reign is an event that belongs to God's future and not necessarily to the lifetimes of people in his church. Luke is clear that God's reign is glimpsed (though not fully realized) in the life and ministry of Jesus, and in that fact his audience would find comfort (Ringe, 1995: 139). To avoid the suggestion that special apocalyptic effects are required to validate Jesus' messianic mission Luke omits Mark's words "in/with power" (Danker, 1988: 195).

The final saying of the group, in contrast to the previous two verses, suggests a positive result for some who are present: they will not die before they see the kingdom of God. The reference may be to the group of disciples who witness the Transfiguration, presented in the following verses (Lk 9:28-36; Trites, 1987: 77; Danker, 1988: 187; Liefeld, 1995: 130; Green, 1997: 376). More likely, however, verse 27 refers to those who accept Jesus' call to discipleship as opposed to those who attempt to "save" their lives and therefore lose them instead (York, 1991: 82).

e. The Transfiguration (Lk 9:28-36)

Three accounts of the Transfiguration appear in the Gospels—Mk 9:2-8; Mt 17:1-8; Lk 9:28-36. There is an almost general scholarly consensus that Matthew and Luke have used the earlier Markan account and edited it for their own purposes (Schürmann, 1969: 552-567; Neirynck, 1973: 253-265; Trites, 1987: 72-73; but see also Niemand, 1989). The supposed agreements between Luke and Matthew against Mark are very few and most are only apparent and superficial (Reid, 1993: 90-93). That Luke has a variant tradition on which he is dependent is not clear, despite the attempts of some writers to show this. Where Luke's text differs from Mark, the vast majority of the differences can be traced either to Lukan redaction or to Lukan composition (Fitzmyer, 1981: 791-792). A fourth account is found in 2 Pet 1:16-18. While this account differs markedly from the Synoptic accounts, it does not seem to be independent, but, rather, seems to depend upon the earlier Synoptic Gospels (Neyrey, 1980: 509).

The *unity* of the Markan narrative is still a matter of debate. Some earlier scholars thought the narrative was composed of two originally separate parts, one part being modeled on the theophany on Mount Sinai (Exodus 24) and the other part being modeled on the shining of Moses' face as a result of his nearness to God. However, the failure to find a seam in the story where the two parts were sewn together has greatly weakened that theory. More recent redaction critics have tried to separate Markan redactional additions from an original pre-Markan story. Unfortunately, there is very little agreement among the critics. One of the few points on which redaction critics do agree is the existence of a pre-Markan narrative that Mark incorporated into his Gospel.

Today most critics agree that the Markan narrative possesses a certain unity and a definite focus—the focus being the message of the heavenly voice. In the text of Mark, the climax of the narrative is not in the metamorphosis of Jesus and the radiance of his clothing, but in the heavenly voice (Kee, 1972: 139; Stegner, 1998: 110-111).

Another critical issue that continues to divide the scholars is the proper classification of the *form* of the narrative. The form of a story is important because form and meaning are closely related. Hence, it makes a difference whether the narrative is a resurrection story projected back into the ministry of Jesus, or an epiphany that reveals the divine essence of Jesus, or an apocalyptic vision that unveils the future.

Recent scholarship has tended to reject the classification that the Transfiguration is a resurrection story and that it is an epiphany story (Stein, 1976: 79-96; Kee, 1972: 135-152; Reid, 1993: 7-15) in favor of the view that in some way it portrays the future. Some scholars hold the view that the narrative *in form* is an apocalyptic vision: it is, so to speak, a preview of coming attractions. The narrative shares certain characteristics with other visions such as the sudden fading away of Moses and Elijah (Mk 9:8) and the use of the same Greek term translated as "there appeared" (Mk 9:4a; Rowland, 1982: 366-367 and note 40). It also shares certain characteristics with that literary stereotype of an apocalyptic vision in Daniel 10 (Sabbe, 1962: 67; Reid, 1993: 21-24).

Another reason for classifying the narrative as an apocalyptic vision is the exegetical tradition associated with Mount Sinai, the literary archetype of the Transfiguration. Mount Sinai came to be interpreted apocalyptically and figured in some descriptions of the approaching end-of-the-world drama. Thus Mount Sinai became a proper vehicle for conceiving an apocalyptic vision. This will become clearer in working with the tradition associated with Mount Sinai (Stegner, 1997: 111-112).

Throughout biblical tradition and in early Jewish literature, stories abound in which angels figure. It is also clear that *andres*, "men," often in a pair, are understood throughout biblical tradition as angels or messengers of God. One has suggested that in Luke's source the two figures, *andres duo*, were originally anonymous angels, "explaining angels" (Murphy-O'Connor, 1987: 17) and that the Transfiguration should be classified as a *predictive angelophany*—as distinguished from mandatory angelophany, in which the divine messenger is seen and delivers a command from God, and interpretative angelophany, in which angels impart to human beings the divine interpretation of past or present happenings. Predictive angelophanies follow essentially the same form as interpretative angelophanies but are distinct from the latter in that the event being interpreted is future, rather than past or present.

Lk 9:28-33a,36b is precisely in the form of a predictive angelophany. (1) The introduction in verse 28 sets the stage for (2) the appearance of the two heavenly beings in verses 30-31. Appearing as men, they are recognizable as angels by their glorious appearance. (3) The element of prostration or fear is not found in this story. It is inappropriate for Jesus to fear or bow down before angels (see Heb 1:5-14). (4) The prediction and divine interpretation are found in verse 31, where the two envoys speak of Jesus' "exodus" that is to be fulfilled in Jerusalem. (5-6) The elements of questioning and reassurance are lacking. Luke reserves these for his agony scene, where Jesus kneels and prays that the cup be taken away from him. An angel appears to strengthen him (Lk 22:41-43). (7) The witnesses are Peter and those with him (verse 32; in verse 28 "those with him" were identified as John and James). (8) The departure of the angels is related in verse 33a. In its final form, however, Luke's account is no longer purely a predictive angelophany. By his redactional activity (the combination of Lk 9:28-33a,36b with 9:33b-35) Luke has eventually converted his narrative into a *pronouncement story* (Reid, 1993: 78-86, 97-98).

A pronouncement story has been defined as "a brief narrative in which the climactic (and often final) element is a pronouncement which is presented as a particular person's response to something said or observed on a particular occasion of the past" (Tannehill, 1981: 1). Six types of pronouncement stories have been identified: (1) correction stories; (2) commendation stories; (3) objection stories; (4) quest stories; (5) inquiry stories; (6) description stories. There are also "hybrids" that combine elements from more than one of the subtypes. Although nobody formerly classified the Transfiguration as a pronouncement story, it does correspond in every way to the first type, the *correction pronouncement story*. In this type of story two attitudes are contrasted. In the stimulus part of the narrative, someone takes a position that may seem innocent or even commendable. The story reaches its culmination as this position is corrected by the responder. Located in the climactic final position, this correction makes the lasting impression, thus inviting the readers or hearers to align their position with that of the corrector. The function of such a story is to challenge one to move from one value stance to another (Tannehill, 1981a: 105).

In Lk 9:28-36, the setting is provided in verses 28-33a. The trip up the mountain, the change in Jesus, and the conversation with Moses and Elijah lead to Peter's statement in verse 33b, "Master, it is good for us to be here; let us make three dwellings, one for you, one for Moses, and one for Elijah." The attitude reflected by Peter's exclamation is that Jesus is on a par with Moses and Elijah. The pronouncement in verse 35, "This is my Son, my Chosen; listen to him," uttered by the voice from the cloud, corrects Peter's position. It challenges him and the subsequent hearers and readers of the Transfiguration story not to see Jesus only as one more in the long line of Jewish prophets and leaders, but to adopt the divine position, understanding Jesus as the unique, chosen one, and to pledge sole allegiance to him (Reid, 1993: 97-99).

The combination of the two texts has been explained in terms of layers of development of the same basic tradition rather than the fusing of entirely separate traditions (Murphy-O'Connor, 1987: 8-21; Reid, 1993: 86-90).

Critics have been so preoccupied by matters of form and redaction criticism that they have not focused on the *Jewish Christian origins of the pre-Markan narrative.* Actually, three lines of evidence lead us to Jewish Christianity. They are the literary form of the narrative, the use of the narrative as a validating formula for church leaders, and the use of the Mount Sinai narrative as a literary archetype. We briefly examine each of these lines of evidence.

Apocalyptic visions are primarily found in late Old Testament books (such as Daniel), in some intertestamental Jewish works, and in some New Testament books. Apocalyptic presupposes a certain view of history which Christianity inherited from Judaism. Therefore, if the Transfiguration is a piece of apocalyptic, its formulators must be sought in Judaism or Jewish Christianity.

The view that this narrative performed a validating function in primitive Christianity is modern and has gained acceptance as scholars have investigated the social function of pieces of literature (Chilton, 1980-1981: 115-124; McGuckin, 1986: 53-57). The three witnesses, Peter and James and John, occupy an important place in the narrative. The statement in Mk 9:2b, "he was transformed before them," further illustrates their importance. They correspond to Aaron, Nadab, and Abihu in literary archetype. These three formed an inner circle among the Twelve and Paul later mentions them as the "pillars" of the Jerusalem church in Gal 2:9. They were leaders of Jewish Christianity, and, as a secondary function, this narrative validated their role by mentioning their names in connection with this significant event. Similarly, the pre-Pauline list of witnesses of the resurrection in 1 Cor 15:3-7 played a validating function for leaders of the primitive Church.

The third line of evidence pointing to Jewish Christianity is the reinterpretation of Exodus 24 in intertestamental

Judaism. Like many other stories in scripture, the story of Mount Sinai was embellished and changed in its many retellings. And like other stories about the wilderness generation, this story too was understood eschatologically and apocalyptically. Sinai becomes the place where the future is revealed. The book of *Jubilees* offers a good example of this retelling. *Jubilees* opens by recalling Exodus 24. Then, the angel of the presence receives tablets recording history "from the day of creation until the day of the new creation..." (*Jub* 1:29). Who else could know about the apocalyptic interpretation of Mount Sinai but Jews and Jewish Christians? We now turn to the use of scripture in this narrative.

In a study of the narrative of the Temptation, it was found that typology played a key role in the use of scripture. There, Old Testament persons, situations, or events foreshadowed similar persons, situations in the New Testament (Stegner, 1997: 99-110). However, the narrative of the Transfiguration does not exemplify typology as it was defined in that study. The narrative is not comparing parallel situations between the life of Jesus and that of the wilderness generation in that Mount Sinai foreshadows an event in the ministry of Jesus (e.g., according to a number of scholars, Mount Sinai foreshadows the Sermon on the Mount for Matthew). Rather, this apocalyptic vision was portraying a future event that had not yet happened. Further, an eschatological and apocalyptic understanding of Exodus 24 is used to picture the eschatological event being enacted in the conclave of Moses, Elijah, and Jesus (Kee, 1972: 147). Rather than speak of Mount Sinai as a type foreshadowing the Transfiguration, it is preferable to say that the Transfiguration was modeled upon the apocalyptic understanding of Exodus 24.

Even the statement that the Transfiguration was modeled upon the apocalyptic understanding of Exodus 24 needs further qualification. The relationship between the two stories is complicated by the presence of words from other Old Testament stories, most of which were related to Mount Sinai and were also interpreted eschatologically. Thus, the apocalyptically interpreted Mount Sinai story in Exodus 24 acted as a kind of literary magnet that attracted other stories associated with it.

An examination of the details that are common to both stories (Stegner, 1997: 114-115) leads to the conclusion that at the level of tradition and redaction, it is beyond reasonable doubt that the Transfiguration is fundamentally a visionary representation of the Sinai motif of Exodus 24 (Chilton, 1980-1981: 119). In addition to Exodus 24, words from other Old Testament stories are found in the Transfiguration, as there are Deut 18:15 ("listen to him"), Ex 34:29-35 (the story about the shining of Moses' face after "talking with God"), etc. The use of scripture in the Transfiguration is determined primarily by its being modeled upon one Old Testament passage—Exodus 24—as a literary archetype (Stegner, 1997: 115-117).

Recently the Transfiguration has also been interpreted as Jesus and three disciples experiencing an altered state of consciousness (ASC) or trance or waking vision, in which Jesus is probably focused on an internal object (communion with the Father), and the disciples on Jesus (face, garments, etc.). People in the Mediterranean world of past and present slip readily and easily into various altered states of consciousness. They do so for a variety of reasons, a major one being the need to find an answer to a question or a resolution to a problem. What function does this ecstatic vision perform for Jesus? It is a key vehicle of revelation that confirms his status as Beloved or Chosen Son and authorizes his role to proceed to Jerusalem, the cross, and ultimate honorable vindication. What function does it perform for the disciples? The ASC is also a vehicle of revelation for them that lessens confusion about Jesus' identity: not Elijah, nor Moses, nor one of the prophets, nor the Baptist, but rather the Chosen or Beloved Son. It calms them down in the face of the frightening destiny that awaits Jesus but already begins to emerge ominously in the growing number of powerful enemies made by Jesus' victories in challenge and riposte encounters (Pilch, 1995: 58-63).

In the Transfiguration story the answer given to Herod's question is both implicit and explicit. The explicit answer is provided by the heavenly voice from the overshadowing cloud: "This is my Son, my Chosen" (Lk 9:35). He may be God's Messiah and suffering Son of Man, but he is also "Son" and "Chosen One." The implicit answer, and indeed a subsidiary and minor one, is contained in the narrative itself, viz., in the appearance of Moses and Elijah in glory with him, as they discuss with him his "departure" (*exodos*), his transit through passion and death to him who calls him "Son." Their eventual disappearance and their leaving him "alone," together with the charge from the heavenly voice, "Listen to him" (probably an echo of Deut 18:15), clearly identifies Jesus as the one who now has to be heard in place of Moses and Elijah. In effect, he is the New Moses and the New Elijah. The "New Moses" is really not an operative motif in the Third Gospel, as it is in the First; it is found here because it is retained from the Markan source (Mk 9:4, with the same charge used there). The appearance of Elijah, however, is different. Even though he already was present in the pre-Lukan source, his appearance fits a theme of the Third Gospel in which Jesus is presented in a role similar to Elijah, or possibly even as a "New Elijah." In addition to the popular identification of Jesus as such (recorded in Lk 9:9,19), the evangelist plays on the relation of Jesus to Elijah in several places in the Gospel (Lk 4:25; 9:54,62). What is puzzling in this regard, however, is Luke's omission of the Saying about the Coming of Elijah found in the Markan source (Mk 9:9-13). It is an episode that creates its own problems, which need not detain us here. We can speculate about the Lukan omission of it

(Conzelmann, 1960: 59), but in any case the omission height-ens the identification of Jesus as the New Elijah implicitly suggested by this episode; it too supplies an answer to Herod's question. The christological affirmation here is that all that Moses and Elijah meant for Israel of old is now summed up in Jesus and that he is the one—as Messiah and suffering Son of Man—to whom all must now listen. The Transfigu-ration scene reveals Jesus for what he is; heaven identifies him. And the irony of it all is that the disciples, having heard the instruction, "Listen to him," "kept silent and in those days told no one any of the things they had seen" (Lk 9:36; Fitzmyer, 1978: 146-147).

Verse 28:   Now about eight days after these sayings
              Jesus took with him Peter and John and James,
              and went up on the mountain to pray.

The opening of Luke's narrative differs considerably from that of Mark. Luke and Mark use their own typical opening (Reid, 1993: 45-46). Luke's note on the passage of time is less precise than "after six days" in Mk 9:2 and Mt 17:1. Several unsuccessful attempts have been made to give a theological motivation for Luke's supposed change to "eight days" (Trites, 1979: 70; Reid, 1993: 100-102). Commenta-tors have not agreed as to any specific reason for the differ-ent wording. Luke is more precise than the other Synoptics in linking the Transfiguration with Jesus' preceding "say-ings." The expression "sayings" connects the Transfigura-tion story both with the preceding sayings in Lk 9:21-27, where a similar phrase is found in verse 26 ("my words"), and with the instruction that follows in Lk 9:43-45, which contains the other instance of "these sayings" in Luke's Gospel (Lk 9:44; Reid, 1993: 47,99-100).

Five times in Luke's Gospel the trio Peter, John, and James are named. In two instances (Lk 5:10; 6:14) Luke has the same order of the names as Mark: Peter, James, and John. It is probable that in these examples Luke simply adopted this order from the Markan tradition. This same order is also found in Lk 9:54, in a pericope peculiar to Luke. In Lk 9:28, as in Lk 8:51, the order differs from Mark's in that John's name precedes James'. This same sequence is also found in Acts 1:13, and there are eight times in Acts when Peter and John are named together. The order of the disciples' names, Peter, John, and James, appears to be deliberately constructed by Luke (Reid, 1993: 50-51).

Once again Luke mentions that Jesus is at prayer, an observation repeated in verse 29 but absent from Mark and Matthew (Liefeld, 1995: 132). The focus is on Jesus' action of ascending the mountain to pray. This is accomplished by the use of the verb *anebē*, "went up," in the singular (Feldkamper, 1978: 134) and the subsequent description of what happens to Jesus. Whether or not there is an allusion to Mount Sinai, "the mountain" does connote a place of close proximity to God. The mention of "the mountain" can also carry an apocalyptic connotation. Lk 23:30 speaks of mountains in an apocalyptic context. In the Transfiguration narrative, "the mountain" can be regarded as one of the many apocalyptic elements, among which are also apparitions, brilliant clothing, a heavenly voice, mysterious dialogues, sleep, and divine esteem for elect visionaries (Reid, 1993: 102-103).

Luke says that Jesus went up on the mountain "to pray." This is a deliberate addition. It excludes the idea that Jesus went up with the three disciples to manifest himself to them (Fitzmyer, 1981: 798). For Luke it is impossible to understand the meaning of this event apart from prayer (Trites, 1979: 74).

Verse 29:   And while he was praying
             the appearance of his face changed,
             and his clothes became dazzling white.

The only agreement between Lk 9:29 and Mk 9:2b-3 is that they both speak of Jesus' clothing becoming white. Luke omits the actual word "transfigured" (*metemorphōthē*, used in Mk 9:2; Mt 17:2), possibly to avoid a term that might have suggested Hellenistic ideas of an epiphany, the appearance of a god [but this claim becomes less persuasive in the light of the cultural and psychological anthropological background discovered by social-scientific studies (Pilch, 1995: 63)]. Instead he describes the remarkable alteration of Jesus' face and the dazzzling whiteness of his clothing (Liefeld, 1995: 132). The noun *eidos* occurs one other time in Luke's Gospel, in Lk 3:22, at Jesus' baptism, where the Holy Spirit descends upon him in bodily form (*sōmatikōi eidei*). In that example as well as in Lk 9:29, *eidos* denotes "form, outward appearance," "the total visible appearance; what may be perceived and known by others." The whole phrase, *to eidos tou prosōpou autou heteron* in Lk 9:29 says simply that the visible appearance of Jesus' face changed (Reid, 1993: 105-106,107). Several examples of similar expressions in the Septuagint describe a change of countenance as a result of prayer or encounter with God. The most famous instance is that of Moses' radiant face (Ex 34:29-30) following his meeting with God on Mount Sinai. Against the background of this and other examples, Luke's expression can be understood as saying that a physical alteration of Jesus' facial expression took place that reflected a change in Jesus' inner being. This change is said to be visible to, and observable by, the three disciples who accompanied Jesus to the hill country. The clues to the cause of this change in Jesus and its significance may be detected in the references to prayer in verses 28,29 and in the content of the conversation between Jesus, Moses, and Elijah in verse 31.

The change in Jesus occurs in the context of prayer, a time when Jesus explicitly seeks communion with God. Often one's relationship with God is expressed in terms of God's face and the face of the one praying. God's face connotes God's presence (e.g., Ps 21:7). Prayer itself is referred to as seeking God's face (Ps 27:8; 105:4), and also as turning one's face to God (Dan 9:3). Seeing God face to face is an expression that is used to describe intense encounters with the divine, such as those of Jacob at Peniel (Gen 31:30) and Moses on Mount Sinai (Deut 5:4; 34:10).

The examples from the Old Testament and early Jewish literature that juxtapose a change of face with prayer give an interpretive clue for understanding the phrase, "the appearance of his face changed." It is likely that Luke is indicating that the alteration in Jesus' countenance reflected something that transpired between himself and God during his prayer. The subject of the exchange between Jesus and God in Luke's Transfiguration story is not made explicit, although the context of Lk 9:28-36 and the content of the conversation between Jesus, Moses, and Elijah in verse 31 provide the clues to what Luke supposed it to be. The location of the episode, as the hinge between Jesus' Galilean and Jerusalem ministries, is an indication that Luke considered Jesus' mission to be the subject of his prayer at the Transfiguration. Like the accounts of his baptism and agony, this time of prayer is depicted at a critical moment of the transition in Jesus' mission (Reid, 1993: 109,110-111).

In close connection with the Transfiguration pericope, at the beginning of the Travel Narrative (Lk 9:51,53) Luke emphatically speaks of Jesus' face. Jesus has set his face to go to Jerusalem. Beside the term "face," the Transfiguration pericope and the beginning of the Travel Narrative are connected by means of the following: (a) by the two terms *exodos* (Lk 9:31) and *analēmpsis*, "assumption" (Lk 9:51) that occur only in Luke and in their ambiguity mean the death as well as the ascension of Jesus; (b) by the motif of fulfillment in the cognate verbs *plēroun* (Lk 9:31) and *sumplērousthai* (Lk 9:51); (c) by Jerusalem (Lk 9:31, 51, 53), as the place where the *exodos* and the *analēmpsis* will take place. The correspondences allow us to interpret the change of Jesus' face in light of Lk 9:51,53. Consequently we interpret Lk 9:29 as follows: In the transformation of Jesus' face appears

—while he is at prayer—his determination to go the way to Jerusalem, the place of his suffering and ascension (Feldkämper, 1978: 136-137).

The story does not elaborate on precisely what was the change in Jesus' face. But in the final form of the story, with its Mosaic and apocalyptic overtones, the references to *doxa*, "glory," and the description of Jesus' clothing becoming flashing white, the phrase, "the appearance of his face changed," evokes an image of a radiant change in Jesus' countenance. The notion that the perfected righteous will have radiant faces (the ultimate change of countenance) occurs frequently in apocalyptic literature. *2 Esdras* 7:97 says of those who have kept the ways of the Most High, "Their face is to shine like the sun." That this radiance of the faces of the righteous is a reflection of the divine glory is made explicit in *1 Enoch* 18:4, "They shall not be able to look on the faces of the righteous because the Lord of spirits shall cause his light to shine on the faces of the saints and the elect righteous." It is not only the face of the righteous one that shines with the radiance of God, but the whole being, as in Dan 12:3, "And those who are wise shall shine like the brightness of the firmament..."

The extension of the radiance goes even further to include the clothing. *1 Enoch* 62:15 asserts, "The righteous and elect ones ... shall wear the garments of glory." It is possible that Luke had these apocalyptic notions in mind when he connected the phrase, "and his clothes became dazzling white" to "the appearance of his face changed." Part of Luke's intent, then, would be to portray Jesus as God's righteous one, with a changed face and garments of glory. In the final form of the story, the joining of these two phrases creates an aura of an event that is not merely natural (Reid, 1993: 111,112,113,114).

There are many references to garments in Luke and at times they have a symbolic meaning. The adjective *leukos*, "white," occurs twice in Luke's writings, here and in Acts

1:10. In both instances it is used of clothing in a description of a supernatural sort. What Luke says about Jesus' clothes in the Gospel carries important symbolism about his person (see, e.g., Lk 2:7,12; 23:11; Karris, 1985: 85-87).

In such a schema, one may expect that the flashing, white clothing of Jesus in Lk 9:29 also carries important symbolism that is revelatory of his person. The primary symbolism conveyed by Jesus' white clothing in Lk 9:29 is that he is a heavenly being. Although it is no secret in Luke that Jesus is the Son of God (e.g., Lk 1:32; 3:22), the meaning of this must be worked out in the course of the Gospel. In the context of Lk 9:21-22 and 9:43-45, where Jesus speaks to his disciples about his coming death, the white clothing is a confirmation of his heavenly status, his righteousness, and his ultimate victory over death. The apocalyptic associations with white clothing introduce a future dimension to the understanding of Jesus' victory and heavenly status. And yet, the Transfiguration is narrated in the context of a happening during Jesus' earthly ministry. In this way, Luke conveys the message that Jesus' heavenly status and glory are both present and yet to come.

In the final form of Lk 9:28-36, there is a parallelism between the dazzling white clothes of Jesus (verse 29) and the glorious appearance of the two heavenly interpreters (verse 31). It has been demonstrated that heavenly figures that appear in human form are identified as divine messengers by their glorious apparel. Jesus, shown here as a man in dazzling white clothing, is portrayed as God's ultimate interpreter. That his life is the pinnacle of divine communication with human beings is the message given in verse 35: "listen to him" (Reid, 1993: 114-115).

Luke describes the appearance of Jesus' garments in a way similar to that of the two men in the resurrection pericope (Lk 24:4) and the ascension (Acts 1:10). Thus, in Lk 9:29, the theme of the suffering and death as well as the exalta-

tion of Jesus belong to the focal point of Luke's interest—
at least by way of allusion (Feldkamper, 1978: 137).

The phrase "before them" (Mk 9:2) places the focus on
the disciples in the Markan tradition. Luke omits the phrase
and, unlike the Markan version, focuses on Jesus. The si-
multaneity of prayer and transfiguration should be emphasized. What is reported here happened, like at Jesus' baptism, while he was praying. Jesus' companions, however, were
not involved in either Jesus' prayer or his transfiguration,
as is clearly stated in Lk 9:32 (Feldkämper, 1978: 136).

Verse 30:   Suddenly they saw two men,
              Moses and Elijah, talking to him.

The phrase "two men" is regarded by most commentators as a secondary addition by Luke. Few, however, offer
an explanation as to why Luke would add this phrase. Those
who do, see it as Luke's intent to make the connection
with the two men at the empty tomb in Lk 24:4 and at the
ascension in Acts 1:10 (Dillon, 1978: 22-25; Danker, 1988:
199-200). According to some scholars, the difficulties encountered in explaining "two men" as a Lukan addition suggest
a different solution: that the phrase "Moses and Elijah" is
the secondary addition, not "two men." It is much more
likely that the two men were anonymous in the special Lukan
tradition behind verses 28-33a. It was only when Luke joined
this to the Markan tradition that he attempted to identify
the two with Mark's figures (Murphy-O'Connor, 1987: 15;
Reid, 1993: 37-40,59-60).

There is no other instance in the New Testament in
which Moses and Elijah are named together, nor does either figure ever function as a heavenly messenger as in Lk
9:30 (Reid, 1993: 61-62). Scholars debate the significance
of Moses' and Elijah's presence.

The old view that they represent the Law and the Prophets respectively (e.g., Marshall, 1978: 384; see Reid, 1993:
121-122) does not do justice to the rich associations each

name has in Jewish thought. Moses had a mountaintop experience at Sinai; his face shone (Ex 34:30); he was not only a lawgiver but also a prophet. Elijah was not only a prophet but was also related to the Law of Moses as symbolizing the one who would one day turn people's hearts back to the covenant. In Jewish thought, Elijah was an eschatological figure, that is, one associated with the end times. Each man was among the most highly respected Old Testament figures; both had one distinctive thing in common—their strange departure from this world. Elijah was taken up to heaven in a whirlwind (2 Kgs 2:11), and Moses was buried by the Lord (Deut 34:6). In summary, it seems that the presence of Moses and Elijah on the Mount of Transfiguration draws attention, first, to the place of Jesus in continuing the redemptive work of God from the Exodus to the future eschatological consummation; second, to the appropriateness of Jesus' association with heavenly figures; and third, to the superiority of Jesus over even these great and divinely favored heroes of Israel's past (Liefeld, 1995: 132-133).

Other scholars point out that both Moses and Elijah were prophets who suffered rejection and persecution, yet each was vidicated by God. Thus, another interpretation of the presence of Moses and Elijah at the Transfiguration is to confirm Jesus' prediction of his own suffering (Lk 9:21-22), but also to assure his future vindication (Pamment, 1980-1981: 338-339). They were for Luke the right persons for the conversation with Jesus about his *exodos* in Jerusalem while they themselves as rejected prophets were "figures of suffering." At any rate, that is how Luke saw them. In the Moses-section of Stephen's discourse (Acts 7:17-34) he develops the idea that Moses, sent by God as ruler and liberator (Lk 7:35), was rejected by Israel (Acts 7:27,35,39). In the redaction of Lk 13:3ff., a text that is important for the theological meaning of Jesus' journey to Jerusalem, Luke

probably alludes to the situation of the rejected and persecuted Elijah (Feldkämper, 1978: 138-139).

Some scholars have pointed out some common elements
between Lk 9:28-36 and the account of the women at the
tomb (Lk 24:1-9), notably the description of the two heavenly messengers and the vocabulary used which allow us to
establish thematic correspondences: the theme of the heavenly messengers (which occurs also in Acts 1:10), the theme
of the radiant garments, and the theme of the "exodus" at
Jerusalem (Guillaume, 1979: 38-41).

Verse 31:   They appeared in glory and were speaking of his
              departure,
              which he was to accomplish at Jerusalem.

The verb *ōphthē*, "appeared," is used three other times
by Luke for supernatural apparitions. It is used of the angel
of the Lord who appeared to Zechariah in Lk 1:11; of the
strengthening angel at the agony scene in Lk 22:43 [the
authenticity of Lk 23:43-44 remains a highly debated question; Ehrman and Plunkett, 1983: 401-416]; and of the risen
Jesus in his appearance to Simon in Lk 24:34. There are
nine similar examples in Acts. Each of these instances occurs in material peculiar to Luke.

Doxa, "glory," is a favorite noun of Luke. It appears
thirteen times in his Gospel and four times in Acts, as compared with only three times in the Gospel of Mark, and the
use of *doxa* here is in close accord with other references to
it in Luke's Gospel (Trites, 1987: 76-77). Three times Luke
retained *doxa* from his source, six times it occurs in material peculiar to Luke, and twice it is peculiar to Luke's redaction of his source. The whole phrase "they appeared in
glory" makes clear that the two men are heavenly messengers.

The unusual noun *exodos* occurs only twice elsewhere
in the New Testament (Heb 11:22; 2 Pet 1:15), and nowhere else in Lukan writings (Trites, 1979: 74-75; Reid,

1993: 63,125). There are several interpretations of the noun *exodos*. In Heb 11:22, it refers to the Exodus, the historic saving event in which God brought the Israelites out of Egyptian bondage and into the promised land. The noun *exodos* also denotes "death," and is so used in 2 Pet 1:15. A difficulty with this interpretation for Lk 9:31 is that in the context of Lk 9:18-27, which contains very blunt speech about Jesus' coming death, the use of *exodos* as a euphemism for death seems unlikely. Another meaning is "departure," and this is the one that best explains *exodos* in Lk 9:31. Taken in this broad sense, it includes the whole complex of events that forms Jesus' transit to God: his passion, death, burial, resurrection, and ascension/exaltation (Fitzmyer, 1981: 167; Feuillet, 1977: 181-206). This interpretation fits well with Luke's whole concept of salvation history and with his geographical perspective. Luke presents salvation history as a course of events following a schedule of times set by God and moving along the "way" leading to the Gentiles (Robinson, 1964: 39-43). Accordingly, Luke depicts Jesus' entire life and ministry as a course or a "way" (Marshall, 1978: 384-385; Reid, 1993: 125-126).

The *exodos* does not only mean Jesus' death fate, but also his consummation in resurrection and ascension (Plummer, 1977: 251; Tiede, 1988: 188). It is a very condensed expression that summarizes the Lukan understanding of Jesus' death as transition to his exaltation (Lk 24:26,46; Conzelmann, 1960: 196). For the word *exodos* belongs to the Lukan terminology as appears from the similarity of Lk 9:31 to Acts 13:25 ("as John was finishing his work") and Acts 20:24 ("if only I may finish [RSV: accomplish] my course"). This spatial sense of *plēroun*, "to fulfill," is found only in Luke. That Luke also thinks of the fulfillment of scripture can be surmised since it is Moses and Elijah who speak with Jesus about his *exodos*, "departure." For the first time Jerusalem is mentioned here emphatically as the place of fulfillment of Jesus' *exodos*. From here on Luke recalls again and again the goal of Jesus' journey (Lk 9:51,53; 13:23, 33f.; 17:11; 18:31; 19:11,28; Dietrich, 1972: 111; Feldkämper, 1978: 139-140).

The question as to from where Luke got the content of the conversation between Jesus and the two Old Testament figures has received various answers: Some take it to be a variant tradition, others a Lukan redaction of Mark. But all agree that the conversation with Jesus during the descent from the mountain (Mk 9:9-13; Mt 17:9-13), which Luke did not take over from the tradition, contains the "stuff" of the conversation with Moses and Elijah (Conzelmann, 60: 58-59). That conversation deals with the suffering (Mk 9:12) as well as the resurrection (Mk 9:9) of the Son of Man. Luke has united these two statements in the pithy term *exodos*, and has defined the fate of Jesus as the fate of a prophet by the mention of Moses and Elijah as his conversation partners. Since "they spoke" in verse 31 undoubtedly refers back to "talked with" in verse 30, the contents of the conversation, which Jesus himself had already communicated to his disciples in Lk 9:22, is no longer a new revelation (Conzelmann, 1960: 57). We deal here much more with a confirmation of the announcement of suffering and death (Lk 9:22) by the presence and the conversation of the heavenly figures (Creed, 1957: 134; Feldkämper, 1978: 140-141; Ringe, 1995: 141).

The city of Jerusalem plays an important role in the geographical schema of Luke-Acts (Reid, 1991: 20-24). In Lk 9:31 it becomes the city of destiny for Jesus' "exodus" (Reid, 1993: 128).

Verse 32: Now Peter and his companions were weighed down with sleep;
but since they had stayed awake,
they saw his glory and the two men who stood with him.

In this verse, the presence of Peter and his companions is recalled. They were last mentioned in verse 28 and have been peripheral in the story so far. Before reintroducing them into the narrative, Luke explains their lack of participation by their having been asleep (Reid, 1993: 128). In verse 32 then is emphatically said what was already indicated earlier (Lk 9:29,31): overcome by sleep, Jesus' companions have no active part in what has happened until now.

Since the motif of sleep is introduced here from the Mount of Olives pericope (Lk 22:45), more is said by it than that the event reported took place at night (Conzelmann, 1960: 58-59). When they wake up the companions see only the *doxa* of Jesus and of the two men with him; they have not heard the conversation about Jesus' *exodos* in Jerusalem. Thus the sleep motif means: The suffering of Jesus as the way to glory which he enters at his resurrection (Lk 24:26,46; Ellis, 1966: 143) remains for them as of now a secret that they meet only with lack of understanding (Lk 9:44; 18:34; 24:25). At their awakening they see only the end of the way of Jesus in the resurrection, not the way that leads to it through suffering and death. The occurrence of *doxa* in Lk 9:32 is the only instance in the Synoptic Gospels in which *doxa* is used of Jesus where it is not explicitly spoken of as a future glory into which he will enter.

By the expression "they saw his glory" "seeing" is contrasted with "hearing": The companions have not heard the conversation about Jesus' *exodos*; therefore, in Lk 9:35 they are urgently summoned to listen. Thereby Lk 9:32, that has no parallel in Mark/ Matthew, prepares the continuation of the narration: the lack of understanding of Jesus' companions that is shown in the mistaken reaction of Peter (Lk 9:32) and in the silence about the event (Lk 9:36) as well as in the urgent summons to "hear" (Lk 9:35; Feldkämper, 1978: 141).

Verse 33:   Just as they were leaving him, Peter said to Jesus,
                  "Master, it is good for us to be here;
                  let us make three dwellings,
                  one for you, one for Moses, and one for Elijah"—
                  not knowing what he said.

Having been reintroduced in verse 32, the disciples now become active participants in the story. The shift in focus from Jesus to the disciples that occurs in Lk 9:33 and the swing back to Jesus in verse 36 is explained by some scholars by means of the hypothesis that Luke welded together two separate pieces of tradition at these points. In one tradition (L) Jesus is the center of attention and in the other (Markan) the focus is on the disciples. The suggestion that verse 36b, which focuses on Jesus, was originally connected with verse 33a is quite interesting. The sentence would have read: "Just as they were leaving, Jesus was found alone."

Only Luke mentions that it was as Moses and Elijah "were leaving" Jesus [this is the only use of the verb *diachorizō* in the New Testament] that Peter made the suggestion to make three dwellings. Peter's address to Jesus is *epistata*, "Master," as compared with *rabbi* in Mk 9:5. Luke never uses the title rabbi in his Gospel. In the two other instances in which there is a Lukan parallel to a pericope in which Mark uses *rabbi* as an address to Jesus, Luke does not employ it. The term *epistatēs* is peculiar to Luke in the New Testament and occurs only in the vocative. Twice it is found in material unique to Luke (Lk 5:5; 17:13), and twice Luke substitutes it for the Markan *didaskale* (Lk 8:24; 9:49). There is one instance in which Luke adds *epistatēs* where the Markan parallel does not have any title of address (Lk 8:45). These data support the assertion that Luke consciously avoids the title "rabbi" and that he substituted his preferred *epistatēs* in Lk 9:33 for the title he found in the Markan tradition (Reid, 1993: 69).

Already prepared by the mention of "Peter" by name in verse 32, he appears as the spokesperson of the threesome in verse 33. As several times before (Lk 5:8; 8:45), he speaks from purely human considerations and motives, without understanding what is really happening. His misplaced re-mark ("not knowing what he said") is caused by the fact that the two men who are standing with Jesus intend to leave. By his proposal to build three dwellings/booths Peter wants to hold on to the scene of glory and to let it last (Schürmann, 1969: 560; Dietrich, 1973: 113; Trites, 1979: 76). His suggestion that they set up three "dwellings" may also evoke memories of the account of Israel's *exodos*. The word translated "dwellings" is *skēnē*, used in the Septuagint for the "booths" that are symbols of the Feast of Taber-nacles (Lev 23:33-43; Danker, 1988: 198; see Reid, 1993: 134-136). Despite its origins as a harvest festival, by Jesus' time (and certainly in Luke's day after the destruction of the Temple of Jerusalem), the Feast of Tabernacles was a festival of pilgrimage celebrating Israel's wanderings through the wilderness to freedom. With or without that connec-tion, Peter's suggestion also refers to the poignant human longing to somehow mark the places and preserve the mo-ments where one has encountered God (Ringe, 1995: 141-142; Feldkämper, 1978: 141-142).

The narrator breaks into the story at this point to in-form the reader that Peter had no comprehension of the meaning of the occasion. This comment leads the reader to draw certain conclusions about Peter and the disciples. In the pericope immediately preceding that of the Transfigu-ration, Peter had the right answer; he said the right thing. The juxtaposition of this passage with Peter's confession, however, forces the reader to re-evaluate Peter's insight. Although Peter knows that Jesus is the Messiah, perhaps his conception of Jesus' messiahship is flawed. The reader's doubt about the knowledge of the disciples is molded even more as the disciples are unable to heal an afflicted boy (Lk 9:37-43) or understand Jesus' passion prediction (Sheeley, 1992: 111).

The phrase "not knowing what he said" is strikingly close to Lk 22:60, "I do not know what you are talking about," Peter's assertion to the man in the courtyard who tries to identify Peter with Jesus after the latter's arrest. It may be that Luke's phrasing in Lk 9:33 is a foreshadowing of Lk 22:60. In both instances it is Peter who does not know what is being said. Central to the scene in both cases is Jesus' identity as the Messiah who must suffer and the attendant implications of this for the disciples. In both Lk 9:33 and 22:60 the Lukan formulation differs from Mark's and can be attributed to Luke's editorship. Luke has moved the element of fear (Mk 9:6, "for they were terrified") to verse 34, associating it with the cloud rather than giving it as the motive for Peter's not knowing what to say. In verse 32, with the inclusion of the detail of the sleepiness of the disciples, Luke has already suggested an explanation for Peter's not knowing what he was saying (Reid, 1993: 70-71).

It has recently been argued that the Synaitic background of the Transfiguration account makes it particularly difficult to agree with the common understanding of Peter's remark regarding the building of the *treis skēnas* ("three dwellings") as a longing to prolong the experience through the building of booths used in the celebration of the Feast of Booths. It has been suggested that the fear which the Transfiguration scene generated in Peter could only have been brought to mind by the tabernacle in the wilderness, thus eliciting his offer to build "three dwellings" as a means of protection from the display of divine glory (Otto, 1997: 101-112).

Verse 34: While he was saying this,
a cloud came and overshadowed them;
and they were terrified as they entered the cloud.

The expresion, "while he was saying this," at the beginning of the verse links closely the preceding comments of Peter with the next event, the coming of the cloud. While

Peter is speaking, there appears a cloud that overshadows the group. The cloud, like other elements in this narrative, can symbolize more than one thing (Reid, 1993: 136-137), but above all the cloud symbolizes the glorious presence of God (Ex 19:16; Trites, 1979: 75). This is notably true in the passage so clearly recalled by the Transfiguration (Ex 24:15-18). Though the disciples enter the cloud, a sense of the transcendence of God is retained as the voice comes "from" the cloud (Liefeld, 1995: 134). The action of the overshadowing does not have the same role in Mark as it is given in Luke (Reid, 1993: 71).

The fear of the three companions (different from Mark/ Matthew) is to be understood in a similar way as verse 33: they begin to fear the separation since Moses and Elijah start to enter into the cloud (Grundmann, 1966: 195; Lohfink, 1971: 190f.).

Verse 35:   Then from the cloud came a voice that said,
                "This is my Son, my Chosen; listen to him!"

With the symbolism of the overshadowing cloud in verse 34, the disciples have been drawn into the encounter with the divine. In verse 35 Peter and his companions remain those for whom the action is intended, as the message from the cloud is specifically directed to them (Reid, 1993; 138).

The voice from the cloud is substantially a reprise of the voice in Lk 3:22. The theme of Jesus' special status as God's Son is replayed, but in a different key. In Lk 9:35 the voice is directed to the disciples, whereas at the baptism scene Jesus is the one to whom it is directed. The message for the disciples is both a confirmation of Peter's declaration of Jesus' messiahship (Lk 9:20) and a corrective of his misunderstanding of what that entails (Lk 9:33; Reid, 1993: 139).

The voice from the cloud addresses itself to Jesus' companions with their double misunderstanding (concerning the necessity of Jesus' fate as a necessary transition to his glory, and the function of the presence of the two heavenly figures) and not to Jesus himself. It proclaims Jesus and commands them to listen to him. The command to "listen" contains in the immediate and wider Lukan context a strong emphasis and its own nuance: It confirms Jesus' appeal and gives it a very special urgency; the voice from the cloud calls attention to the fact that after the "temporariness" of Moses and Elijah, it is now Jesus to whom they should listen; in light of the preceding as well as the following context, the voice from heaven appeals to the disciples to listen to Jesus especially when he explains the secret of his suffering (Conzelmann, 1960: 591; Schürmann, 1969: 562; Feldkämper, 1978: 143-144).

The Transfiguration, and particularly Lk 9:35, is of great christological value as Luke uses the Old Testament to define more precisely his christological understanding. The christological meaning of Lk 9:35 turns on a revealing Lukan alteration. Luke uses "my Chosen" to replace the baptismal "the Beloved." This saying is also in the third person instead of the baptism's second person so that the testimony is clearly made directly to the disciples. The baptism scene is intensified (Schürmann, 1969: 562) as the Transfiguration begins to point the reader's attention forward to what Jesus will accomplish, and who he really is. Moses' presence points typologically to the pattern Jesus steps into; a new exodus begins with Jesus (Bock, 1987: 15-116).

Most interpreters argue that the words, "This is my Son, my Chosen," or "This is my beloved Son," like those at the baptism, are quoted from Ps 2:7 and designate the Messiah. There is certainly a special relationship between this episode and the baptism-scene in the Lukan Gospel. The latter has inaugurated the Galilean ministry, with a heavenly voice identifying Jesus as "Son." Now that identification is repeated in close conjunction with the journey that is to be taken to the city of destiny (Lk 9:51). The assertion of verse 35 is precisely what is affirmed by Luke and questioned by others, as the ultimate honor status of Jesus (Malina-Rohrbaugh, 1992: 343).

It is clear that in the Lukan Gospel the heavenly identification of Jesus just before the *exodos* begins is clearly parallel to the heavenly identification at the baptism. But to give "Son" (or even "Son of God") in the Lukan Gospel exclusively the meaning of Messiah is simply not convincing. On the other hand, it is not necessary to load it with the explicit affirmation of divine sonship that it acquires in the patristic writings or in the definition of the Council of Nicaea (A.D. 325; Fitzmyer, 1981: 793-794).

It has also been argued that the words "beloved Son" are words spoken by another voice from heaven recorded in Gen 22:2,12 and 16 (Stegner, 1989: 17-20). The presence of "beloved Son" in Genesis 22, the absence of the word "beloved" in the Septuagint version of Ps 2:7, the inappropriateness of the term "beloved" as a description for the Messiah, and the uncertain date of the Targum that might account for the term—these four points support the thesis that the voice from the cloud is quoting Genesis 22 (Stegner, 1997: 116).

If those who believe that the climax of the narrative is found in the words of the voice out of the cloud, the central christological passage is found in the words: "This is my beloved Son [This is my Son, my Chosen]; listen to him." However, what freight of meaning did the title "beloved Son" convey for Jewish Christians? Fitzmyer seems to be on the right track in saying: "Here the Synoptic tradition has made use of a title that is pre-Pauline and has connotations other than messiah" (Fitzmyer, 1981: 793). It has previously been shown that the voice is quoting Genesis 22 rather than Ps 2:7. Accordingly, the passage is citing an Isaac/Jesus typology. As Isaac was the beloved son of Abraham, so Jesus is the beloved Son of God. Also, in Jewish Christian ears the word "beloved Son" possibly echoed Jesus' prayer life ("Abba") and the consciousness of an intimate relationship with God.

In addition, the title "beloved Son" is partially defined by the context in which it is set. In the Temptation narrative, the title "Son of God" depicted one whose obedience to God enabled him to overcome the devil and, consequently, demonstrate his sonship. Here, the Son of God is pictured in another role. In form, the narrative is an apocalyptic vision. In its apocalyptic re-interpretation, Sinai is the place where the future is revealed. In this scene the Father assigns to the Son the role of "spokesman for the endtime" by telling the audience to listen to him" (Kee, 1972: 123; Stegner, 1997: 117-118).

A secondary thrust of the words "listen to him" is probably polemical. In Deut 18:15 Moses speaks these same words to the people concerning the prophet like himself whom God will raise in the latter days. In this narrative the function of the prophet-like-Moses in the eschatological drama, together with the subordination of Moses to Jesus in the rest of the narrative, probably reflects theological purpose of early Jewish Christianity.

In addition to serving a christological function, a polemical function, and a validating function, this narrative probably also served an apologetic function. The century in which Jesus lived was a time of heightened eschatological expectations. In this narrative one aspect of the end itself is depicted. By gathering together and exploiting the common symbols/expectations of the endtime—Mount Sinai, Elijah, the prophet-like-Moses, the Feast of Booths—the story would appeal to the hopes not only of Jewish Christians, but also of the wider Jewish audience (Stegner, 1997: 118-119).

Verse 36:   When the voice had spoken, Jesus was found alone. And they kept silent and in those days told no one any of the things they had seen.

All three Synoptic Gospels state that at the end of the Transfiguration only Jesus was there with the disciples. So the scene ends with Jesus at the center of their attention. Luke's statement is concise and ends emphatically with the word "alone." Luke thus underlines the "aloneness" and—according to what has been said above—the uniqueness of Jesus even more than the Markan/Matthean parallels, since the indirect reference to Moses and Elijah (Mark/Matthew: "no one...any more" "no one except Jesus himself alone") is lacking. On the other hand, the references to the departure and the entrance of both men into the cloud prepared for the "aloneness" of Jesus.

Instead of the summons addressed to his companions, not to say anything to anyone about the event before the Son of Man's resurrection from the dead (Mk 9:9//Mt 17:9), Luke concludes the pericope by saying that they kept silent about it (on their own initiative) and did not say anything about it to anyone "in those days," that is, during Jesus' ministry (Fitzmyer, 1981: 803-804). For Luke it most probably meant that because the Transfiguration foreshadowed Easter, it would not be appropriate to tell about it until Easter (C.A. Evans, 1990: 154). If this "silence" expresses the lack of understanding of the secret of suffering, then it is in Luke even more radical than in Mark and Matthew. They do not need Jesus' summons! On the other hand, by the expression "in those days" it is characterized as a provisional silence respectively lack of understanding (Dillon, 1978: 40-41; Fitzmyer, 1981: 804). In due time, after the resurrection, they will remember, understand, and not feel heavy. In fact, they will tell it broadly as good news (Craddock, 1990: 135).

f. Healing of an Epileptic Boy (Lk 9:37-43a)

Lk 9:37-50 is a transition section between the introduction of the subject of death and the turn toward Jerusalem in Lk 9:51. Lk 9:37-50 previews that journey in that both Jesus' passion and his teaching the disciples govern all four brief episodes. The four subunits are really four vignettes in which the disciples are revealed as lacking: in power (Lk 9:37-43a), in understanding (Lk 9:43b-45), in humility (Lk 9:46-48), and in sympathy/"hospitality" (Lk 9:49-50). The first episode (Lk 9:37-43a) occurs the day after the Transfiguration (Craddock, 1990: 136).

The Cure of the Possessed Boy is an episode that Luke has probably borrowed from Mark. He presents this story in a much shorter form (seven and a half verses) than the latter (sixteen verses). The following are lacking in his version: First, the detailed introduction with the dispute (Mk 9:14: "arguing") between the disciples and the scribes, and Jesus' inquiry (Mk 9:14-16, "What are you arguing about with them?"). Second, Jesus' question addressed to the father and the immediately following conversation about faith as a requirement for healing (Mk 9:21-24). Third, the disciples' question concerning the ground of their incapability, and Jesus' answer concerning the necessity and power of prayer (Mk 9:28f.). This shows that Luke was not interested in the conversation part of this pericope. But the narrative parts of the pericope are also abbreviated. The four descriptions of the symptoms of possession (Mk 9:18,20,22a,26) are reduced to two (Lk 9:39 and 42a; Sterling, 1993: 472).

Moreover, the structure of the pericope in Luke is different from that in Mark. Among the many differences, the following are especially important. First, the request of the father is found in Mark approximately in the middle of the story (Mk 9:22f.), that means, after the description of the illness (Mk 9:18a) and the reference to the powerlessness of the disciples (Mk 9:18b). It sounds very fainthearted and doubting (Mk 9:22: "if you are able"; Mk 9:24: "help my unbelief"), as if the father is already discouraged by the powerlessness of the disciples. By his request he asks forthwith if Jesus can heal this case. Luke, however, presents the request at the beginning (Lk 9:38); the description of

the illness of the boy (Lk 9:39) and the information about
the futile attempt at exorcism on the part of the disciples
(Lk 9:40) follow the request and give the ground why the
father addresses himself with his request to Jesus. Second,
instead of the instruction in Mark/ Matthew—unique as a
conclusion of a Synoptic miracle story—Luke has a typical
miracle story (Held, 1963: 187-188). The structure and con-
ciseness allow the reader to recognize that Luke is mainly
concerned with the contrast between Jesus' power and the
powerlessness of the disciples (Schürmann, 1969: 567-568;
Marshall, 1978: 389-390).

Luke takes over the motif of the powerlessness of the
disciples (Lk 9:40) from the tradition. With the immediately following complaint about the "faithless generation"
(Lk 9:41) only the disciples can be meant (Tiede, 1988:
192). But Luke does not make them into an object of explicit reflection as Mark (Mk 9:22-24; verse 24: unbelief;
9:28f.) and Matthew (Mt 17:19-20: "Little faith"; "faith as
a grain of mustard seed"). The notice and the complaint
about the powerlessness of the disciples serves him to illustrate Jesus' power "contrapunctally" (Schürmann, 1969: 569;
Feldkamper, 1978: 144-146).

As the miracle story stands in the Lukan Gospel, it is
not a miracle of faith (despite the implication of verse 41).
It is a miracle of compassion, similar to that of the raising
of the widow's son at Nain (Lk 7:11-17; Fitzmyer, 1981:
807). Since the healing of the possessed boy is the last miracle
story before the Travel Narrative (Lk 9:51-19:44), the summary constitutes a retrospective view of the entire first part
of the Gospel. A similar—synthesizing and retrospective—
summary statement is found at the end of the Travel Narrative shortly before the entry into Jerusalem (Lk 19:37).

How comprehensive this retrospective is intended to be
can be derived from the concluding verse as well as from a
few redactional peculiarities of the pericope itself. In the
description of the reaction Luke reaches back to a vocabu-

lary by which he has described the first reactions to Jesus' ministry in the synagogues of Nazareth and Capernaum (Lk 4:22, "They were amazed"; Lk 4:32, "They were astounded"). But whereas there and then the people were astonished about his teaching (Lk 4:22, "at his words"; Lk 4:32, "at his teaching, because he spoke with authority"), one is here astonished about the grandeur of God that manifests itself in Jesus' deeds. Word and deed together (compare Lk 24:19; Acts1:1), that is, the powerfully active word is meant in this summary of Jesus' deeds that looks back at the first part of the Gospel. To this also refers the redactional statement, Lk 9:42, "he healed the boy," which reminds us of Lk 7:7, "But only speak the word, and let my servant be healed." Although Lk 9:37-43 deals with an exorcism, Luke nevertheless speaks of "healing" (Lk 9:42). The use of the terminology of healing for an exorcism is also found elsewhere in Luke-Acts (Lk 6:18; 7:21; 8:2; Acts 10:38). The last text is of special importance in our context, since it expresses very clearly that Jesus acts in the power of God.

Finally, in our pericope occurs a clear reference to the resurrection of the dead. Luke may have been instigated by Mk 9:26f. (compare to this Lk 9:9,10). There the healer is revealed as "the one who someday will actually raise the dead" (Schweizer, 1970: 189; Feldkämper, 1978: 147).

Verse 37:   On the next day,
              when they had come down from the mountain,
              a great crowd met him.

Although verse 37 begins a fresh narrative unit, its relation to the Transfiguration scene is marked emphatically by dual chronological and topographical markers. That previous episode may have been concluded, but it has some obvious connection with the present one. Only as this scene unfolds will it become clear how the Transfiguration scene places its stamp on this one. Only as this scene unfolds will it become clear how important it is that Jesus' followers

learn to integrate into their understanding of the one divine purpose these seemingly disparate elements: dishonor,
rejection, and even death, on the one hand, the exercise of
divine authority, elevated status before God, and service in
the salvific mission, on the other (Green, 1997: 387).

In contrast to Mk 9:14, which gives the impression that
this cure takes place on the same day as the Transfiguration (Stein, 1992: 288), Luke dates it to the following day.
This could further suggest that for him the Transfiguration
took place at night (Danker, 1988: 202; Nolland, 1993:
508,511; Bock, 1994: 880). But some think that the sketch
of the situation is too general to indicate whether Luke
thought the Transfiguration took place at night (C.F. Evans,
1990: 422). The incident takes place "when they had come
down from the mountain," that is, the unnamed mountain
of Lk 9:28. This detail has been borrowed from Mk 9:9a,
even though Luke omits the rest of the passage (verses 9c-
13). The silence of Mk 9:9b has already been used in verse
36. The "great crowd" must be thought of as awaiting his
arrival because the rest of his disciples were there. Luke
makes no mention of the scribes in the crowd (see Mk 9:14),
or of a debate (Fitzmyer, 1981: 807-808).

Verse 38:   Just then a man from the crowd shouted,
                "Teacher, I beg you to look at my son;
                he is my only child.

The "man from the crowd" "shouted" in desperation.
He reminds us of Jairus (Lk 8:40-42), while the fact that
this afflicted son is his "only child" reminds us of the widow
of Nain (Lk 7:11-17; C.A. Evans, 1990: 155). Jesus is referred to here as "teacher." Mark also used "teacher," but
Mt 17:15 has "Lord." The verb epiblepein, "to look at," "to
have regard for" (Bovon, 1991: 496), is predicated of God's
compassion in the Magnificat (Lk 1:48). Luke adds the words
"only child" to emphasize the father's plight (see Lk 7:12;
8:42; Danker, 1988: 203; Tiede, 1988: 191; Stein, 1992: 288).

The father is a classic peasant victim. Since his son could not marry, the father faced the end of the family line, the loss of its land, and hence its place in the village. All members of his extended family were thus imperiled (Malina-Rohrbaugh, 1992: 344).

Verse 39:   Suddenly a spirit seizes him,
             and all at once he shrieks.
             It convulses him until he foams at the mouth;
             it mauls him and will scarcely leave him.

Luke uses *pneuma*, "spirit," without any of the usual modifiers. The parallel in Mk 9:17 has "having a dumb (or mute) spirit." In Lk 9:42 the "spirit" will be referred to as a "demon" and as an "unclean spirit." To any modern reader who scrutinizes the details in the Markan description of the boy's condition, it is clear that the child is an epileptic (see RSV: "he is an epileptic"; Van der Loos, 1965: 401-405; Page, 1995: 160-166). "Epilepsy" is derived from the Greek *epilepsia*, "attack, seizure." For Luke's mention of the cries and of the extended nature of the attacks, compare from Mark's account the details of the exorcism (Mk 9:26; not used by Luke). For the emphasis on suddenness, note the attack as the boy is being brought to Jesus (Nolland, 1993: 509).

Today epilepsy is regarded as a chronic nervous disorder involving changes in consciousness and motion resulting from either an inborn effect that produces convulsions of greater or lesser severity or an organic lesion of the brain (by tumor, toxic agents, or injury; Fitzmyer, 1981: 808; Marshall, 1978: 391). The unique Lukan reference to the spirit's not easily (*mogis*) leaving him pictures situation's severity (Bock, 1994: 882).

Verse 40:   I begged your disciples to cast it out,
             but they could not."

Only slight changes to Mark's wording occur in this verse.

For another instance in the Gospel in which Jesus is recognized as having disciples in the ministry, see Lk 5:30. The thrust of "they could not" suggests that the disciples' inability is stressed in contrast to Jesus' own mighty power. It is the literary contrast of apprentices and the master thaumaturge. Recall Gehazi's inability apart from Elisha in 2 Kgs 4:31 (Fitzmyer, 1981: 809). The failure of the disciples will be a foil for Jesus' success (Nolland, 1993: 509,511).

Verse 41:   Jesus answered, "You faithless and perverse
                generation,
             how much longer must I be with you
             and bear with you?
             Bring your son here."

"You faithless and perverse generation" (see Deut 32:20) is the first of such explicit, pejorative descriptions of Jesus' contemporaries in Luke; see another in Lk 11:29. A less pointed reference has already been made to "this generation" in Lk 7:31. The exclamation is derived from Mk 9:19, but Luke has added to it the second adjective "perverse." According to some scholars the words refer to the disciples (Schürmann, 1969: 570; Ellis, 1966: 144; Tiede, 1988: 192), but according to others they are addressed to a larger audience, the father and the crowds (Plummer, 1901/1977: 255; Creed, 1957: 136). However, the "all" of verse 43b would seem to indicate that Luke was referring to both the disciples and the others. Jesus' words are enigmatic in that they generalize a criticism of "this generation" (Fitzmyer, 1981: 809; Stein, 1992: 289). Jesus' reply is not, as in Mk 9:19, directed specifically to the disciples but it is a general statement on the type of response his message encounters (Danker, 1988: 203).

Jesus' words "how long must I be with you and bear with you," that is, "how long must I put up with you," have been read as an allusion to Yahweh's putting up with Israel in Isa 46:4LXX (Schürmann, 1969: 570), but this is unlikely, because the context there is positive and here negative (Nolland, 1993: 510). This statement prepares for Lk 9:43b-45 (Fitzmyer, 1981: 809; Stein, 1992: 289). Indeed, Luke creates a close link between Lk 9:37-43a and 43b-45. Both the proleptic glory of the Transfiguration and the un-paralleled power over the demonic must give way to the necessary suffering fate of the Son of Man already (Nolland, 1993: 506,510). Readers of the Gospel know that Jesus' de-parture is already determined (C.F. Evans, 1990: 424).

Verse 42:   While he was coming,
              the demon dashed him to the ground in convulsions.
              But Jesus rebuked the unclean spirit,
              healed the boy, and gave him back to his father.

In the description that follows, Luke omits Mark's re-cital about the father's faith (Mk 9:21-24). Luke may have considered it irrelevant, for the problem is the disciples' inability to carry out the injunctions given them by Jesus not long before the Transfiguration (Lk 9:1-2). It was their task to proclaim the kingdom of God and to heal, yet on the mountain they wanted to prepare tents for Jesus, Moses, and Elijah. They wished to retain Elijah, but like Gehazi, the servant of Elijah's successor Elisha (see 2 Kgs 4:29-31), they could not carry out instructions (Danker, 1988: 203). With what is in Luke's Gospel a rare outburst of irritation and frustration (verse 41), Jesus does what the disciples have proven unable to do (Ringe, 1995: 143). After healing the boy, Jesus "gave him back to his father" (see Lk 7:15). The note of compassion comes strongly to the fore. Luke uses the language of healing for exorcisms, but this does not mean that he confuses illness and exorcism (Nolland, 1993: 510). Luke's omission of prayer is interesting, for he normally stresses it.

Verse 43a: And all were astounded at the greatness of God.

This verse records a typicaly Lukan reaction to the miracle, being present in neither Mark nor Matthew. The

reaction probably means no more than that the people recognized that what Jesus had done was done as God's agent.
Jesus is the one in whom God's salvific power is manifested;
or to put it more in the words of the episode itself, Jesus is
the one in whom the majesty of God is made manifest
(Grundmann, 1966: 266; Schürmann, 1969: 570; Danker,
1988: 203-204). "And all were astounded at the greatness
of God" (Lk 9:43a). This is again a distinctly Lukan comment, present in neither the Markan nor the Matthean
parallels (Fitzmyer, 1978: 147-148; 1981: 810).

In the request of the father (Lk 9:38) and the "chorus
conclusion" (Lk 9:43) Luke clearly expresses that it is God
himself who is at work in the powerful deeds of Jesus. The
request contains the rare verb *epiblepō*, "to look at" (in the
New Testament only here, in Lk 1:48 and Jas 2:3) which
in the Septuagint means God's care. According to Luke's
presentation the father requests from Jesus what one otherwise requests from God.

To this corresponds the redactional "chorus conclusion"
(Lk 9:43) with its comparison of God's greatness and Jesus'
work. In Jesus' deed God's grandeur is shown (compare Acts
2:11,22), God is at work in Jesus' powerful deeds, "for God
was with him" (Acts 10:38). So ultimately we are dealing
here with the epiphany of the power of God in Jesus (Held,
1963: 182).

But the concluding verse clarifies still something else:
Luke does not understand this miracle story as a single case,
but as "typical" for Jesus' powerful deeds (Schürmann, 1969:
568). This is indicated by the generalization and intensifi-
cation that are characteristic for summaries: "And *all* were
astounded at the greatness of God ... while everyone was
amazed at all that he was doing" (Lk 9:38a and 38b;
Feldkämper, 1978: 146).

Luke's omission of Mk 9:28-29 at the end of the story
softens the criticism of the disciples (who fail to comprehend that this sort of demon is cast out only by prayer;
Fitzmyer, 1981: 810).

g. The Second Prediction of the Passion (Lk 9:43b-45)

The disciples lack not only the power to control the demon but also comprehension of the nature of this Jesus whom they are following: They just don't get it. How could someone who can command demons fall prey to human power? (Ringe, 1995: 143).

The first and second predictions of the Passion serve as framework for the account of the Transfiguration and the accompanying recital of exorcism (Danker, 1988: 204). The Second Announcement of the Passion is another pre-Lukan identification of Jesus, again most likely derived from Mark (Mk 9:30-32) in its substance. There is no certain evidence of the influence of a variant tradition (Schürmann, 1969: 574; Ernst, 1977: 309; Schneider, 1977: 220). It is undoubtedly retained by Luke as part of the triple announcement in the gospel tradition. It also supplies a further answer to Herod's question: He is the Son of Man who is to be handed over to his enemies. Noteworthy is the Lukan modification of this episode, which eliminates the reference to Galilee (Mk 9:30; Conzelmann, 1960: 60), emphasizes the incomprehension of the disciples, and strips away the mention of Jesus' death and resurrection. Coming after the impression that was made by the Cure of the Possessed Boy, it obviously serves again as an answer corrective to the crowd's astonishment. Contrast also the "handing over" of Jesus here with the prayer on the cross (Lk 23:46; Fitzmyer, 1978: 148).

The disciples are unable to understand Jesus' prophecy of his own death in Lk 9:43b-44 (the omission of reference to the resurrection serves to emphasize Jesus' death) and the reader is told that the meaning of Jesus' words "was concealed from them, so that they could not perceive it" (Lk 9:45). Ironically, the disciples were filled with such fear that they could not even ask Jesus what he meant. This aside begins the process of putting distance between the narrator and the reader, on the one hand, and the disciples, on the other. The reader is able to grasp the significance of Jesus' words, perhaps because the reader has some indication of the way in which the story is to end. The disciples, however, are completely in the dark; that they have misunderstood the words of Jesus is made abundantly clear by their argument over who is to be the greatest in the coming kingdom (Lk 9:46). The distance will grow greater until the crucifixion, when the reader will stand at the foot of the cross with the women and the centurion, while the disciples have drawn off to a safe distance from the scene. The aside also reinforces the sense of superiority that the narrator and the reader feel over the disciples by reminding the reader that the disciples were unable to understand what the reader has understood (Sheeley, 1992: 109-110).

Verses 43b-44:   (43b) While everyone was amazed at all that
                          he was doing,
                          he said to his disciples,
                    (44) "Let these words sink into your ears:
                          The Son of Man is going to be betrayed
                          into human hands."

Luke's introduction is unique, for he omits any geographical note like that found in Mk 9:30//Mt 17:22 (Bock, 1994: 887). The Second Prediction of the Passion follows the Transfiguration where Jesus' messianic status was affirmed by Peter. The glorious appearance of Jesus confirms that confession along with the voice from heaven. Jesus, God's Messiah, is also the suffering Son of Man. In the immediately previous context all the people are amazed and marvelling at the exorcism Jesus accomplishes where his disciples had failed. By joining the passion prediction to the crowds' marvelling—a contrast absent from Mk 9:31 and
Mt 17:22 (Marshall, 1978: 392; C.A. Evans, 1990: 157)—the narrator highlights the people's inadequate understanding of Jesus. In view of Luke's economy of statement elsewhere, his repetition of the astonishment of the crowd is

noteworthy (Danker, 1988: 204). With the transition he forges in verse 43b, Luke maximizes the contrast between the all-powerful exorcist of Lk 9:37-43a and the soon to be trapped Son of Man of verses 43b-45. The amazement of all is a statement about the sheer impressiveness of Jesus' deeds, not a statement about any particular kind of personal response from the crowds (Nolland, 1993: 512,513).

It is not coincidental that the two realities concerning the person and ministry of Jesus—his exalted status and his impending dishonor—are set side by side. Rather, there is a studied transition from one to the other, so that Jesus' words of doom to his disciples are spoken "while everyone was amazed." Together, then, verses 43-44 again demonstrate the necessity of the integration in the disciples' conceptualization of Jesus' messianic identity, of his elevated status vis-à-vis the divine purpose, and his rejection at the hands of humans. But it is this integration, or collocation of terms, that the discples do not grasp (Green, 1997: 390).

Jesus' command to the disciples introducing the passion prediction to "let these words sink into your ears" (that is, "listen carefully") draws the reader to the importance of the announcement and highlights the disciples' subsequent failure to understand its meaning (Marshall, 1978: 393). The second prediction is briefer than the first, omitting any reference to resurrection. The prediction focuses on the impending ("is going to be") betrayal of the Son of Man into human hands (Tiede, 1988: 192). Again "Son of Man" is the subject of the passion as in Lk 9:22, and the line ties the two predictions together. But this saying focuses on *paradidosthai*, "to be handed over." Luke commonly uses *paradidōmi* in the context of persecution. In the Gospel, of the seventeen occurrences, eleven refer to the persecution of Jesus. Two other times the reference is to the persecution of disciples. In Acts the same word will be frequently used in the context of the persecution of the witnesses (seven out of thirteen times). Whereas in other texts Luke supplies the subject of the "handing over," in Lk 9:44; 18:32 and 24:7 no mention is made of who will hand Jesus over. They probably are "theological" passives with God being the implied subject. The implication then is that Jesus' being given over to judgment and death is accomplished in God's plan and ultimately by God himself, though through human agency (cf. Acts 2:22-23; 4:27-28). Even though Jesus' fate was completely within the divine plan, the disciples themselves did not understand Jesus' saying. This is underscored by the threefold repetition in Lk 9:45 (Cunningham, 1997: 88-90).

Verse 45:   But they did not understand this saying;
              its meaning was concealed from them,
              so that they could not perceive it.
              And they were afraid to ask him about this saying.

The aside in Lk 9:45 comments on the disciples' inability to understand the meaning of Jesus' passion prediction. While its more important function is that of commenting on the story in such a way as to prepare the reader for the reactions of the disciples to follow, it is also true that the narrator has allowed the reader to glimpse the inner thoughts and reactions of the disciples. The reader learns not only that the disciples have misunderstood Jesus but that they recognized their confusion and were too afraid to try to clear it up. As with the inside view in Lk 7:29-30 the importance of this aside transcends the information it contains to impinge upon the relationship between narrator and reader (Sheeley, 1992: 115).

The Lukan curtailment of the announcement ("this saying") brings it about that the disciples' incomprehension focuses on the necessity of Jesus to suffer rather than on his resurrection (Fitzmyer, 1981: 814).

If "so that" should be read as indicating purpose, then it means that it was God's will that the disciples not understand Jesus' passion announcement at this time. On the other hand, if "so that" should be read as indicating result, then the disciples did not grasp Jesus' meaning simply because they were slow to catch on. The latter interpretation is favored by the fact that the disciples were afraid to ask what Jesus meant (Stein, 1992: 291). The disciples' fear is a mark of partial understanding: whatever it is that Jesus is saying, it disturbs acutely their sense of how things should be (Nolland, 1993: 514).

h. *Dispute about Greatness* (Lk 9:46-48)

The depth of the disciples' confusion becomes even clearer when, in the wake of their failure, they quarrel over who is the greatest. A squabble over honor status would be typical within any ancient Mediterranean grouping (Malina-Rohrbaugh, 1992: 344). It is a debate that recurs in the context of the Last Supper (Lk 22:24) apparently representing a problem Luke encounters in many guises in the Church for which he writes (Ringe, 1995: 143-144). Given that Lk 9:46-48 follows a passage about the disciples' misunderstanding, the idea may be that rivalry hinders the disciples from the understanding of God's plan (Fitzmyer, 1981: 815; Tannehill, 1986: 254-255; Bock, 1994: 891).

The fear of verse 45 is not the awe or astonishment expected in a theophanic scene, but constitutes at least skepticism (see Lk 24:38) and more probably, in this context, a denial of faith. The debilitating presence of such fear recasts the disciples not as helpers of the divine mission, but as opponents. This adversarial role is furthered now by Luke's dual reference to the disciples' considerations, their inner thoughts, using language normally, though not exclusively, associated with Jesus' opponents. The content of their deliberations betrays them even further. Even though persons in any gathering in Greco-Roman antiquity would naturally be concerned with questions of relative status (and behavior appropriate to one's place with regard to the station of others), Jesus' message has been oriented against such maneuvering and positioning. As he reveals their inner thoughts with one another (see Lk 2:35), he displays their marked failure to embody in their relations with one another the central tenets of his message (Green, 1997: 391).

The Dispute of the Disciples about Greatness (Lk 9:46-48) gives no explicit answer to the question of Herod. It is retained from the Markan source (Mk 9:33-37) and abbreviated; it at most identifies Jesus as "someone sent," indicating that he is to be welcomed with the openness of a child (Leaney, 1954-1955: 91-92). The use of traditional material here and the farther one gets from the question of Herod both make it more difficult to see the episode as a direct answer to it (Fitzmyer, 1978: 148).

In combining the two pronouncements of Mk 9:35,37 into one, Luke has reversed their order, situating "welcome this child in my name" first and "the least of all is the greatest" second (Marshall, 1978: 395). This places emphasis on the second saying and the theme of lowliness. It also produces a more consistent and uniform text (Kodell, 1987: 419).

Verses 46-48: (46) An argument arose among them
                        as to which one of them was the greatest.
                  (47) But Jesus, aware of their inner thoughts.
                        took a little child and put it by his side,
                  (48) and said to them,
                        "Whoever welcomes this child in my name
                              welcomes me,
                        and whoever welcomes me
                        welcomes the one who sent me;
                        for the least among all of you is the greatest."

Luke omits the change of location (Mk 9:33) in order to emphasize the jarring contrast between the second passion prediction and the attitude of the disciples in their dispute over greatness (Lk 9:44). Luke has explicitly formulated the question at issue. Mk 9:33 only hints at it and notes the disciples' embarrassed silence, when Jesus questions them about their discussion on the road to Capernaum. The term *dialogismos*, "argument," may be chosen because each disciple thinks perhaps he is the greatest (Plummer, 1901/1977: 257; Bock, 1994: 894). As formulated in Lk 9:46, it would refer to greatness within the group of disciples (Stein, 1992: 293). Mt 18:1 introduces Matthew's own nuance with "in the kingdom of heaven" (Fitzmyer, 1981: 817). Luke's version of the saying of Jesus (verse 48) stresses receptivity and humility. The idea of service, though implied in openness, is not explicitly included here—perhaps because it is stressed in the supper dispute about greatness (Lk 22:24-30), but also because the themes of lowliness and receptivity are central here.

Two Lukan touches in verse 47 are the word *epilabomenos* (twelve times in Luke-Acts; six in the rest of the New Testament) and the omission of the embrace (Fitzmyer, 1981: 816). For Mark's "one such child" (Mk 9:37), Luke has "this child." The saying is concerned not with an attitude toward children as such, but with the present attitude of the disciples toward the child before them: which of them is ready to receive this child (= Jesus)? (Marshall, 1978: 396).

Verse 48 is a good example of step parallelism in which the first thought (child—me) is raised a step higher in the second thought (me—him who sent me). Even as a child is received as a representative of Jesus, so Jesus is received as a representative of God (see Lk 10:16. There is a strong emphasis here that Jesus' mission originated with God (Stein, 1992: 293). The humility taught is by means of the practice of hospitality (Craddock, 1990: 137). The hospitality believers receive reveals the attitude people have toward Jesus (see Acts 16:33-34; Stein, 1992: 293). But this is not merely a moral instruction advising Christians to be humble. It is a revelation of where and how the reign of God is present in all of its greatness (Tiede, 1988: 194).

Luke does not comment immediately, as in Mk 9:35b; rather, his first reaction is symbolic. He associates with himself the smallest and weakest member of human society, giving him/her a place of honor beside himself. The phrase "in my/your name" is the catchword linking the saying to the following episode of the exorcist (Stein, 1992: 292).

i. The Strange Exorcist (Lk 9:49-50)

Matthew has omitted the exorcist story, connecting the saying on receiving a child (Mt 18:5; Mk 9:37) directly to the saying on scandal derived from Q (Mt 18:6-7; Lk 17:1-2). Instead of "in the name of," Matthew uses "child" as a catchword to connect with "one of these little ones" (Mt 18:6). Luke has done just the opposite, retaining the exorcist story because of its suitability to his purposes and postponing the Q material until a later time (Lk 17:1-2; Kodell, 1987: 421). Verses 49-50 bring to an end the section that Luke has devoted to preparing for the journey to Jerusalem (Nolland, 1993: 525).

Like the previous episode, the Saying about the Strange Exorcist (Lk 9:49-50) is retained because of the Markan source (Mk 9:38-41), although Luke does adapt it. The one title that it contains, "Master" (*epistatēs*), used of Jesus by John (son of Zebedee), replaces the Markan counterpart, "Teacher" (*didaskalos*), a title that Luke does not eschew for Jesus (see Lk 9:38), but which he has altered for one that he uses elsewhere and that is used by him alone (Lk 5:5; 8:24,45; 9:33; 17:3). Though it is not a significant title for New Testament Christology nor a real answer to Luke's identification of Jesus, it does imply some authority that he has. Falling into the line-up of other identifications, it serves in its own small way as an identification of him and an answer to Herod's question (Fitzmyer, 1978: 148-149).

Verse 49:   John answered,
            "Master, we saw someone casting out demons in
                your name,
            and we tried to stop him, because he does not
                follow with us."

The level of incomprehension of the disciples is exemplified by one of their number, John. Why John is the spokesman here, and not Peter, is hard to say. John's condemnatory attitude is manifest again in Lk 9:54 (together with James; C.F. Evans, 1990: 429; Nolland, 1993: 524). He, and the other disciples, denied an "outsider" permission to work in Jesus' name. That is, they had engaged in boundary-making on the basis of conventional notions of perceived honor. He did not belong to the community around Jesus, so his behavior was disallowed. It is a question of union rights. Did others, besides the apostles, have the privilege of exorcising? (Danker, 1988: 206). The irony is that this unnamed exorcist had been working in the name of Jesus—just as Jesus' disciples had been instructed to do (verse 48; see verse 24)—and he had been successful in the very arena of salvific activity in which the disciples had just been found wanting (verse 40). The implication here is indeed that this non-disciple succeeded in expelling demons in Jesus' name (Nolland, 1993: 525). The failure of the disciples is represented at its most basic level in this: Jesus had implored the disciples to honor those of no status at all (Lk 9:46-48), but they have refused partnership with one who did not share the status they assumed for themselves (Green, 1997: 392). To "stop" (*kōluō*) is used here as an antonym of to "welcome" (*dechomai*; Koenig, 1985: 31). The imperfect tense *ekōluomen* describes the disciples' efforts and may suggest that they repeatedly tried to get this man to stop (Arndt, 1956: 270; Bock, 1994: 897).

Verse 50:   But Jesus said to him,
            "Do not stop him; for whoever is not against you is
                for you."

The pronouncement in verse 50 is clear; it is a contradiction of John's point of view. Though Jesus may have given to the Twelve "power and authority over all demons" (Lk 9:1), he does not restrict the use of his powerful name only to them (and that goes also for their "successors"!). Their ministry is not a copyrighted monopoly (Bock, 1996: 278).

The Twelve, who should have celebrated the fact that the influence of Jesus was spreading, especially in view of their own recent failure (Lk 9:40), manifest a spirit of exclusivism. Apparently that spirit entered the Church quite early and it has certainly stayed late. Where leaders compete, it follows that they will also seek to exercise control over the membership of the communities they lead (Craddock, 1990: 137-138). Coming on the heels of Lk 9:46-48, with its emphasis on the reception of the "little child" with esteem, this episode explicitly extends that attitude even to those who are outside the group of disciples. Jesus' answer to John's implied question is given in the form of a proverb. It sounds like a contradiction of the "Q" saying, "Whoever is not with me is against me" (Lk 11:23a/Mt 12:30a). But the saying in Lk 11:23 is a warning to the individual Christian disciple against neutrality and is meant as a test of *oneself*, whereas the form used here is a norm for the attitude of disciples toward *others* who are outsiders (Fitzmyer, 1981: 819-820; Creed, 1957: 139; Danker, 1988: 206; Bock, 1994: 898).

BIBLIOGRAPHY

(The books and articles presented in the bibliographies of Volume 1 and Volume 2-a are not repeated here.)

Annen, Franz. *Heil für die Heiden. Zur Bedeutung und Geschichte der Tradition vom besessenen Gerasener (Mk 5,1-20 parr.).* Frankfurt-am-Main: Verlag Jozef Knecht, 1976.

Arlandson, James Malcolm. *Women, Class, and Society in Early Christianity: Models from Luke-Acts.* Peabody: Hendrickson, 1997.

Arndt, W. F. *The Gospel According to St. Luke.* St. Louis: Concordia Publishing House, 1956.

Bachmann, Michael. "Johannes der Taüfer bei Lukas: Nachzügler oder Vorlaufer?" in Haubeck, Wilfrid and Michael Bachmann. eds. *Wort in der Zeit. Festgabe für Karl Heinrich Rengstorf zum 75. Geburtstag.* Leiden: E.J. Brill, 1980. 123-155.

Barrett, Charles. ed. *The New Testament Background: Selected Documents.* New York: Harper, 1961.

Bauckham, Richard. *Jude and the Relatives of Jesus in the Early Church.* Edinburgh: T. & T. Clark, 1990.

_____. "The Brothers and Sisters of Jesus: An Epiphanian Response to John P. Meier," *Catholic Biblical Quarterly* 56 (1994), 686-700.

Beck, Norman A. *Anti-Roman Cryptograms in the New Testament: Symbolic Messages of Hope and Liberation.* New York: Peter Lang, 1997.

309

Bock, Darrell L. "Proclamation from Prophecy and Pattern: Luke's Use of the Old Testament for Christology and Mission," in Evans, Craig A. and Werner Stegner, eds. *The Gospels and the Scriptures of Israel*. Sheffield: Sheffield Academic Press, 1994b.

_____. *Luke*. The NIV Application Commentary. Grand Rapids: Zondervan, 1996.

Bourguignon, Erika. *Possession*. San Franciso: Chandler and Sharp, 1976.

Braumann, Georg. "Die Schuldner und die Sünderin: Luk. VII.36-50," *New Testament Studies* 10 (1964), 487-493.

Brawley, Robert L. *Centering on God: Method and Message in Luke-Acts*. Louisville, KY: Westminster/John Knox Press, 1990.

Brock, Ann Graham. "The Significance of *phileō* and *philos* in the Tradition of Jesus' Sayings and in the Early Christian Communities," *Harvard Theological Review* 90 (1997), 393-409.

Brodie, Tom L. "Towards Unravelling Luke's Use of the Old Testament: Luke 7:11-17 as an Imitatio of 1 Kings 17.17-24," *New Testament Studies* 32 (1986), 247-267.

_____. "Not Q but Elijah: The Saving of the Centurion's Servant (Luke 7:1-10) as an Internalization of the Saving of the Widow and Her Child (1 Kgs 17:1-16)," *Irish Biblical Studies* 14 (1992), 54-71.

Brown, John P. "Techniques of Imperial Control: The Background of the Gospel Event," in Gottwald, Norman. ed. *The Bible and Liberation: Political and Social Hermeneutics*. San Francisco: Community for Religious Research and Education, 1976. 73-83.

Büchele, Anton. *Der Tod Jesu im Lukasevangelium. Eine redaktionsgeschichtliche Untersuchung zu Lk 23*. Frankfurt am Main: Verlag Josef Knecht, 1978.

Cameron, Ron. "'What Have You Come Out To See?' Characterization of John and Jesus in the Gospels," *Semeia* 49 (1990), 35-69.

Catchpole, David R. "The Centurion's Faith and Its Function in Q," in Van Segbroeck et alii. eds. *The Four Gospels 1992 - Festschrift Frans Neirynck.* Louvain: Leuven University Press, 1992. 517-540.

Chilton, Bruce D. "The Transfiguration: Dominical Assurance and Apostolic Vision," *New Testament Studies* 27 (1980-1981), 115-124.

Claudel, Gérard. *La Confession de Pierre. Trajectoire d'une péricope évangélique.* Etudes Bibliques. Paris: Gabalda, 1988.

Cotter, Wendy J. "The Children in the Market-Place," *Novum Testamentum* 24 (1987), 289-304.

_____. "Children Sitting in the Agora: Q (Luke) 7:31-35," *Forum* 5 (1989), 63-82.

_____. "'Yes, I Tell You, and More Than a Prophet': The Function of John in Q," in Kloppenborg, John S. ed. *Conflict and Invention: Literary, Rhetorical, and Social Studies on the Sayings Gospel Q.* Valley Forge, PA: Trinity Press International, 1995. 135-150.

Cunningham, Scott. *"Through Many Tribulations": The Theology of Persecution in Luke-Acts.* Sheffield: Sheffield Academic Press, 1997.

Danker, Frederick W. *Benefactor: Epigraphic Study of a Graeco-Roman Semantic Field.* St. Louis: Clayton Publishing House, 1982.

Darr, John A. "'Watch How You Listen': Jesus and the Rhetoric of Perception in Luke-Acts," in McKnight, Edgar V. and Elizabeth Struthers Malbon. eds. *The New Literary Criticism and the New Testament.* Valley Forge, PA: Trinity Press International, 1994. 87-107.

Dauer, Anton. *Johannes und Lukas: Untersuchungen zu den johanneisch-lukanischen Parallelperikopen Joh 4:46-54/Lk 7:1-10—Joh 12:1-8/Lk 7:36-50,10:38-42.* Wurzburg: Echter Verlag, 1984.

Dautzenberg, G. *Sein Leben bewahren: Psyche in den Herrenworten der Evangelien.* Munich: Küsel-Verlag, 1966.

Davies, Stevan L. *The Revolt of the Widows: The Social World of the Apocryphal Acts*. London: Feffer & Simons, 1980.

Delobel, Joel. "L'onction par la pécheresse: La composition littéraire de Luc 7,36-50," *Ephemerides Theologicae Lovanienses* 42 (1966), 415-475.

_____. "Encore la pécheresse. Quelques réflexions critiques," *Ephemerides Theologicae Lovanienses* 45 (1969), 180-183.

de Meeus, Xavier. "Composition de Lc. XIV et genre symposiaque," *Ephemerides Theologicae Lovanienses* 37 (1961), 847-870.

Denova, Rebecca I. *The Things Accomplished Among Us. Prophetic Tradition in the Structural Pattern of Luke-Acts*. Sheffield: Sheffield Academic Press, 1997.

Derrett, J. Duncan M. "The Anointing at Bethany and the Story of Zacchaeus," in *Law in the New Testament*. London: Darton, 1970.

_____. *New Resolutions to Old Conundrums: A Fresh Insight into Luke's Gospel*. Shipton-on-Stour: Peter I. Drinkwater, 1986.

Dibelius, Martin. *From Tradition to Gospel*. New York: Charles Scribner's Sons, 1971.

Dillon, Richard J. *From Eye-Witnesses to Ministers of the Word*. Analecta Biblica 82. Rome: Biblical Institute Press, 1978.

Drury, John. "The Sower, the Vineyard and the Place of Allegory in the Interpretation of Mark's Parables," *Journal of Theological Studies* new series 24 (1973), 367-379.

Du Plessis, I.J. "Contextual Aid for an Identity Crisis: An Attempt to Interpret Luke 7:35," in Petzer, J.H. and P.J. Hartin, eds. *A South African Perspective on the New Testament*. Festschrift Bruce M. Metzger. Leiden: Brill, 1986. 112-127.

Dupont, Jacques. "Le Phariséen et la pécheresse (Lc 7,36-50)," *Communautés et Liturgies* 4 (1980), 260-268.

_____. "La lampe sur le lampadaire dans l'evangile de Luc (Lc 8,16; 11,33)," in *Etudes sur les Evangiles synoptiques*. Louvain: Leuven University Press, 1985. 1031-1048.

Ehrman, Bart D. and Mark A. Plunkett. "The Angel and the Agony: The Textual Problem of Luke 22:34-44," *Catholic Biblical Quarterly* 45 (1983), 401-416.

Evans, Craig A. *To See and not Perceive: Isaiah 6:9-10 in Early Jewish and Christian Interpretation*. Sheffield: Academic Press, 1993.

Evans, Craig A. and J.A. Sanders. *Luke and Scripture: The Function of Sacred Tradition in Luke-Acts*. Minneapolis: Fortress Press, 1993.

Fanon, Frantz. *The Wretched of the Earth*. New York: Ballantine, 1963.

Feuillet, André. "Les perspectives propres á chaque évangeliste dans les récits de la Transfiguration," *Biblica* 39 (1958), 281-301.

_____. "'L'exode' de Jesus et le déroulement du mystère rédempteur d'apres S. Luc et S. Jean," *Revue Thomiste* 77 (1977), 181-206.

Fischbach, Stephanie M. *Totenerweckungen: Zur Geschichte einer Gattung*. Forschung zur Bibel. Wurzburg: Echter Verlag, 1992.

Fitzmyer, Joseph A. "The Composition of Luke, Chapter 9," in Talbert, Charles H. ed. *Perspectives on Luke-Acts*. Danville, VA: Association of Baptist Professors of Religion, 1978. 139-152.

Fletcher-Louis, Crispin H.T. *Luke-Acts: Angels, Christology and Soteriology*. WUNT 2. Series, 94. Tübingen: Mohr Siebeck,1997.

Fonrobert, Charlotte. "The Woman with a Blood-Flow (Mark 5:24-34) Revisited: Menstrual Laws and Jewish Culture in Christian Feminist Hermeneutics," in Evans, Craig A. and James A. Sanders, eds. *Early Christian Interpretation of the Scriptures of Israel: Investigations and Proposals*. Sheffield: Sheffield Academic Press, 1997. 121-140.

Friedrich, Gerhard. "*prophētēs*," in Friedrich, Gerhard, ed. *Theological Dictionary of the New Testament*. Volume VI. Grand Rapids: Eerdmans, 1968.

Friedrichsen, T.A. "Luke 9:22—A Matthean Foreign Body?" *Ephemerides Theologicae Lovanienses* 72 (1996), 398-407.

Fuchs, Albert. "Schrittweises Wachstum: Zur Entwicklung der Perikope Mk 5:21-43 par Mt 9:18-26 par Lk 8:40-56," *Studien zum Neuen Testament und seiner Umwelt* 17 (1992), 5-53.

Gagnon, Robert A.J. "Statistical Analysis and the Case of the Double Delegation in Lk 7:3-7a," *Catholic Biblical Quarterly* 55 (1993), 709-731.

_____. "Luke's Motives for Redaction in the Account of the Double Delegation in Luke 7:1-10," *Novum Testamentum* 36 (1994), 122-145.

Garrett, Susan R. "Exodus from Bondage: Luke 9:31 and Acts 12:1-24," *Catholic Biblical Quarterly* 52 (1990), 656-680.

_____. "'Lest the Light in You be Darkness': Luke 11:33-36 and the Question of Commitment," *Journal of Biblical Literature* 110 (1991), 934-105.

Genest, Olivette. "De la fille à la femme à la fille (Luc 8,40-56)," in Legaré, Clément, et al., eds. *De Jésus et des femmes. Lectures sémiotiques*. Recherches N.S. 14. Paris/Montreal: Editions du Cerf/Editions Bellarmin, 1987. 105-120.

Gerhardsson, Birger. "The Parable of the Sower and Its Interpretation," *New Testament Studies* 14 (1967-1968), 165-193.

Gils, Félix. *Jésus prophéte d'après les évangiles synoptiques*. Louvain: Leuven University Press, 1957.

Glöckner, Richard. *Neutestamentliche Wundergeschichten*. Walberberger Studien. Mainz: Matthias-Grünewald-Verlag, 1983.

Goodacre, Mark. "Fatigue in the Synoptics," *New Testament Studies* 44 (1998), 45-58.

Grassi, Joseph A. "You Yourselves Give Them to Eat": An Easily Forgotten Command of Jesus (Mk 6:37; Mt 14:16; Lk 9:13)," *The Bible Today* n. 97 (October 1978), 1704-1709.

Green, Joel B. *The Gospel of Luke.* The New International Commentary on the New Testament. Grand Rapids: Eerdmans, 1997.

Guelich, Robert. *Mark 1:1-8:28.* Word Biblical Commentary, 34A. Dallas: Word Books, 1989.

Guillaume, Jean-Marie. *Luc interprète des anciennes traditions sur la Résurrection de Jésus.* Etudes Bibliques. Paris: J. Gabalda, 1979.

Hahn, Ferdinand. *Mission in the New Testament.* London: SCM Press, 1965.

Harris, Murray J. "'The Dead Are Restored to Life': Miracles of Revivification in the Gospels," in Wenham, David and Craig Blomberg, eds. *Gospel Perspectives.* Volume 6: *The Miracles of Jesus.* Sheffield: JSOT Press, 1986. 295-326.

Harris, Xavier. "Ministering Women in the Gospels: Jesus' Female Disciples," *The Bible Today* 29 (1991), 109-112.

Hartin, Patrick J. "'Yet Wisdom Is Justified by Her Children' (Q 7:35): A Rhetorical and Compositional Analysis of Divine Sophia in Q," in Kloppenborg, John S. ed. *Conflict and Invention: Literary, Rhetorical, and Social Studies on the Sayings Gospel Q.* Valley Forge, PA: Trinity Press International, 1995. 151-164.

Hendrickx, Herman. "Peter and the Rock," in Villegas, Socrates B. ed. *The Way of the Shepherd: Studies in Theology Offered to His Eminence Cardinal L. Sin.* Makati, MM: Salesiana Publishers, 1992. 61-83.

Hennecke, Edgar, Wilhelm Schneemelcher, and R. McL. Wilson. *New Testament Apocrypha 2.* Philadelphia: Westminster Press, 1964.

Hofius, Otfried. "Fusswasschung als Erweis der Liebe: Sprachliche und sachliche Anmerkungen zu Lk 7,44b," *Zeitschrift für die neutestamentliche Wissenschaft* 81 (1990), 171-177.

Hoffmann, Paul. *Studien zur Theologie der Logienquelle.* Neutestamentliche Abhandlungen. Neue Folfge 8. Münster: Aschendorff, 1982.

Hofrichter, Peter Leander. *Modell und Vorlage der Synoptiker: Das vorredaktionelle "Johannesevangelium."* Hildesheim - Zurich - New York: Georg Olms Verlag, 1997.

Hollenbach, Paul W. "Jesus, Demoniacs, and Public Authorities: A Socio-Historical Study," *Journal of the American Academy of Religion* 49 (1981), 567-588.

Imbach, Josef. "Die Ture nicht zuschlagen," *Geist und Leben* 64 (1991), 7-16.

Jonsson, Jacob. *Humor and Irony in the New Testament.* Leiden: E.J. Brill, 1985.

Judge, Peter J. "Luke 7:1-10: Sources and Redaction," in Neirynck, Frans. ed. *L'Evangile de Luc - The Gospel of Luke.* Louvain: Leuven University Press, 1989. 473-490.

Juel, Donald. *Luke-Acts: The Promise of History.* Atlanta: John Knox Press, 1983.

Kariamadam, Paul. "Transfiguration and Jesus' Ascended Glory (An Explanation of Luke 9:28-36)," *Bible Bhashyam* 23 (1997), 1-13.

Karris, Robert J. *Invitation to Luke.* A Commentary on the Gospel of Luke. Image Books. Garden City, New York: Doubleday, 1977.

_____. *Luke, Artist and Theologian.* New York: Paulist Press, 1985.

Kee, Howard C. "The Transfiguration in Mark: Epiphany or Apocalyptic Vision?," in Reumann, John. ed. *Understanding the Sacred Text.* Valley Forge, PA: Judson Press, 1972. 135-152.

_____. *Community of the New Age: Studies in Mark's Gospel.* Philadelphia: Westminster Press, 1972.

_____. "Jesus: A Glutton and a Drunkard," *New Testament Studies* 42 (1996), 374-393.

Kellenbach, K. von. *Anti-Judaism in Feminist Religious Writings.* Atlanta: Scholars Press, 1994.

Kertelge, Karl. *Die Wunder Jesu im Markusevangelium: Eine redaktionsgeschichtliche Untersuchung.* Munich: Kosel-Verlag, 1970.

_____. *Das Markusevangelium.* Die Neue Echter Bibel. Wurzburg: Echter Verlag, 1994.

Khiok-Khng, Yeo. "The Mother and Brothers of Jesus (Lk 8:19-21; Mk 3:31-35; Mt 12:46-50)," *Asia Journal of Theology* 6 (1992), 311-317.

Kilgallen, John J. "John the Baptist, the Sinful Woman, and the Pharisee," *Journal of Biblical Literature* 94 (1985), 675-679.

_____. "A Proposal for Interpreting Luke 7:36-50," *Biblica* 72 (1991), 305-330.

_____. "Forgiveness of Sins (Luke 7:36-50)," *Novum Testamentum* 40 (1998), 105-116.

Kirk, Alan. "Some Compositional Conventions of Hellenistic Wisdom Texts and the Juxtaposition of 4:1-13; 6:20b-49; and 7:1-10 in Q," *Journal of Biblical Literature* 116 (1997), 235-257.

Klauck, Hans-Josef. *Allegorie und Allegorese in synoptischen Gleichnistexten.* Münster: Aschendorff, 1978.

Klein, Hans. *Barmherzigkeit gegenuber den Elenden und Geächteten: Studien zur Botschaft des lukanische Sonderguts.* Neukirchen-Vluyn: Neukirchener Verlag, 1987.

Kluge, Jürgen. "'Die Auferstehung des Jünglings zu Nain' oder 'Der Auferstehungsglaube und die Frage nach Leben und Tod,'" in Kakuschke, Reimar. ed. *Auferstehung - Tod und Leben. Analysen und Projekte zum Religionsunderricht.* Göttingen: Vandenhoeck & Ruprecht, 1978. 202-220.

Knowles, Michael P. "Abram and the Birds in Jubilees: A Subtext for the Parable of the Sower?" *New Testament Studies* 41 (1995), 145-151.

Kodell, Jerome. "Luke and the Children: The Beginning and End of the Great Interpolation (Luke 9:46-54; 18:9-23)," *Catholic Biblical Quarterly* 49 (1987), 415-430.

Koenig, John. *New Testament Hospitality*. Philadelphia: Fortress Press, 1985.

Krämer, Michael. *Die Gleichnisrede in den synoptischen Evangelien. Eine synoptische Studie zu Mt 13,1-52; Mk 4:1-34; Lk 8:4-21*. Egelsbach/Cologne/New York: Verlag Hansel-Hohenhausen, 1993.

Kratz, Reinhard. *Rettungswunder: Motiv-, traditions- und formkritische Aufarbeitung einer biblischen Gattung*. Europäische Hochschulschriften. Series XXIII: Theologie 123. Frankfurt am Main/Bern/Las Vegas: Peter Lang, 1979.

Kurz, William S. "Hellenistic Rhetoric in the Christological Proof of Luke-Acts," *Catholic Biblical Quarterly* 42 (1980), 170-195.

Lachs, Samuel Tobias. *A Rabbinic Commentary on the New Testament: The Gospels of Matthew, Mark, and Luke*. New York: Ktav, 1987.

Lafon, Guy. "Le repas chez Simon," *Etudes* 377 (1992), 651-660.

Lamarche, P. "Le possédé de Gérasa (Mt 8,28-34; Mc 5,1-20; Lc 8,26-39)," *Nouvelle Revue Theologique* 100 (1968), 581-597.

Lampe, G.W. "The Holy Spirit in the Writings of St. Luke," in Nineham, Dennis. ed. *Studies in the Gospels: Essays in Memory of G.H. Lightfoot*. Oxford: Basil Blackwell, 1955. 159-200.

LaVerdiere, Eugene. *Dining in the Kingdom of God: The Origins of the Eucharist According to Luke*. Chicago: Liturgy Training Publications, 1994.

Laurentin, René. *Structure et Theologie de Luc I-II*. Etudes Bibliques. Paris: Gabalda, 1957.

Leaney, Robert. "Jesus and the Symbol of the Child (Lc 9:46-48)," *Expository Times* 65 (1954-1955), 91-92.

Lee, D.A. "Women as 'Sinners': Three Narratives of Salvation in Luke and John," *Australian Biblical Review* 44 (1996), 1-15.

Legaré, Clément. "Analyse sémiotique de Luc 7,36-50: Jésus et la pécheresse," in Legaré, Clement et al., eds. *De Jésus et des femmes. Lectures sémiotiques.* Paris/Montreal: Editions du Cerf/Editions Bellarmin, 1987. 59-104.

Lehmann, Karl. *Auferweckt am tritten Tage nach der Schrift.* Quaestiones Disputatae 38. Freiburg: Herder, 1968.

Leroy, Herbert. "Vergebung und Gemeinde nach Lukas 7.36-50," in Feld, Helmut and Josef Nolte. eds. *Wort Gottes in der Zeit: Festschrift fur Karl Hermann Schelkle.* Dusseldorf: Patmos Verlag, 1973. 85-94.

Lewis, I.M. *Ecstatic Religion: An Anthropological Study of Spirit Possession and Shamanism.* Baltimore: Penguin, 1971.

Liefeld, Walter L. *Luke:* The Expositor's Bible Commentary. Grand Rapids: Zondervan Publishing House, 1995.

Lohfink, Gerhard. *Die Himmelfahrt Jesu: Untersuchungen zu den Himmelfahrts- und Erhohungstexten bei Lukas.* Munich: Kösel-Verlag, 1971.

Lohmeyer, Ernst. *Das Evangelium des Markus.* Göttingen: Vandenhoeck & Ruprecht, 1959.

Love, Stuart L. "Women and Men at Hellenistic Symposia Meals in Luke," in Esler, Philip L. ed. *Modelling Early Christianity: Social-scientific Studies of the New Testament in Its Context.* London/New York: Routledge, 1995. 198-210.

Luz, Ulrich. *Das Evangelium nach Matthaus 8-17.* Gütersloh: Neukirchener Verlag, 1989.

Mack, L. Burton. "The Anointing of Jesus: Elaboration Within a Chreia," in Mack, Burton L. and Vernon K. Robbins. *Patterns of Persuasion in the Gospels.* Sonoma, PA: Polebridge Press, 1989. 85-106.

Malina, Bruce J. "'Let Him Deny Himself' (Mark 8:34 & Par.): A Social-Psychological Model of Self-Denial," *Biblical Theology Bulletin* 24 (1994), 106-119.

Malina, Bruce and Jerome H. Neyrey. *Calling Jesus Names: The Social Value of Labels in Matthew.* Sonoma, CA: Polebridge Press, 1988.

Mann, C.S. *Mark: A New Translation with Introduction and Commentary.* Anchor Bible 27. New York: Doubleday, 1986.

Manns, Frederic. "Luc 4,47 et les traditions juives sur Rahab," *Revue des Sciences Religieuses* 61 (1987), 1-16.

Mattill, A.J. *Luke and the Last Things: A Perspective for the Understanding of Lukan Thought.* Dillsboro, NC: Western North Carolina Press, 1979.

McBride, Denis. *The Gospel of Luke: A Reflective Commentary.* Northport, NY: Costello Publishing, 1982.

McGuckin, J.A. *The Transfiguration of Christ in Scripture and Tradition.* Lewiston, NY: Edwin Mellen Press, 1986.

McHugh, John. *The Mother of Jesus in the New Testament.* Garden City, NY: Doubleday, 1975.

McIver, Robert K. "One Hundred-Fold Yield - Miraculous or Mundane? Matthew 13:8,23; Mk 4:8,20; Lk 8:8," *New Testament Studies* 40 (1994), 606-608.

McKenna, Megan. *Not Counting Women and Children: Neglected Stories from the Bible.* Makati: St. Paul's Philippines, 1997.

Meier, John P. *A Marginal Jew: Rethinking the Historical Jesus. I: The Root of the Problem and the Person.* New York: Doubleday, 1991.

_____. "The Brothers and Sisters of Jesus in Ecumenical Perspective," *Catholic Biblical Quarterly* 54 (1992), 1-28.

_____. "On Retrojecting Later Questions from Later Texts: A Reply to Richard Bauckham," *Catholic Biblical Quarterly* 59 (1997), 511-527.

_____. "The Circle of the Twelve: Did It Exist during Jesus' Public Ministry?," *Journal of Biblical Literature* 116 (1997a), 601-612.

Menken, Maarten J.J. "The Position of *Splagnizesthai* and *splagchna* in the Gospel of Luke," *Novum Testamentum* 30 (1988), 107-114.

Metzger, Bruce. "Seventy or Seventy-Two Disciples," *New Testament Studies* 5 (1958-1959), 299-306.

Milgrom, Jacob. *Leviticus 1-16: A New Translation with Introduction and Commentary.* Anchor Bible. New York: Doubleday, 1991.

Moessner, David P. "Luke 9:1-50: Luke's Preview of the Journey of the Prophet Like Moses of Deuteronomy," *Journal of Biblical Literature* 102 (1983), 575-605.

_____. *Lord of the Banquet: The Literary and Theological Significance of the Lukan Travel Narrative.* Minneapolis: Fortress Press, 1989.

Moloney, Francis J. "Reading Eucharistic Texts in Luke," *Proceedings of the Irish Biblical Association* n. 14 (1991), 25-45.

Moxnes, Halvor. *The Economy of the Kingdom: Social Conflict and Economic Relations in Luke's Gospel.* Philadelphia: Fortress Press, 1988.

_____. "The Social Context of Luke's Community," in Kingsbury, Jack Dean. ed. *Gospel Interpretation: Narrative-Critical and Social-Scientific Approaches.* Harrisburg, PA: Trinity Press International, 1997. 166-177.

Muhlack, Gudrun. *Die Parallelen von Lukas-Evangelium und Apostelgeschichte.* Frankfurt-am-Main: Peter Lang, 1979.

Murphy-O'Connor, Jerome. "What Really Happened at the Transfiguration?," *Bible Review* 3 (1987), 8-21.

Mussner, Franz. "Der nicht erkannte Kairos (Mt 11:16-19 = Lk 7:31-35)," *Biblica* 40 (1959), 599-612.

Navone, John. "The Lucan Banquet Community," *The Bible Today* n. 50 (1970a), 155-162.

Neirynck, Frans. "Minor Agreements Matthew-Luke in the Transfiguration Story," in Hoffmann, Paul, et al., eds. *Orientierung an Jesus: Zur Theologie der Synoptiker: Für Josef Schmid.* Freiburg-Basel-Vienna: Herder, 1973. 253-265.

_____ and T.A. Friedrichsen. "Note on Luke 9:22. A Response to M.D. Goulder," *Ephemerides Theologicae Lovanienses* 65 (1989), 390-395.

Neyrey, Jerome H. "The Apologetic Use of the Transfiguration in 2nd Peter 1:16-21," *Catholic Biblical Quarterly* 42 (1980), 504-519.

Niemand, Christoph. *Studien zu den Minor Agreements der synoptischen Verklärungsperikopen.* Europäische Hochschulschriften. Frankfurt am Main: Peter Lang, 1989.

Noel, Filip. *De compositie van het Lucasevangelie in zijn relatie tot Marcus.* Verhandelingen van de Koninklijke Academie voor Wetenschappen, Letteren, and Schone Kunsten van Belgie. Brussel: Paleis der Academien, 1994.

Nolland, John. *Luke 9:21-18:34.* Word Biblical Commentary 35b. Dallas, TX: Word Books, 1993.

Obeng, E.A. "The Significance of the Miracles of Resuscitation and its Implication for the Church in Africa," *Bible Bhashyam* 18 (1992), 83-95.

Okorie, A.M. "Meals as Type-Scenes in the Third Gospel," *Melita Theologica* 47 (1996), 17-26.

Osborne, Grant R. "Women in Jesus' Ministry," *Westminster Theological Journal* 51 (1989), 259-291.

Otto, R.E. "The Fear Motivation in Peter"s Offer to Build treis skenas," *Westminster Theological Journal* 59 (1997), 101-112.

Paffenroth, Kim. *The Story of Jesus According to L.* JSNT Supplement Series 147. Sheffield: Sheffield Academic Press, 1997.

Pamment, M. "Moses and Elijah in the Story of the Transfiguration," *Expository Times* 92 (1980-1981), 338-339.

Page II, Charles R. *Jesus and the Land.* Nashville: Abingdon Press, 1995.

Payne, Philip B. "The Order of Sowing and Ploughing in the Parable of the Sower," *New Testament Studies* 25 (1978-1979), 123-129.

Penney, John Michael. *The Missionary Emphasis of Lukan Pneumatology*. Sheffield: Sheffield Academic Press, 1997.

Pesch, Rudolf. "The Markan Version of the Healing of the Gerasene Demoniac," *Ecumenical Review* 23 (1971), 348-376

_____. *Der Besessene von Gerasa: Entstehung und Überlieferung einer Wundergeschichte*. Stuttgart: Katholisches Bibelwerk., 1972.

Pettem, M. "Luke's Great Omission and His View of the Law," *New Testament Studies* 42 (1996), 35-54.

Petzke, Gerd. "Historizität und Bedeutsamkeit von Wunderberichten. Möglickeiten und Grenzen des religionsgeschichtlichen Vergleiches," in Betz, Hans Dieter and Luise Schottroff, eds. *Neues Testament und Christliche Existenz*. Festschrift für Herbert Braun. Tübingen: J.C.B. Mohr (Paul Siebeck), 1973. 367-385.

_____. *Das Sondergut des Evangeliums nach Lukas*. Zürcher Werkkommentare zur Bibel. Zurich: Theologischer Verlag, 1990.

Pilch, John J. "The Transfiguration of Jesus: An Experience of Alternate Reality," in Esler, Philip F. ed. *Modelling Early Christianity: Social-Scientific Studies of the New Testament in Its Context*. London/New York: Routledge, 1995. 47-64.

_____. *The Cultural World of Jesus: Sunday by Sunday, Cycle C*. Collegeville: The Liturgical Press, 1997.

Pitt-Rivers, Julian. "The Stranger, the Guest and the Hostile Host: Introduction to the Study of the Laws of Hospitality," in Peristany, J.G. ed. *Contributions to Mediterranean Sociology*. Paris: Mouton & Co, 1968. 13-30.

Price, Robert M. *The Widow Traditions in Luke-Acts: A Feminist-Critical Scrutiny*. Alpharetta, GA: Society of Biblical Literature, 1996.

Ravens, D.A.S. "The Setting of Luke's Account of the Anointing: Luke 7:2-8:3," *New Testament Studies* 34 (1988), 282-292.

_____. "Luke 9:7-62 and the Prophetic Role of Jesus, *New Testament Studies* 36 (1990), 119-129.

Rauscher, Johann. *Das Bildwort von der Ollampe in der synoptischen Tradition: Eine Auslegung von Mk 4:21f. par. Lk 4:16f.; Mt 5:15; Lk 11:33.* Desselbrun: Apud Auctorem, 1994.

Rebell, W. "'Sein Leben verlieren' (Mark 8:35 parr.) als Strukturmoment vor- und nach-osterlichen Glaubens," *New Testament Studies* 35 (1989), 202-218.

Reid, Barbara E. "The Centerpiece of Salvation History: Jerusalem in the Gospel of Luke," *The Bible Today* 29 (1991), 20-24.

_____. *The Transfiguration: A Source-and Redaction-Critical Study of Luke 9:28-36.* Paris: J. Gabalda, 1993.

Reiling, S. and J.L. Swellengrebel. *A Translator's Handbook on the Gospel of Luke.* Leiden: Brill, 1971.

Reinhardt, Wolfgang. *Das Wachstum des Gottesvolkes. Biblische Theologie des Gemeindewachstums.* Göttingen: Vandenhoeck & Ruprecht, 1995.

Resseguie, James L. "Automatization and Defamiliarization in Luke 7:36-50," *Journal of Literature & Theology* 5 (1991), 137-150.

Robbins, Vernon K. "The Woman Who Touched Jesus' Garment: Socio-rhetorical Analysis of the Synoptic Accounts," *New Testament Studies* 33 (1987), 502-515.

Robinson, William C. "On Preaching the Word of God (Luke 8:4-21)," in Keck, Leander E. and J. L. Martyn, eds. *Studies in Luke-Acts. Essays presented in honor of Paul Schubert.* Nashville/New York: Abingdon Press, 1968. 131-138.

Rochais, Gérard. *Les Récits de Résurrection des Morts dans le Nouveau Testament.* Cambridge: Cambridge University Press, 1981.

Rohrbaugh, Richard L. "The Pre-Industrial City in Luke-Acts," in Neyrey, Jerome H. ed. *The Social World of Luke-Acts: Models for Interpretation.* Peabody: Hendrickson, 1991), 125-149.

Rolland, Philippe. "Je vous envoie (Mt 10:1-42; Mc 6,7-13; Lc 9,1-6; Lc 10,1-12)," *Spiritus* 29 (n. 113, 1988), 359-365.

Rosen, George. *Madness in Society: Chapters in the Historical Sociology of Mental Illness.* Chicago: University of Chicago Press, 1968.

Roth, S. John. *The Blind, the Lame, and the Poor. Character Types in Luke-Acts.* Sheffield: Sheffield Academic Press, 1997.

Rowland, Christopher. *The Open Heaven: A Study of Apocalyptic in Judaism and Early Christianity.* New York: Crossroad, 1982.

Ruch, E. "One More Look at 'Hiding the Light' in Luke 8:16-18 and Mark 4:21-25," *Notes on Translation* 10 (1996), 11-17.

Ruether, Rosemary. *New Woman New Earth.* New York: Seabury Press, 1975.

Ryan, Rosalie. "The Women from Galilee and Discipleship in Luke," *Biblical Theology Bulletin* 15 (1985), 56-59.

Sabbe, Maurice. "La rédaction du récit de la transfiguration," in *La vue du Messie.* Recherches Bibliques 6; Louvain: Leuven University Press, 1962. 65-100.

Sabourin, Leopold. *The Gospel According to St. Luke.* Bandra, Bombay: St. Paul Publications, 1984.

_____. *L'Evangile de Luc.* Introduction et commentaire. Rome: Gregorian University, 1985.

Schenke, Ludger. *Studien zur Passionsgeschichte des Markus.* Forschung zur Bibel 4. Würzburg: Echter Verlag, 1971.

_____. *Die wunderbare Brotvermehrung: Die neutestamentlichen Erzählungen und ihre Bedeutung.* Würzburg: Echter Verlag, 1983.

Schmithals, Walter. *Das Evangelium nach Markus, Kapitel 1:1-9:1.* Ökumenischer Taschenbuch-Kommentar zum Neuen Testament 2.1. Gütersloh: Gütersloher Verlaghaus/Gerd Mohn, 1979.

Schnider, Franz. *Jesus der Prophet.* Freiburg: Universitatsverlag, 1973.

Schnyder, Christoph. "Jesus erweckt den einzigen Sohn einer Witwe vom Tode (Lukas 7,11-17)," in Steiner, Anton and Volker Weymann, eds. *Wunder Jesu: Bibelarbeit in der Gemeinde: Themen und Materialen.* Basel/Zurich-Köln: Friedrich Reinhardt Verlag/Benziger Verlag, 1978. 77-87.

Schottroff, Luise. "Women as Followers of Jesus in New Testament Times: An Exercise in Social-Historical Exegesis of the Bible," in Gottwald, Norman K. ed. *The Bible and Liberation, Political and Social Hermeneutics.* Maryknoll, NY: Orbis Books, 1989. 418-427.

_____. *Befreiungserfahrung: Studien zur Sozialgeschichte des Neuen Testaments.* Munich: Chr. Kaiser Verlag, 1990.

Schürmann, Heinz. "Lukanische Reflexionen über die Wortverkündigung in Lk 8:4-21," in *Ursprung und Gestalt. Erörterungen und Besinnungen zum Neuen Testament.* Düsseldorf: Patmos, 1970. 29-41.

Schutz, Frieder. *Der leidende Christus. Die angefochtene Gemeinde und das Christuskerygma der lukanischn Schriften.* Stuttgart: Kohlhammer Verlag, 1969.

Schweizer, Eduard. *The Good News According to Mark.* Atlanta: John Knox Press, 1976.

_____. *The Good News According to Matthew.* London: SPCK, 1975.

Seethaler, Angelika. "Die Brotvermehrung — ein Kirchenspiegel?," *Biblische Zeitschrift* N.F. 34 (1990), 108-112.

Selvidge, Marla J. *Woman, Cult and Miracle Recital: A Redactional Critical Investigation on Mark 5:24-34.* London/Toronto: Associated University Presses, 1990.

Sévin, Marc. "L'approche des textes bibliques," *Lumen Vitae* 50 (1995), 253-260.

Siegman, E.F. "Teaching in Parables (Mk 4:10-12; Lk 8:9-10; Mt 13:10-15)," *Catholic Biblical Quarterly* 23 (1961), 161-181.

Sim, David C. "The Women Followers of Jesus: The Implications of Luke 8:1-3," *Heythrop Journal* 30 (1989), 51-62.

Steele, E. Springs. *Jesus' Table-Fellowship with Pharisees: An Editorial Analysis of Luke 7:36-50, 11:37-54, and 14:1-24.* Notre Dame: University of Notre Dame, 1981.

Stegner, William Richard. *Narrative Theology in Early Christianity.* Louisville: Westminster/John Knox Press, 1989.

_____."The Use of Scripture in Two Narratives of Early Jewish Christianity (Matthew 4:1-11; Mk 9:2-8)," in Evans, Craig A. and James A. Sanders. eds. *Early Christian Interpretation of the Scriptures of Israel: Investigations and Proposals.* Sheffield: Sheffield Academic Press, 1997. 98-123.

Stein, Robert H. "Is the Transfiguration (Mark 9:2-8) a Misplaced Resurrection-Account?" *Journal of Biblical Literature* 95 (1976), 79-96.

Sterling, Gregory E., "Jesus as Exorcist: An Analysis of Matthew 17:14-20; Mark 14-29; Luke 9:37-43a)," *Catholic Biblical Quarterly* 55 (1993), 467-493.

Suriano, Thomas M. "Christian Faith and the Miracles of Jesus," *The Bible Today* n. 92 (November 1977), 1358-1364.

Swartz, S.M. "Hiding the Light: Another Look at Luke 8:16-18," *Notes on Translation* 8 (1994), 53-59.

Swidler, Leonard. *Biblical Affirmations of Women.* Philadelphia: Westminster Press, 1979.

Talbert, Robert C. *The Narrative Unity of Luke-Acts: A Literary Interpretation.* Volume One: *The Gospel According to Luke.* Philadelphia: Fortress Press, 1986.

Tannehill, Robert C. "Introduction: The Pronouncement Story and Its Types," *Semeia* 20 (1981), 1-13.

_____. "Varieties of Synoptic Pronouncement Stories," *Semeia* 20 (1981a), 101-119.

Taylor, Vincent. *The Gospel According to St. Mark*. London: Macmillan & Co, 1957.

Ternant, Paul. "La résurrection du fils de la veuve de Nain," *Assemblées du Seigneur* 41 (1971), 69-79.

Trites, Allison. "The Transfiguration of Jesus: The Gospel in Microcosm." *Evangelical Quarterly* 51 (1979), 67-79.

_____. "The Transfiguration in the Theology of Luke: Some Redactional Links," in Hurst, L.D. and N.T. Wright, eds. *The Glory of Christ in the New Testament: Studies in Christology in Memory of George Bradford Caird*. Oxford: Clarendon Press, 1987. 71-81.

Trummer, Peter. *Die blutende Frau: Wunderheilung im Neuen Testament*. Freiburg/Basel: Herder, 1991.

Turner, Max. *Power from on High: The Spirit in Israel's Restoration and Witness in Luke-Acts*. Sheffield: Sheffield Academic Press, 1996.

Vaage, Leif E. "Q1 and the Historical Jesus: Some Peculiar Sayings (7:33-34; 9:57-58,59-60; 14:26-27)," *Forum* 5 (1989), 159-176.

_____. "More Than a Prophet and Demon-Possessed: Q and the Historical John." in Kloppenborg, John S. ed. *Conflict and Invention: Literary, Rhetorical, and Social Studies on the Sayings Gospel Q*. Valley Forge, PA: Trinity Press International, 1995. 181-202.

van Cangh, Jean-Marie. *La multiplication des pains et l'Eucharistie*. Lectio Divina 86. Paris: Editions du Cerf, 1975.

van Iersel, Bas. "Die wunderbare Speisung und das Abendmahl," *Novum Testamentum* 7 (1964-1965), 167-194.

Vogels, Walter. "A Semiotic Study of Luke 7:11-17," *Eglise et Théologie* 14 (1983), 273-292.

Wagner, J. Ross. "Psalm 118 in Luke-Acts: Tracing a Narrative Thread," in Evans, Craig A. and James A. Sanders, eds. *Early Christian Interpretation of the Scriptures of Israel: Investigations and Proposals*. Sheffield: Sheffield Academic Press, 1997. 154-178.

Wanke, Joachim. *Beobachtungen zum Eucharistieverständnis des Lukas auf Grund der lukanischen Mahlberichte*. Erfurter Theologische Schriften. Leipzig: St. Benno-Verlag, 1973.

Wegner, Uwe. *Der Hauptmann von Kafarnaum (Mt 7, 28a; 8,5-10,13 par Lk 7,1-10). Ein Beitrag zur Q-Forschung*. WUNT 2. Reihe, 14. Tubingen: J.C.B. Mohr (Paul Siebeck), 1985.

Weren, Huub. "Zaaien, groeien en oogsten (Lk 8:1-21; 13:1-9; 20:9-19)," JOTA 3 (1989), 14-24.

Wilkens, W. "Die Auslassung von Mark. 6:45-8:26 bei Lukas im Licht der Komposition Luk 9:1-50," *Theologische Zeitschrift* 32 (1976), 193-200.

Wink, Walter. "Jesus' Reply to John: Matt 11:2-6/Luke 7:18-23," *Forum* 5 (1989), 121-128.

Witherington. Ben. "On the Road with Mary Magdalene, Joanna, Susanna, and Other Disciples—Luke 8:1-3," *Zeitschrift für die neutestamentliche Wissenschaft* 70 (1979), 243-248.

Zeller, Dieter. "Die Bildlogik des Gleichnisses Mt 11:16/Lk 7:31," *Zeitschrift für die neutestamentliche Wissenschaft* 68 (1977), 252-257).

Zerwick, Max. *Biblical Greek*. Rome: Scripta Pontificii Instituti Biblici, 1963.